PICTURESQUE PALESTINE

SINAI AND EGYPT

VOL. I

PICTURESQUE

PALESTINE

SINAI AND EGYPT

PICTURESQUE PALESTINE

SINAI AND EGYPT

EDITED BY

SIR CHARLES WILSON, R.E., K.C.B., F.R.S.

FORMERLY ENGINEER TO THE PALESTINE EXPLORATION SOCIETY

ASSISTED BY THE MOST EMINENT PALESTINE EXPLORERS
ETC.

WITH NUMEROUS ENGRAVINGS ON STEEL AND WOOD

IN FOUR VOLUMES

VOL. I

REVIVISCIMUS

SAN RAFAEL CA

Second, facsimile editions
by Reviviscimus
2010

For information, address:
Reviviscimus Press, P.O. Box 151011
San Rafael CA 94915
reviviscimuspress.com

Printed in the
United States of America

Library of Congress Cataloging-in-Publication Data

Picturesque Palestine, Sinai and Egypt /
edited by Sir Charles Wilson.—2nd, complete facsim. ed.

p. cm.

"Assisted by the most eminent Palestine explorers etc.; with numerous engravings on steel and wood; in four volumes."
"First edition, J. S. Virtue and Co., Limited, London, 1881"—T.p. verso.
Includes bibliographical references and index.
ISBN 978-1-59731-455-8 (4-volume pbk. set: alk. paper)
ISBN 978-1-59731-456-5 (vol. 1: pbk.: alk. paper)
ISBN 978-1-59731-457-2 (vol. 2: pbk.: alk. paper)
ISBN 978-1-59731-458-9 (vol. 3: pbk.: alk. paper)
ISBN 978-1-59731-459-6 (vol. 4: pbk.: alk. paper)
1. Palestine—Description and travel. 2. Sinai (Egypt)—Description and travel.
3. Egypt—Description and travel. I. Wilson, Charles William, Sir, 1836–1905.
DS 107.P65 2010
915.69404'34—dc22 2010022142

JERUSALEM, FROM SCOPUS.

CONTENTS.

VOL. I.

LIST OF ILLUSTRATIONS.

VOL. I.

ENGRAVINGS ON STEEL.

ENGRAVINGS ON WOOD.

INTRODUCTION.

THE writers on sacred geography may be divided into three classes. There was first the class of pilgrims, beginning with the Empress Helena, and continuing through the whole period of the Middle Ages, almost down to our own time. The writings of this class contain much that is curious in the way of legend and of fancy, but in the way of historical, geographical, or philosophical investigation they contain almost nothing.

Next, in the seventeenth century, supervened the class of travellers, few and far between, who wandered from the beaten track, partly in pursuit of adventure, partly for the sake of investigating these countries scientifically, and who, advancing onwards to the present time, included amongst their number some few who have acquired a widespread fame—amongst others, first and foremost, the Emperor Napoleon, who, in his brief Notes on Syria, founded on his military expedition, has laid the basis of all the subsequent scientific descriptions of Palestine. But these travellers were hardly ever gifted with a sense of the perception either of natural scenery, or of imaginative and devotional sentiment. Jerusalem, as was expressed by that great genius of whom we have just spoken, did not lie within the line of their operations.

The third group partly resembled these, but may be distinguished as the literary class. Châteaubriand was the first. He described—inaccurately, but still with a sense of what he saw before him—something of the peculiar conformation of the outlines of the country. He was the first who spoke of that long line of mysterious hills beyond the Jordan which now impresses every traveller who visits those scenes.

These literary travellers were finally united with that more scientific group which preceded them in the person of one who must be called for all practical purposes the discoverer of Palestine. It was Dr. Robinson, the American traveller, who first brought to the geography of Palestine a previous knowledge worthy of the subject and an eye capable of observing it. From that time forward the two streams of literary and of scientific investigators have been continued, sometimes apart, sometimes united. The crowd of visitors who hang on the outskirts of the literary class, and who have published their travels, are well-nigh countless. Their books are amongst the least worthy of the noble theme of any that have appeared on this or any other country. But the class which may be called scientific have more or less kept before their minds the ideal which advanced knowledge and the seriousness of the subject demanded; and it is to their work that this volume is chiefly owing. It represents the results of their travels—in Egypt, so far as it concerns the Chosen People; in Arabia, so far as Arabia is connected with the giving of the Law and the wanderings of the Israelites; in Palestine, as it includes not only the sacred history, both Jewish and Christian, but also the monuments of the Crusaders and the Saracen princes of a later time.

The engravings and the descriptions must be left to speak for themselves. A few words only need here be added to express the value of such an addition to our knowledge of the Holy Land, or rather, we may say, of the Holy Lands. Of Egypt it is enough to say that its transitory connection with the slavery and migration of the children of Israel, although very slightly indicated in the Egyptian history or monuments, yet deserves any light which can be thrown by the recent investigations which have taken place with regard to Heliopolis or the neighbourhood of Suez. The desert of Mount Sinai is more closely bound up with the sacred history. A few incidents in the wanderings of the Chosen People, the identification of Paran and of the Giving of the Law with the magnificent scenery of Serbal and the Gebel Mousa, and the conjectural identification of Petra with Kadesh, or, at any rate, with Mount Hor, furnish the only links of direct relationship; but the general atmosphere, the natural history, and the unique configuration of the granite mountains which form the peculiar charm of the desert, cannot fail to quicken the appreciation with which we read the accounts of the "great and terrible wilderness," and the thunders and lightnings of Mount Horeb, the palm-trees of Elim, and the springs of Rephidim and Kadesh.

But in Palestine the connection of the history and the geography is so intimate and so compact as to exceed that of any other country, with the exception of Greece. The beauty, the variety, the marked features of the Grecian landscape, cannot be rivalled by any other part of the world, and are so interwoven with every stage of the mythology and history of the marvellous people which inhabited it, as to place its historical geography in a superlative degree above that of any other nation or locality.

Next to Greece, however, Palestine stands supreme. The extraordinary rift of the Jordan valley, deeper than any similar fissure on the surface of the earth, the innumerable questions, historical or scientific, which that valley suggests in the overthrow of the five cities in the passage of the Jordan, would of itself render Palestine peculiar amongst the countries of the globe. The caves with which its limestone rocks are perforated are features which cannot be destroyed or altered by time, and represent a series of adventures and hiding-places from the time of Abraham and David down to the heroic insurgents of the age of Josephus. The wells and springs, which are so remarkable an element in all Eastern lands, and which ally themselves alike with the early history of the Patriarchs and with the recorded discourses of Him who by the well of Sychar proclaimed the great truth of the spirituality and universality of His religion, still remain as living witnesses to the history of which they are the expression, and justify with singular force the striking words of a well-known traveller, "There is no event so permanent as that which is writ in water." The fragments of buildings which overspread the whole country, and which date from almost every age, recall the prehistoric times of those old aboriginal tribes whose names appear only to be blotted out by the successive tides of invasion which have swept over the country; and the manifold vestiges of Jerusalem, Samaria, Caesarea, and Baalbec carry us on, like the broken arches of a majestic aqueduct, through the Herodian, the Syro-Roman, and the Crusading periods, so as to leave upon the mind the impression, even more than Greece or Italy, of a land of ruins. The mountains, if unlike Greece, where, by reason of the variety of form and colour,

> "Each old poetic mountain
> Inspiration breathes around,"

yet, by the general elevation of the whole country, have given form and substance to the peculiar diction of Prophet and Psalmist, and have also lent themselves to that long succession of celebrated views with which no other history can compare. They, and they alone, made possible the view of Abraham from Bethel; the view of Jacob from the rocky defile of Jabbok; the view of Moses from the top of Pisgah; the survey of Balaam from that same spot over the country which lay beneath his feet; the parting view of the exile of the forty-second Psalm, as he mounted the hills of Gilead and looked back on the beloved sanctuary of his home; the view of a greater than Abraham, or Moses, or David, from a mountain "exceeding high," over "all the kingdoms of the world;" or, again, from Hermon, where His garments became as white as snow; or, again, from that spot which, almost alone in Palestine, is consecrated, not by tradition, but by its own intrinsic evidence, as the place where, "when He saw Jerusalem, He wept over it."

Such are some of the scenes which are presented in this volume. It is believed that they will tend, at once by the accuracy of description and of delineation, to produce a livelier sense of the "godly land," and the descending river, and the holy city "with the mountains standing round about it."

In the New Testament they can for the most part only supply the external framework where the grand events occurred and the great truths were proclaimed, which form the substance of the Christian revelation. The events and the truths are too spiritual to be touched by the local and natural position of mountain and valley, of building and vegetation. "He is not here—He is risen." But for the Old Testament, where the name of every plain is significant, where the formation of every glen has wrought itself into a picture, where every stream, spring, and well has intertwined itself with some sacred history, where every bird and beast has almost a voice that speaks, it is not too much to say, "Thy servants take pleasure in her stones and favour the dust thereof."

THE JAFFA GATE.
The chief entrance to the city of Jerusalem, as it appears from within the city walls. The open space within the gate is used as a market-place.

JERUSALEM.

"If I forget thee, O Jerusalem, let my right hand forget her cunning."—Ps. cxxxvii. 5.

JERUSALEM is emphatically a mountain city. Situated in the heart of the hill country which extends from the great plain of Esdraelon to the southern extremity of the Promised Land, surrounded on all sides by limestone hills whose surface is broken by countless ravines, and only approached by rough mountain roads, its position is one of great natural strength. This peculiarity in the situation of the Holy City is frequently alluded to in the Bible, and we may infer from the well known words of the Psalmist, "As the mountains are round about Jerusalem, so the Lord is round about his people," that importance was attached to the hills as a barrier or protection against hostile attack.

The modern city stands, as did the ancient one, on the southern extremity of a gently shelving plateau, not more than one thousand acres in extent, which is bordered by two valleys that bear names familiar to us from childhood: one is the Valley of the Brook Kedron, the other the Valley of Hinnom. These two valleys, at first mere shallow depressions in the ground, take their rise within a few yards of each other, and at an altitude of two thousand six hundred and fifty feet above the sea, in the gentle undulation which at that point parts the waters of the Mediterranean from those of the Jordan Valley. Separating at once, they soon take one of those rapid plunges downward so characteristic of the wild glens of Judaea, and, after encircling the plateau, meet again at Bir Eyub (the Well of Job), six hundred and seventy-two feet below their original starting-point; hence, united as the Wady en Nar, "Valley of Fire," they pass by a deep gorge through the Wilderness of Judaea to the Dead Sea.

The eastern or Kedron valley, after running eastward for a mile and a half, turns sharply to the south and forms at its southern extremity the Valley of Jehoshaphat. The western valley, or Valley of Hinnom, which at its head swells out into a large shallow basin, follows a southerly course for one mile and a quarter, and then turns eastward to Bir Eyub, south of the city.

A third ravine, the Tyropoeon, or Valley of the Cheesemongers, which rises near the head of the plateau between the Kedron and Hinnom valleys, runs southward to join the former at Siloam, and divides the ground on which the city stands into two spurs of unequal size, which terminate in abrupt broken slopes. On Mount Moriah, the eastern and smaller spur, once stood the temples of Solomon, Zerubbabel, and Herod, and the palace of Solomon; on the western, which is one hundred and twenty feet higher than Moriah, and of greater area, were situated the "upper city" of Josephus, the stately palace of Herod, and the three great towers Hippicus, Phasaelus, and Mariamne. A fourth and smaller ravine, the rugged nature of which was unsuspected a few years ago, rises near the eastern side of the plateau and falls into the Kedron near the well-known Golden Gate. In the bed of this ravine two large reservoirs were constructed; one of these still exists as the Birket Israil, or Pool of Bethesda.

The sides of the valleys of Kedron and Hinnom are now encumbered with rubbish, but they are still sufficiently steep to be difficult of access, and every here and there places are found where the rock has been cut perpendicularly downwards, in cliffs ten to twenty feet high, to give additional security. It was probably in these natural defences, strengthened by art, which protect the city on the south, east, and west, that the Jebusites put their trust when they boasted to King David, "Thou wilt not come in hither; the blind and lame shall drive thee back." The only side upon which the city could be attacked with any chance of success was the north; and here it was defended by walls of such massive strength as to be capable of offering a determined resistance to the most celebrated armies of the ancient world.

Immediately beyond the Kedron Valley, "before" or to the east of Jerusalem, is the Mount of Olives (see page 8), a long ridge of graceful outline, swelling out ever and again

ENTRANCE TO THE CITADEL.
Showing the rudely constructed wooden bridge across the moat and Turkish sentries on guard.

into rounded knolls which command striking views of the city and the surrounding country. On one of these knolls, opposite Mount Moriah, and two hundred and twenty feet above the Temple Platform, are the Mosque and Church of the Ascension; on another, towards the north, a small ruin marks the spot where, according to tradition, the men of Galilee stood "gazing up into heaven" (Acts i. 11); and still farther northward is Scopus, the brow of the hill whence Titus and his legions looked down upon the doomed city (see Frontispiece).

The ride from Scopus along the crest of Olivet to the Church of the Ascension is one of the greatest interest and beauty: on one side there are ever-changing views of the deep depression of the Jordan Valley and the Dead Sea; on the other, every step brings more prominently to view some spot, or it may be some building, which no thoughtful man can look upon without at least a passing emotion.

The view from the Mount of Olives is one which, from its strange beauty and its extraordinary interest, lingers long and lovingly in the memory of those who have seen it. Away to the north is the minaret-crowned height of Neby Samwil, the Mizpeh, perhaps, of Scripture, whence many a weary pilgrim has caught his first glimpse of the long-looked-for Zion. To the east are grey, bare hills, cut up by a thousand ravines, which descend abruptly to the Jordan Valley, and that strange salt sea which occupies the deepest depression of the earth's surface. The atmosphere is so clear, so transparent, that the placid water seems at times almost within reach, yet it is many miles away, and its surface is no less than three thousand nine hundred feet below the mount. Beyond the Jordan Valley and the Dead Sea, a long mountain wall, which is broken here and there by wild gorges through which the waters of Arnon and other streams find their way to the lower depths, extends from Mount Gilead on the north to the Mountains of Moab on the south (see page 9). In the evening, when the sun is low and the blinding glare from the white hills in the foreground is somewhat subdued, the colouring on the distant mountains is exquisite, and the changing light produces a succession of ever-varying tints which it would be impossible to transfer to canvas.

The view towards the west, which should be seen by morning light, embraces the entire city of Jerusalem; every hill and valley and nearly all the important buildings can be recognised at once, and a general impression of their relative positions obtained. Looking down from his vantage ground on Olivet, the spectator is at once struck by the appearance of ruin and decay which the city presents, and especially by the vast accumulation of rubbish within and around it: the deep gorge of the Tyropoeon, which cut through the heart of the town, is now but a slight depression; the wild ravine in which the Pool of Bethesda was cut is filled to overflowing; Kedron's bed is deeply covered with debris; the precipices which Joab scaled are slopes of earth and stones planted with corn and vegetables; and the Via Dolorosa is forty to fifty feet above the level of the ancient roadway. The extensive cemeteries which hem in the city on almost every side give a mournful aspect to the view, and this effect is heightened by the oppressive silence which broods over the place during the greater portion of the day, and by the sober grey of the dome-roofed houses. How strangely changed from that Jerusalem which the Psalmist once described in loving terms as "Beautiful for situation, the joy of the whole earth!" From the Church of the Ascension the ground shelves down to the dry bed of the Kedron and then rises steeply to the summit of Mount Moriah, on which is now situated the

JERUSALEM FROM THE MOUNT OF OLIVES.

This page is adjacent to a plate and is intentionally left blank.

THE TOWER OF DAVID.—PHASAELUS.
Shewing the moat and bridge of the Citadel, and the gardens of the Armenian monastery, beyond the Turkish barracks.

Haram esh Sherif. The surface of the Haram enclosure is studded with cypress and olive, and its sides are surrounded, in part, by the finest mural masonry in the world, capable, even in its decay, of affecting men's minds more strongly than any other building of the ancient world.
At its southern end is the Mosque el Aksa and a pile of buildings formerly used by the Knights Templar. Nearly in the centre is a raised platform paved with stone, from the centre of which rises the well-known "Dome of the Rock" (Kubbet es Sakhra) (see vignette, title-page). Within this sacred enclosure stood the Temple of the Jews, but all traces of it have long since disappeared, and its exact position has for years been one of the most fiercely contested points in Jerusalem topography.

Beyond Mount Moriah and the Valley of the Tyropoeon, which can be plainly distinguished running down from the Damascus Gate, is the western hill now known as Zion. The ancient city extended over the entire hill, but the southern end is now bare. Within the modern walls the ground is thickly covered with houses, except on the west, where there is an open space occupied by gardens. At the north-west corner, where the road from Jaffa enters the town, is the Citadel with its massive towers, and adjoining them on the south are the principal barracks of the Turkish garrison.

From the Jaffa Gate on the west, a street, following apparently the direction of a small lateral branch of the Tyropoeon Valley, runs eastward, along the northern side of the Zion of today, to the Haram esh Sherif. North of this line stretches the Christian quarter of the town, rising gradually to the north-west till it reaches the corner of the modern wall at Goliath's Castle (Kalat Julud), a ruined castle, supposed by some writers to be the tower Psephinus mentioned by Josephus. Nearly in the centre of this quarter lies the Church of the Holy Sepulchre.

Without the walls towards the north-west is the great Russian establishment, consulate, cathedral, and hospice, which, like some great fortress or barrack, overshadows and completely dominates the Holy City. In the same direction are the less pretentious buildings of the German orphanage for girls, and the Syrian orphanage for boys, as well as the church of the native Protestant community.

Jerusalem is entirely surrounded by a massive wall built by Sultan Suleiman in A.D. 1542. It is provided with numerous flanking towers, and protected on the north by a ditch partly cut in the rock. The form of the city is that of an irregular quadrangle, and the total extent of the walls is about two and a half miles. There are ten gates in the walls, five of which are open and five closed. Of the former, the Jaffa Gate is on the west, the Damascus Gate on the north, St. Stephen's Gate on the east, and the Zion and Dung Gates on the south; of the latter, the Gate of Flowers or of Herod is on the north, the Golden Gate on the east, and the Single, Double, and Triple Gates on the south. From the Jaffa Gate the street of David runs eastward to the "Gate of the Chain," the principal entrance to the Haram esh Sherif. From the Damascus Gate one street traverses the city from north to south, passing near the eastern end of the Church of the Holy Sepulchre and through the bazaars to the vicinity of the Zion Gate, whilst another, named "El Wad," or Valley Street, follows, except where it has to cross the causeway, the general direction of the Tyropoeon Valley to the Dung Gate. From St. Stephen's Gate a street runs past the Pool of Bethesda to the Valley Street, and from the Zion Gate a street leads in an almost direct line to an open space in front of the Jaffa Gate. The principal streets divide Jerusalem, approximately, into four quarters, of which the north-east, including Bezetha and the Upper Tyropoeon Valley, is occupied by Moslems; the north-west and south-west, or Zion and the western hills, by Christians; and the south-east, comprising the eastern slope of Zion and the Lower Tyropoeon, by Jews.

The Jaffa Gate, or Gate of Hebron (Bab el Khalil), is the principal entrance to the city, and its immediate neighbourhood is generally enlivened by a throng of passers-by, and by the groups of muleteers, packers, and idlers who spend a large portion of their time lounging about the cafes without the gate (see page 1).

South of the Jaffa Gate is the Citadel, and beyond it are the barracks and the extensive gardens of the Armenian monastery (see page 5). This portion of the western hill was covered in part, or perhaps entirely, by Herod's Palace, with its gardens, and by the three towers which adjoined it on the north. Josephus has left us a glowing account of the royal palace, which "was entirely surrounded by a wall thirty cubits high, with decorated towers at equal intervals, and contained enormous banqueting halls, besides numerous chambers richly adorned." The towers were built of blocks of white stone of great size, "so exactly joined together that each tower appeared to be one mass of rock;" and they played a prominent part during the memorable siege by the Romans. These towers were left standing by Titus when he destroyed the city, to protect the legion left to garrison the place and prevent any insurrectionary movements on the part of the Jews.

Any remains which may now exist of Herod's Palace are buried beneath a mass of rubbish more than thirty feet deep; but two at least of the towers, Phasaelus and Hippicus, can be recognised in the works of the modern Citadel. The Citadel, remodelled in the fourteenth century, and again repaired in the sixteenth century, consists of five square towers and other buildings, surrounded by a ditch (see page 3). It has a commanding position, and before the introduction of fire-arms must have been of great strength. Even now the solid masonry of the lower portion would resist for some time any artillery that could be brought against it.

The Tower of David (see page 5) appears to be the oldest portion of the Citadel, and its dimensions and mode of construction agree well with those of the tower Phasaelus as described by Josephus. The substructure consists of a solid masonry escarp, rising from the bottom of the ditch at an angle of about forty-five degrees, with a pathway, or *chemin des rondes,* round the top. Above this the tower rises in a solid mass for a height of twenty-nine feet, and then comes the superstructure. The escarp retains to some extent its original appearance, but time and hard treatment have worn away much of the finer work, and the repairs have been executed in the usual slovenly manner of the Turks. The old work, where it can be

THE MOUNT OF OLIVES.
From a house-top at the south-west corner of the Pool of Hezekiah, looking eastward.

seen, is equal, if not superior, to the best specimens of masonry in the far-famed wall of the Temple Platform; the faces of the stones are dressed with an astonishing degree of fineness, and the whole, when perfect, must have presented a smooth surface difficult to escalade, and, from the solidity of the mass, unassailable by the battering ram. The masonry of the solid tower is rougher; the faces of the stones project, and they are pitted with a number of deep square holes which have long

THE SOUTHERN SLOPES OF OLIVET AND THE MOUNTAINS OF MOAB.
From the same spot, overlooking David Street, crowded with people; the large domed quadrangle on the right is the Synagogue of the Ashkenazim Jews.

puzzled the antiquary. The superstructure contains several chambers, and a cistern for the collection of rain-water. In one of the rooms a "mihrab" marks the place where, according to Moslem tradition, David composed the Psalms, and another chamber is pointed out as the reception room of the same king. The Tower of David was the last place to yield when Jerusalem was captured by the

Crusaders; and when the city walls were destroyed by the Moslems in the thirteenth century, it was for some reason—probably its solidity—spared, to come down to our own time as a fine example of the mural masonry of the Jews.

The remaining towers of the Citadel have suffered far more severely, from the battering

THE ZION GATE, OR GATE OF THE PROPHET DAVID.
In the foreground, outside the Gate, are a group of Bethlehemites and a water-carrier.

they have undergone during numerous sieges, and without extensive excavation it would be impossible to determine their original form. The tower, however, which guards the Jaffa Gate, though its dimensions are somewhat smaller than those given by Josephus, is satisfactorily identified with the tower of Hippicus by the discovery of an aqueduct twelve feet below the level of the present conduit, which is probably that by which, according to the Jewish historian, water was brought into that building.

Within the Citadel there is ruin and rubbish everywhere; without, in the moat, soldiers' gardens, beds of cactus or prickly pear, and filth of every possible description; and on the ramparts a few old cannon, much dreaded by the artillerymen who have to fire them. The view from the top of David's Tower is extensive, embracing the whole town, the Mount of Olives, the Dead Sea, and the Mountains of Moab—a pleasant sight to feast the eyes upon for half an hour before the sun goes down.

In front of the Tower of David is the residence of the late Bishop Gobat, whose stalwart

THE TOMB OF DAVID.
The whole group of buildings is called Neby Daûd, which signifies the Sanctuary of the Sepulchre of the Prophet David.

form and kind, homely manner will not soon be forgotten. Not far from it, opposite the Citadel, on the east side, of Armenian Street, which leads to the Zion Gate, is Christ Church, the English Protestant church. The foundation stone of this church was laid in 1842 by Bishop Alexander, a Jewish proselyte, who in the previous year had been consecrated first bishop of the United Church of England and Ireland in Jerusalem. The church owes its existence to the efforts of the English Society for Promoting Christianity among the Jews, which has had resident missionaries in the city since 1824.

Proceeding southward along Armenian Street, we have on the right the fine gardens of the Armenian Monastery, and on the left the monastery itself, and the Church of St. James. The monastery is the largest and most comfortable building of its class in Jerusalem, and has, attached to it, schools and dormitories for the accommodation of students preparing themselves for the priesthood, and also an extensive range of buildings capable of containing three thousand pilgrims. It was founded by the Georgians as early as the eleventh century, but when their fortunes declined and they were unable to satisfy the claims made upon them by the Turks, it was sold by them to the Armenians in the fifteenth century. The Georgians attached as a condition to the sale that the monastery should be restored to them when they were again able to support it; and upon this condition the Greek Church has based a claim to the buildings, which may some day swell into one of those quarrels respecting the holy places which have led to such serious consequences. The refectory or dining-hall of the monastery retains much of its old character—a step divides the patriarch and bishops from the rest of the clergy; the tables are fine slabs of white marble; the pavement is of what is known as "Santa Croce" marble; there is some pretty inlaid work; and on the walls, amidst much that is modern, are some fine old porcelain tiles.

The Church of St. James is, with the exception of that of the Holy Sepulchre, the largest within the city, and is the richest in gilding, decoration, and pictures. On the north side of the church is a chapel dedicated to St. Stephen, in which is preserved the font used on the occasion of the baptism of the first Jew converted to Christianity. The walls of the church and its chapels are covered with porcelain tiles of comparatively modern date and of inferior pattern.

A short distance beyond the monastery is the Zion Gate, or the Gate of the Prophet David, Bab en Neby Daûd (see page 10), leading out to the group of buildings called Neby Daud, which stand on the waste portion of the modern Mount Zion (see page 11). The gate itself dates from the reconstruction of the walls by Suleiman in 1539—42 A.D. Close to the Zion Gate is an Armenian monastery called the House of Caiaphas, in which are shown the prison of Our Lord and the stone that once closed the Holy Sepulchre. In the quadrangle of the monastery are the tombs of the Armenian patriarchs of Jerusalem. A short distance beyond are the "cœnaculum," or chamber of the Last Supper, and the Tomb of David, contained in one building. The tomb, or cenotaph shown as such, occupies the eastern end of a chamber which appears to have been the crypt of an old church erected during the Frank kingdom of Jerusalem, probably that called the Church of St. Mary.

We must now return to the market-place in front of the Jaffa Gate, and, proceeding for a short distance eastward down David Street, turn to the left into the street of the Christians to gain the Church of the Holy Sepulchre. Passing along this last street, we have, at first, on the left the large reservoir known as Hezekiah's Pool, and on the right the Greek Church and Monastery of St. John the Baptist. Hezekiah's Pool, or, as it is called by the people, "The Pool of the Patriarch's Bath," is an open tank surrounded by houses, which is supplied with

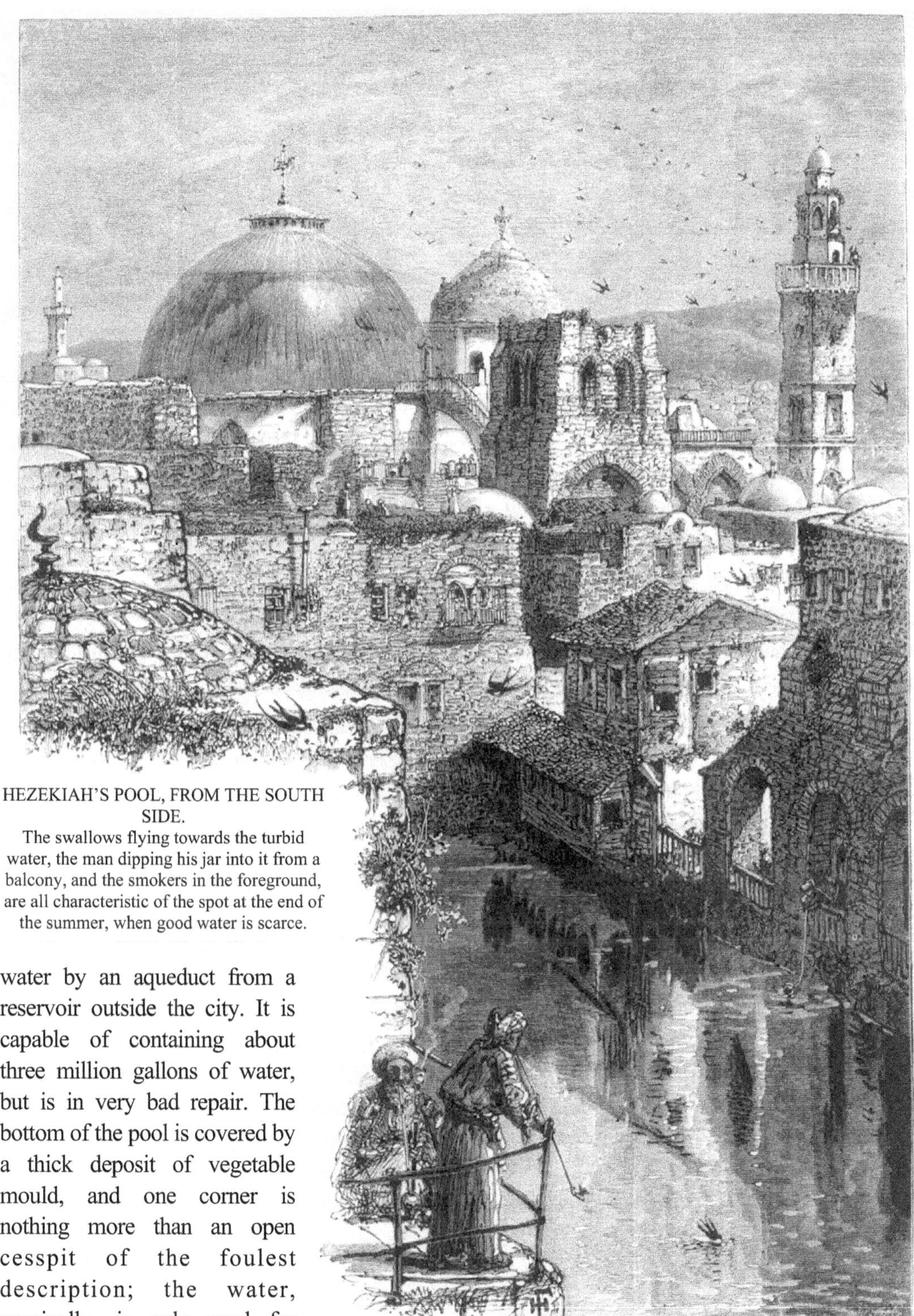

HEZEKIAH'S POOL, FROM THE SOUTH SIDE.
The swallows flying towards the turbid water, the man dipping his jar into it from a balcony, and the smokers in the foreground, are all characteristic of the spot at the end of the summer, when good water is scarce.

water by an aqueduct from a reservoir outside the city. It is capable of containing about three million gallons of water, but is in very bad repair. The bottom of the pool is covered by a thick deposit of vegetable mould, and one corner is nothing more than an open cesspit of the foulest description; the water, nominally, is only used for washing purposes, but the poorer classes often draw it for drinking during summer, and hence arises much fever and sickness. The Church of St. John the Baptist, or " Forerunner," has been built above a much older church, which is half-filled with rubbish, but in a good state of preservation. The floor of this old church is twenty-five feet below the present level of the "Street of the Christians"—a good proof of the great accumulation of rubbish in this part of the city. At Easter time Christian Street is thronged with pilgrims passing to and fro, or making purchases at the numerous shops, and presents an appearance of life and animation which it is far from possessing during the autumn and winter months. On the left-hand side of the street, near the Church of the Holy Sepulchre, is the great Greek Monastery, celebrated for the library and manuscripts which it contains. Five churches—of which the oldest is that of St. Thecla—are included in the monastery, and there is considerable accommodation for the monks and for pilgrims who visit Jerusalem. On the right-hand side of the street a narrow passage and flight of steps lead down to the courtyard in front of the entrance to the Church of the Holy Sepulchre (see page 16). The open court is the favourite resort of pedlars from Bethlehem, who expose their wares for sale on the pavement, and drive a thriving trade in rosaries, mother-of-pearl ornaments, olive-wood trinkets, and other small articles, which the pilgrims purchase as mementoes of their visit to the Holy City.

A discussion of the many difficult questions connected with the site of the Holy Sepulchre would be beyond the scope of the present work; it will be sufficient here to state briefly the nature of the theories which have been advanced, and to give a slight sketch of the history of the church. The three principal theories are:—First, that the Sepulchre of our Lord was beneath the Sakhra "Rock," in the Haram esh Sherif, and that the noble building above it, the "Dome of the Rock," is the Church of the Resurrection erected by the Emperor Constantine in the fourth century. According to this theory, of which Mr. James Fergusson is the well-known author and able exponent, the tradition relating to the site of the sepulchre was transferred to the present tomb in the eleventh century. Second, that the Church of the Holy Sepulchre occupies the ground once covered by the churches of Constantine, and that it contains within its walls the tomb of Christ. Third, that the true sepulchre was to the north of the city without the present walls, and was never found, but that the present "Holy Sepulchre" is the tomb "miraculously discovered" by Constantine, and that over which he built his church.

The first question that arises is whether Constantine really found the "new sepulchre wherein was never man yet laid," which Joseph of Arimathaea "had hewn out in the rock" in his own garden. What is historically certain is that Constantine erected on the "discovered ground" a magnificent group of buildings, which were completed and dedicated in 335 A.D.

In 614 A.D., when the Persians captured Jerusalem, the Great Basilica, or Martyrion, was wholly or partially destroyed by fire, but it was rebuilt about 626 A.D. by Modestus, Superior of the Monastery of Theodosius. The buildings, which are fully described by a French bishop, Arculf, who saw them about 700 A.D., then consisted of the Anastasis, or Church of the Resurrection which contained the Holy Sepulchre; the Basilica, or Martyrion, a five-aisled building with a circular apse and an opening towards the east; the square Church of St. Mary; and a very large church on the east of the sepulchre, called the Church of Golgotha.

In 936, and again in 969, when the Fatimite Caliphs gained possession of the city, portions of the churches were damaged by fire; and in 1010 they were partially destroyed by El Hakim, the third Fatimite Caliph. This wild fanatic commenced a systematic persecution of the Christians, drove them from their churches, and even attempted to destroy the Holy Sepulchre. About the middle of the eleventh century the Christians began to return to Jerusalem (1048 A.D.) and commenced the rebuilding of the churches; and it is to this period that Mr. Fergusson ascribes the transference of the site of the Holy Sepulchre from the Sakhra in the Haram esh Sherif to its present position. During the last half of the eleventh century Jerusalem fell under Turkish rule, and the Christians were much oppressed; they were robbed and maltreated even whilst worshipping in their churches, and the pilgrims had to submit to every species of insult. Among those who suffered was Peter the Hermit, whose burning eloquence on his return to Europe roused the indignation of Western Christendom and brought about the First Crusade. On the 15th July, 1099, the Crusaders captured Jerusalem, and, after putting to death most of the Turkish population, entered the Church of the Holy Sepulchre barefooted and singing hymns of praise. They soon, however, found the building too insignificant, and commenced to remodel it and add new shrines. An English monk named Saewulf, who made a pilgrimage to Jerusalem about 1103, has left an account of the buildings as they then existed, and a description of the numerous "Holy Places," many of which have been handed down by tradition to the present day. When Saladin took the city in 1187, and also in 1244, when the Christians were finally driven from Jerusalem, the church and the sepulchre were injured, but with these exceptions the buildings remained nearly in the state in which the Crusaders left them until the great fire of 1808. The church, except the eastern portion, was almost entirely destroyed; the dome fell in, crushing the Chapel of the Holy Sepulchre; the marble columns of the Rotunda were cracked and calcined; images, altars, pictures, were consumed in the general conflagration; and there was a mass of ruin from the Chapel of Helena to the rock-hewn tomb of Joseph of Arimathaea.

In the intrigues which followed at Jerusalem and Constantinople in connection with the rebuilding of the church, the Greeks secured for themselves the greater portion of the buildings, and during the execution of the repairs two noble monuments of the Latin or Frank kingdom, the tombs of Godfrey de Bouillon and his brother Baldwin, disappeared. The work was completed and the renovated church consecrated in 1810, a certain Greek, Commenos by name, being architect.

The only entrance to the church at present is on the south side, from the open court or quadrangle which has been alluded to above. South of the court is the Greek Monastery of Gethsemane, occupying the site of the residence of the Grand Master of the Knights of

ENTRANCE TO THE CHURCH OF THE HOLY SEPULCHRE.
Pilgrims buying rosaries and other relics in the forecourt.

St. John; in front of this building are the bases of three columns, probably the remains of some porch or screen. On the east side are the Greek Monastery of Abraham, containing a small chapel in which is shown the spot, close to Golgotha, where Abraham was on the point of

THE SHRINE OF THE HOLY SEPULCHRE.
The enormous candles at the entrance are only lighted on important festivals.

sacrificing Isaac; the Armenian Church of St. John; and the Coptic Chapel of the Angel St. Michael, whence a passage leads to the Coptic Monastery. On the west side are the Chapel of St. James, the brother of our Lord; the Chapel of the "Forty Martyrs," or of the "Ointment Bearers"—originally the Chapel of the Trinity—where all marriages and baptisms were conducted, and which contains a very beautiful font; and the Chapel of St. John, in the basement story of the great tower. The façade of the church occupies the entire northern side of the court. There are two doorways, one open and one closed by the masonry of the Chapel of Calvary, and above each door is a window. The whole dates from the twelfth century, and forms part of the work of the Crusaders when they remodelled the church. Some of the ornamentation is very similar to that which may be seen in many churches in Normandy at the present day, and a bas-relief over one of the doors, representing with much spirit the entrance of Christ into Jerusalem, is supposed to have been executed in France. The string courses above the doors and windows are partly made up of blocks of stone belonging to a very beautiful cornice of classical design, almost identical with that of the cornice of the Golden Gate in the east wall above the Haram esh Sherif. At the north-east corner of the court is a small chapel dedicated to St. Mary of Egypt. Above this chapel is another called the Chapel of the Agony, which is adjacent to Mount Calvary, and belongs to the Latins. In the north-east corner of the court is the fine Campanile or Bell Tower, projecting from the facade, and once standing free, but now incorporated with the church. The tower was erected towards the close of the Latin occupation of Jerusalem, about 1170, and as late as 1678, consisted of five stories. There are at present only three stories, so that the striking effect which must have been produced by the tower when it was in its original state is quite lost.

On entering the church we pass at once into the south transept of the Church of the Crusaders, which, in consequence of the changes made in 1808, has now the appearance of a vestibule. Here, on the left-hand side, some members of the Moslem family which has charge of the keys will always be found seated when the church is open; and the visitor has directly in front of him the "Stone of Unction," which is said to mark the spot on which our Lord's body was laid when it was anointed after having been taken down from the cross. The stone, a large slab of limestone, is raised a few inches above the level of the floor, and is said to have been placed in its present position when the church was rebuilt. A few paces to the left of the stone is the spot where the Virgin Mary and the other women stood when the body of Christ was anointed, and beyond it lies the Rotunda, which is sixty-seven feet in diameter. The Rotunda formerly had twelve large columns which supported the dome, but there are now eighteen piers which carry a clerestory and a dome open at the top. A vaulted aisle with three apses, now walled up and divided into chambers, runs round the western half of the Rotunda.

In the centre is the Shrine of the Holy Sepulchre (see page 17), built, in the very worst taste, of the ruddy coloured limestone known at Jerusalem as "Santa Croce" marble. The building is about twenty-six feet long and eighteen feet wide. Its western end is polygonal in shape, its eastern, square; and the interior is divided into two chapels, one on the east, known as the Chapel of the Angels, the other containing the Sepulchre of Christ. In front of the

THE CHAPEL OF HELENA, CHURCH OF THE HOLY SEPULCHRE.
Showing the entrance to the Cave of the Cross.

entrance to the Chapel of the Angels are gigantic wax candles, only lighted on certain solemn occasions, and here the pilgrims take off their shoes before venturing to tread on the holy ground within. On either side of the entrance are two holes in the wall through which the "Holy Fire" is given out at the Greek Easter; and in the centre of the chapel itself, encased in marble and resting on a pedestal, is a portion of the stone that was rolled away from the mouth of the Sepulchre. At the western end of the antechamber is a low doorway, the mouth of the tomb, over which is a bas-relief representing the figure of our Lord rising from the grave, with the angel seated on the right-hand side, and the two Marys bringing incense and spices for the anointment on the left. The tomb chamber is entirely lined with marble, and from its roof hang forty-three lamps, of which thirteen belong to the Latins, thirteen to the Greeks, thirteen to the Armenians, and four to the Copts. These lamps are kept burning day and night. The tomb is a raised bench two feet high, six feet four inches long, and three feet wide, covered by a marble slab which has a groove cut transversely across the centre. Above the tomb are three bas-reliefs in white marble representing the resurrection.

A small chapel belonging to the Copts is attached to the western end of the shrine of the Holy Sepulchre, and nearly opposite to it a door leads from the Rotunda to the Chapel of the Syrians, and thence to the chamber which contains the tombs of Joseph and Nicodemus. The tombs are of the kind known as "kokim" (deep horizontal recesses), and there can be no reasonable doubt that the chamber is an ancient Jewish sepulchre containing, when perfect, six "kokim" for the reception of bodies. This would at first sight seem to indicate that the ground upon which the church is built lay without the walls of the ancient city; but we know that some of the kings were buried in Jerusalem, and it is doubtful to what extent the Jews, before the Captivity, buried their dead outside the walls. At the time of the Roman siege one tomb at least lay within the walls, for it is referred to by Josephus as a well-known object.

North of the shrine of the Holy Sepulchre the spot is pointed out where our Lord appeared to Mary Magdalene as a gardener, and a little beyond it is the Latin Chapel of the Apparition, which commemorates the appearance of Christ to his mother after the Resurrection. Behind the chapel is the Monastery of the Franciscans who live within the church, and in the adjacent sacristy are kept the sword and spurs of Godfrey de Bouillon.

Directly east of the Sepulchre is the large Greek church, which occupies the site of the church of the Crusaders, destroyed by fire in 1808. It is profusely decorated, and contains a broken column said to mark the centre or navel of the earth. The church is separated from the aisles that surround it by a partition wall, through which a door leads to the two Greek chapels of the "Prison" and the "Bonds" of Christ. This portion of the church appears to have been little damaged by the fire. Passing along the north aisle, the first chapel belongs to the Greeks, and is dedicated to Longinus, the soldier who pierced Jesus' side with a spear; beyond this is a closed doorway, which once formed the eastern entrance to the church; and then the Armenian Chapel of the "Parting of the Vestments;" still further, at the east end of the south aisle, is the Greek Chapel of the "Crowning with Thorns," which contains the

THE CHAPEL IN THE CAVE OF THE CROSS.
Called "The Chapel of the Invention (i.e. the finding) of the Cross."

"Column of the Derision," a fragment of a granite column on which Christ is said to have sat when he was crowned with thorns and mocked by those that stood near. In the same chapel is also kept a crown of thorns, made from the species of shrub which is supposed by tradition to have been that which supplied the original crown. Between the two last-mentioned chapels a

PILGRIMS OF THE GREEK CHURCH BUYING CANDLES.
To be lighted by the " Holy Fire" in the Church of the Holy Sepulchre, at the celebration of the Easter Festival.

flight of steps leads down from the east aisle to the Chapel of Helena, a portion of the church which does not seem to have suffered during the fire (see page 19). The chapel is divided into three aisles by four stunted columns with heavy-looking capitals, which carry a dome that rises above the level of the courtyard of the Abyssinian Monastery, and gives light to the chapel below. There are two apses containing altars dedicated respectively to St. Helena and the Penitent Thief. The position of the third apse is occupied by an opening through which a flight of steps leads down to the Chapel of the Invention of the Cross (see page 21). In the Chapel of St. Helena the place is pointed out where the Empress sat whilst the workmen were searching for the cross in the cave below, which appears to have been either an old cistern or a natural cavern artificially enlarged. It now contains an altar and a life-size statue of the Empress. According to tradition, the search instituted by the Empress Helena led to the discovery of the three crosses; but, unfortunately, the tablet bearing the inscription had become detached, and it was at first impossible to distinguish the cross upon which our Saviour died. This difficulty was overcome by taking the three crosses to a noble lady of Jerusalem who was afflicted with an incurable illness; the crosses of the thieves had no effect, but on being touched with the true cross her disease left her, and she sprang from her couch whole and well.

Not far from the entrance to the church, and close to the "Stone of Unction," is the Chapel of Adam. Here Adam, and also Melchizedek, are supposed to have been buried. At the entrance to the chapel once stood the tombs of Godfrey and Baldwin; and at its eastern end may be seen the rock of Calvary, with the rent made in it by the earthquake at the time of the Crucifixion. Doubts have frequently been raised with respect to the genuine character of the rock of Calvary, and it has even been stated that it was built up with blocks of granite; but there can hardly be a doubt that the greater portion, if not the whole, is natural rock, the same limestone that is seen at the tombs of Joseph and Nicodemus, and in other places in the church. The floor of the Chapel of the "Exaltation of the Cross" is fifteen feet above that of the Rotunda, and here is shown the summit of Calvary and the hole in which the cross is said to have been placed. By the side of this chapel and on the same level, being supported by vaults, is the Latin Chapel of the Crucifixion, erected where Christ, according to tradition, was nailed to the cross.

No description of the Church of the Holy Sepulchre would be complete without some notice of the ceremony of the "Holy Fire," which, to the disgrace of Eastern Christianity, is enacted at the present day, and we cannot do better than quote the graphic words of Dean Stanley: "The Chapel of the Sepulchre rises from a dense mass of pilgrims, who sit or stand wedged round it; whilst round them, and between another equally dense mass, which goes round the walls of the church itself, a lane is formed by two lines, or rather two circles, of Turkish soldiers stationed to keep order. For the spectacle which is about to take place, nothing can be better suited than the form of the Rotunda, giving galleries above for the spectators and an open space below for the pilgrims and their festival. For the next two hours everything is tranquil. Nothing indicates what is coming, except that two or three pilgrims who have got close to the aperture keep their hands fixed in it with a clench never relaxed. It is about noon that this circular lane is suddenly broken through by a tangled group rushing violently round till they are caught by one of the Turkish soldiers. It seems

VIA DOLOROSA —THE ECCE HOMO ARCH.

to be the belief of the Arab Greeks that unless they run round the Sepulchre a certain number of times the fire will not come. Possibly, also, there is some reminiscence of the funeral games and races round the tomb of an ancient chief. Accordingly the night before, and from this time forward for two hours, a succession of gambols takes place, which an Englishman can only compare to a mixture of prisoner's base, football, and leap-frog, round and round the Holy Sepulchre. First he sees these tangled masses of twenty, thirty, fifty men, starting in a run, catching hold of each other, lifting one of themselves on their shoulders, sometimes on their heads, and rushing on with him till he leaps off, and some one else succeeds; some of them dressed in sheep-skins, some almost naked, one usually preceding the rest as a fugleman, clapping his hands, to which they respond in like manner, adding also wild howls, of which the chief burden is 'This is the tomb of Jesus Christ! God save the Sultan!—Jesus Christ has redeemed us!' What begins in the lesser groups soon grows in magnitude and extent, till at last the whole of the circle between the troops is continually occupied by race, a whirl, a torrent of these wild figures, like the witches' Sabbath in

'Faust,' wheeling round the Sepulchre. Gradually the frenzy subsides or is checked, the course is cleared, and out of the Greek Church on the east of the Rotunda a long procession with

HOUSE OF SAINT VERONICA, IN THE VIA DOLOROSA.
The peasant walking up the street, wearing an embroidered abai, or cloak made of goats' hair, is carrying a plough. On the right sits a seller of fruit under an awning made of his cloak.

embroidered banners, supplying in their ritual the want of images, begins to defile round the Sepulchre.

"From this moment the excitement, which has been before confined to the runners and dancers, becomes universal. Hedged in by soldiers, the two huge masses of pilgrims still remain in their places, all joining, however, in a wild succession of yells, through which are caught from time to time, strangely, almost affectingly, mingled, the chants of the procession— the solemn chants of the Church of Basil and Chrysostom mingled with the yells of savages. Thrice the procession passes round; at the third time the two lines of Turkish

THE HOUSES OF THE RICH AND POOR MAN, DIVES AND LAZARUS.
This is the most picturesque group of buildings in the Via Dolorosa. In the foreground are a Bedouin mounted on a camel laden with forage, and an Ashkenazi Jew conversing with a water-seller.

soldiers join and fall in behind. One great movement sways the multitude from side to side. The crisis of the day is now approaching. The presence of the Turks is believed to prevent the descent of fire, and at this point it is that they are driven, or consent to be driven, out of the Church. In a moment the confusion as of a battle and a victory pervades the Church. In every direction the raging mob bursts in upon the troops, who pour out of the Church at the south-east corner. The procession is broken through, the banners stagger and waver. They stagger, and waver, and fall, amidst the flight of priests, bishops, and standard-bearers hither and thither before the tremendous rush. In one small but compact band the Bishop of Petra (who is on this occasion the Bishop of 'the Fire,' the representative of the patriarch) is hurried to the Chapel of the Sepulchre, and the door is closed behind him. The whole church is now one heaving sea of heads. One vacant spot alone is left—a narrow lane from the aperture

A SHOEMAKER'S SHOP, JERUSALEM.
Jewish shoemakers at work.

on the north side of the chapel to the wall of the church. By the aperture itself stands a priest to catch the fire; on each side of the lane hundreds of bare arms are stretched out like the branches of a leafless forest—like the branches of a forest quivering in some violent tempest . . . .

"At last the moment comes. A bright flame as of burning wood appears inside the hole—the light, as every educated Greek knows and acknowledges, kindled by the bishop within—the light, as every pilgrim believes, of the descent of God himself upon the Holy Tomb. Any distinct feature or incident is lost in the universal whirl of excitement which envelops the church as slowly, gradually, the fire spreads from hand to hand, from taper to taper, through that vast multitude, till at last the whole edifice, from gallery to gallery and through the area below, is one wide blaze of thousands of burning candles. It is now that, according to some accounts, the bishop or patriarch is carried out of the chapel in triumph, on the shoulders of the people, in a fainting state, 'to give the impression that he is overcome by the glory of the Almighty, from whose immediate presence he is supposed to come.' It is now that the great rush to escape from the rolling smoke and suffocating heat, and to carry the lighted tapers into the streets and houses of Jerusalem, through the one entrance to the church, leads at times to the violent pressure which in 1834 cost the lives of hundreds. For a short time the pilgrims run to and fro, rubbing the fire against their faces and breasts to attest its supposed harmlessness. But the wild enthusiasm terminates from the moment that the fire is communicated; and perhaps not the least extraordinary part of the spectacle is the rapid and total subsidence of a frenzy so intense—the contrast of the furious agitation of the area of the Rotunda, the Chapels of Copt and Syrian, the subterranean Church of Helena, the great nave of Constantine's basilica, the stairs and platform of Calvary itself, with the many churches above—every part, except the one Chapel of the Latin Church, filled and overlaid by one mass of pilgrims, wrapt in deep sleep and waiting for the midnight service.

"Such is the Greek Easter—the greatest moral argument against the identity of the spot which it professes to honour—stripped, indeed, of some of its most revolting features, yet still, considering the place, the time, and the intention of the professed miracle, probably the most offensive imposture to be found in the world.

Intimately connected with those historical and legendary events, that have found a local habitation within the walls of the Church of the Holy Sepulchre, are the traditions which during the course of centuries have clustered round certain spots in the narrow, crooked streets that lead from the Turkish Barracks, north of the Haram esh Sherif, to the church—the stations of the Via Dolorosa. The course of the Via Dolorosa depends on the site of the Praetorium, or residence of Pilate, and this has never been satisfactorily ascertained. At one period the Praetorium was supposed to have stood on the eastern hill, Moriah; at another on the western, the modern Sion; and it was not till the close of the crusading period that its present position was assigned to it, and the first station of the Via Dolorosa was located in the above-mentioned Turkish Barracks (see page 30). The second station is in the street below, where, at the foot of the Scala Santa, which led to the Judgment Hall, the cross was laid upon Christ. A few paces westward the street is spanned by the Ecce Homo Arch (see page 24), which marks the spot where Pilate brought Jesus forth "wearing the crown of thorns and the purple robe," and presented Him to the multitude with the memorable words, "Behold the man!" (John xix. 5). The arch has all the appearance of a Roman triumphal arch of the time of Hadrian. It consists of a large central arch, with a smaller one on the north side which has been included in and forms the eastern termination of the Church of the Convent of the Sisters of Sion. Following the street downwards to the valley the third station is reached, a broken column near the Austrian Hospice which indicates the place where Christ fell under the cross. A little lower down is the house of Lazarus (see page 26), and the fourth station, where Christ met the Virgin Mary; and then follow the house of Dives, with its handsome doorway, and the fifth station, where our Lord having fallen for the second time, Simon of Cyrene took up the cross. A short ascent leads to the house of St. Veronica, the sixth station (see page 25). The road now ascends to the street which connects the Bazaars with the Damascus Gate, and here at the crossing is shown the seventh station, the so-called "Porta Judiciaria." The eighth station, where Christ addressed the women who accompanied him with the words, "Daughters of Jerusalem, weep not for me," is at the Monastery of St. Caralombos; the ninth station, where He fell for the third time, is in front of the Coptic Convent; the tenth, within the church, marks the spot where He was undressed; the eleventh where He was nailed to the cross; the twelfth where the cross was raised; the thirteenth where He was taken down from the cross; and the fourteenth the Sepulchre itself. It is, perhaps, needless to add that the buildings along the Via Dolorosa are modern, and that the "stations" themselves have been moved from place to place in the city whenever necessity or convenience required their removal.

Not far from the entrance to the Church of the Holy Sepulchre is the old gateway which formerly led into the pile of buildings belonging to the Knights of St. John, and which now, surmounted by the Prussian eagle, gives access to the ground presented by the Sultan to Prussia on the occasion of the visit of the Crown Prince to Jerusalem in 1869. The arch is semicircular, and when perfect must have been a beautiful specimen of twelfth-century work. Round the arch is a series of figures in stone, now much mutilated, but once representing the months. February is indicated by a man pruning, July by a reaper, August by a thresher, September by a grape-gatherer, &c. In the centre are the sun and moon—"Sol" a half figure holding a disc on high, Luna" a female with a crescent. Above the arch is a cornice enriched with figures of lions and other animals, carved with great spirit, apparently by the same man who cut those in the cornice above the Chapel of the Egyptian Mary, near the door of the Church of the Holy Sepulchre. In the close vicinity of the arch is the minaret of the Mosque of Omar (see page 35), erected 1417 A.D., and supposed to mark the place where Omar prayed when he entered Jerusalem after its capitulation. The mosque occupies the site of the

MASJED EL MAJAHIDIN—MOSQUE OF THE KNIGHTS OF THE CRESCENT.
Turkish Barracks, commonly called the Tower of Antonia. The cactus and caper-bush growing on the wall on the right are especially characteristic of mural vegetation in Jerusalem.

Kubbet Dirka, built by a nephew of Saladin in the thirteenth century. Extensive excavations have been made by the German Government in the old home of the Hospitallers. The church dedicated to the Virgin Mary, known as Maria Latina, the monastery of the same name, and portions of the Hospice of the Knights of St. John, have been cleansed of the rubbish and filth which encumbered them, and much of interest has been brought to light. The south wall has a staircase attached to it which gives access to the cloisters, and to the old refectory recently fitted up as a German Protestant Chapel at the private cost of the German Emperor. The other buildings are being repaired or rebuilt as schools and other establishments for the use of the German community at Jerusalem, and the Church of Maria Latina is to be restored in the original style.

From the Bazaars, which lie immediately east of the old Hospice of the Knights of St. John, a street runs directly to the Bab el Amud (Gate of the Column), commonly known as the Damascus Gate (see page 41). This, the most picturesque of the city gateways, through which passes the great road to Nablus and Damascus, is the work of Sultan Suleiman, and dates from the sixteenth century. The gateway which preceded it was known in the twelfth century as that of St. Stephen, from the Church of St. Stephen, which then stood a few yards distant without the walls, on the place where the first Christian martyr is supposed to have been stoned. The scene of St. Stephen's martyrdom is now shown on the east side of the city without the present St. Stephen's Gate. The Damascus Gate is built over an older gateway, possibly as old as the time of Hadrian, which can just be seen rising above the rubbish. Flanking the gate are two towers built with stones taken from the ancient walls, and perhaps resting on the foundations of the older walls of the city.

*The Bazaars stretch southwards from the Church of Maria Latina to David Street. They are not remarkable for architectural beauty or for the value of the wares offered for sale, but in the early morning they are filled with a busy throng amidst which representatives of almost every nationality may be found. This is especially the case at Easter, when the population of Jerusalem is for two or three weeks apparently doubled by the presence of thousands of pilgrims, Christians and Moslems. For at this season Moslem devotees come from all parts of the Turkish Empire and even from India to pray within the sacred enclosure on Mount Moriah, the Haram esh Sherif, and to visit the reputed Tomb of Moses at the north-west of the Dead Sea. Probably this pilgrimage was instituted to counterbalance the great influx of Christians, especially of the Greek and Oriental Churches, who come from all parts of Russia and Greece and from remote Turkish provinces, to attend the Easter services in the Church of the Holy Sepulchre (see page 22) and to bathe in the river Jordan. This is the harvest time for the people of Jerusalem. Not only is every khan, convent, and hotel crowded, but tents are pitched outside the walls, while in all available open spaces within the city the poorer pilgrims make themselves at home, cooking their simple food in the open air and resting at night under the stars. Men, women, and children, wrapped in their

* The following pages (to page 37), describing the Bazaars and Markets of Jerusalem, are contributed by Miss Mary Eliza Rogers.

travelling rugs, crowd together in family groups till they are hardly distinguishable from their baggage.

A favourite site for a bivouac is the open space just within the Jaffa Gate; but pilgrims and wayfarers who select this spot must move at a very early hour in the morning, to make

A GROCER'S SHOP, JERUSALEM.
Two peasant women seated in the foreground, and a man of Silwan (Siloam) carrying a patched goat's skin filled with water from Job's well.

way for the peasants who come from the neighbouring villages with daily supplies of fruit, vegetables, and poultry for Jerusalem. This open space probably represents the "marketplace" mentioned by Josephus as being situated on the western hill, prior to the capture of the city by the Romans; and here the wholesale fruit and vegetable market is now held every day soon after sunrise. Dusky women of Bethany and Siloam, in long blue or white gowns, with bright-coloured kerchiefs tied round their heads, bring large baskets full of cucumbers, tomatoes and onions, and other garden produce, while from more distant villages, especially Bethlehem and Artas, troops of donkeys come laden with enormous cauliflowers and turnips, guided by boys in white shirts girdled with broad red leather belts. The pleasant-looking

A STREET CAFÉ, JERUSALEM.
A Bedouin and peasant playing at a game called dámeh.

Bethlehem women, wearing crimson and yellow striped or blue gowns with long white linen veils, carry on their heads baskets of grapes, figs, prickly pears, pomegranates, and apricots, or whatever fruit is in season. Sometimes this market-place is almost blocked up with piles of melons, or with oranges and lemons from Jaffa, and in the early summer time roses are sold here by weight to the makers of conserves and attar of roses. Hotel-keepers and servants from the various convents come here to make their bargains, and turbaned greengrocers and itinerant vendors of fruit come to buy their stock for the day. Soon the place is crowded, and the bustle of buying and selling begins. No purchase is effected without a considerable amount of contention. The seller does not usually price the goods, but waits for an offer. The first offer is always absurdly low. The seller then names an exorbitantly high price. For instance, a dignified-looking shopkeeper, wearing a white turban, will offer three piastres for a large basket full of tomatoes. The girl in charge answers indignantly, "I will carry my tomatoes back to Siloam rather than take less than fifteen!" — "O thou most greedy of the greedy, I will give no more than six!" — "O possessor of a tightly closed hand, I will not take less than twelve! How shall I buy the rice for my mother if I give away the fruits of her garden?" Finally she obtains seven and a half piastres for her tomatoes, and goes away perfectly satisfied, having argued with pertinacity for the half piastre.

In an hour or two the market people disperse, and only a few retail sellers of fruit or of rude pottery remain. The illustration on page 1 gives an excellent idea of this place as it appears during the midday hours.

As soon as the market is over the crowds increase in the bazaars. The narrow bazaar, of which a bird's-eye glimpse is shown on page 9, is called David Street. It opens into the market-place, and is paved with shallow steps as smooth as polished marble, descending towards the east, and generally littered with vegetable refuse. The shops on each side of the way are like large cupboards raised one or two feet from the ground. Within these recesses the shopkeepers sit at their ease gravely smoking in the midst of their wares. Damascus and Aleppo silks, Manchester prints and calicoes, Constantinople and Swiss muslin coloured veils, are displayed, and farther on pipes and hardware and dried fruits may be found. To the right are the bazaars leading to the Jewish quarter, and here most of the busiest workers congregate—tailors, embroiderers, tinsmiths, and shoemakers. The engraving on page 27 gives a good idea of a shoemaker's shop in one of the most narrow but busy bazaars in the city. It is close to an old archway overgrown with cactus and henbane. Two men are engaged at work. The wearer of the earrings, the master, is seated at a bench formed of a solid block of wood, and is vigorously using his mallet to beat into solidity a piece of leather for the sole of a shoe, while from the bowl of the neglected narghileh at his side a long curling column of smoke rises towards the dilapidated roof, and a lesser column issues from the mouthpiece which rests on the edge of the stall. The poor old shortsighted assistant squatting on the floor, and making a bench of his left leg, is patiently plying his awl and his waxed thread. The interior of the shop is fitted up with rude shelves, on which are ranged in rows heavy red shoes with pointed and turned-up toes and a few clumsy-looking lasts. Outside, on the large smooth round stones (which give a fair example of the usual kind of pavement on level ground in Jerusalem), may be seen the shoes of the occupants of the shop, two water-coolers of native pottery, and a roll of leather soaking in a bowl of water.

It must not be supposed that this is the best shoemaker's shop to be found in the city. There is one not far off where rows of large red boots, the pride of the Bedouin chieftain, and red slippers and shoes of all sizes, may be found, and another in which may be purchased delicately made Damascus socks of yellow kid, like boots, to be worn by ladies under their yellow shoes. It is one of the greatest delights of a peasant to put on a pair of new shoes, and

ENTRANCE TO THE HOSPICE OF ST. JOHN AND MINARET OF OMAR.
A muezzin in the balcony chanting the call to prayer. Peasants loading a camel in the foreground, and a townswoman wearing a white izzar and dark veil in the distance.

especially to see all his family newly shod for a fête day. In the same neighbourhood the cotton-cleaners are found, one of whom, a Jew, is represented on page 44, busy at work. Cotton pods are brought to him in a sack. After weighing them, he separates the husks and seeds from the cotton with his bow-string, which he beats vigorously with his mallet. On a tray, mounted on a low stool, the seeds and pods may be seen; these will be weighed with the cotton in the presence of the owner when the task is completed. When there is sufficient space a second bow is used, and thus a double spring is obtained. The smaller bow is attached to a beam overhead, and to this is suspended a large harp-shaped bow, called a mandaf, the long string of which on being beaten into the cotton quickly converts it into fleecy clouds. The labour of holding the bow is avoided by thus suspending it, and the work is accomplished with surprising rapidity.

Cotton-cleaners are frequently employed in private houses to purify and lighten mattresses and divan cushions by the same process.

In every district a grocer's shop may be found, and on page 32 a typical one may be seen. The grocer in his striped gown and coloured turban sits on his shop-board quietly smoking, for it is nearly midday, and there is not much business to attend to. His stock consists of baskets of Egyptian rice and rice from the Jordan, a good supply of loaf sugar and coffee, dried fruits, pistachio nuts, walnuts, olives, salt, pepper, and all kinds of spices. A laden camel is just coming into the picture, making a growling noise and ringing his bells. The right foot of the rider alone is visible. In advance of the camel comes a water-carrier from Siloam, with a patched goatskin filled with water from the Bir Eyub (Job's Well). He rattles his brass cups, and cries out in a shrill voice, "May God compassionate me!" Two peasant women with dishevelled hair and yellow kerchiefs bound round their stiff red cloth caps are resting near the shop. They have rings in their noses and on their fingers, but their feet are bare. Peasant women of Judaea are not generally attractive in appearance. The features of the townspeople are much more refined, and there are many women and girls, both Christian and Moslem, in Jerusalem whose coloured muslin veils hide really pretty faces. Jewesses do not veil themselves, but the younger and prettier among them are kept very much out of sight.

From David Street a turning towards the north, called Christian Street, leads to the Church of the Holy Sepulchre, and here there are a few European shops, kept by Maltese, Italians, and Germans, in the midst of the truly Oriental barbers, pipe-makers, bakers' shops, and cafes. A good example of one of the less important street cafes is shown on page 33. All that is absolutely necessary is a nook in which a fire can be made for the preparation of pipes and coffee, a supply of coffee cups, narghilehs, and long pipes, and a few rush seats; but the proprietor adds greatly to the attractions of his establishment if he can supply a board for the game called dameh, at which a Bedouin and a peasant are represented playing in the illustration. In the evening a story-teller or a singer may generally be found here entertaining a group of smokers.

A turning eastward out of Christian Street leads through dirty crooked streets of stairs and arched passages, dark and dusty, to the most important bazaars and khans, which are in the centre of the city (see page 71). Here, under lofty arcades, the butchers', fruiterers', oil, grain, and leather markets are held. The butchers call out loudly, "Oh, every one that hath money let him come and buy!" and "Oh, such a one, come and buy!" The cry of the sellers of fruit appears to be more disinterested, for they often say to a passer-by, "Take of our fruit without money and without price!" but immediately afterwards they will ask him an exorbitant sum for it!

Leaving the bazaars and turning to the left up David Street, we approach the Haram esh Sherif, one of the most sacred and ancient of all

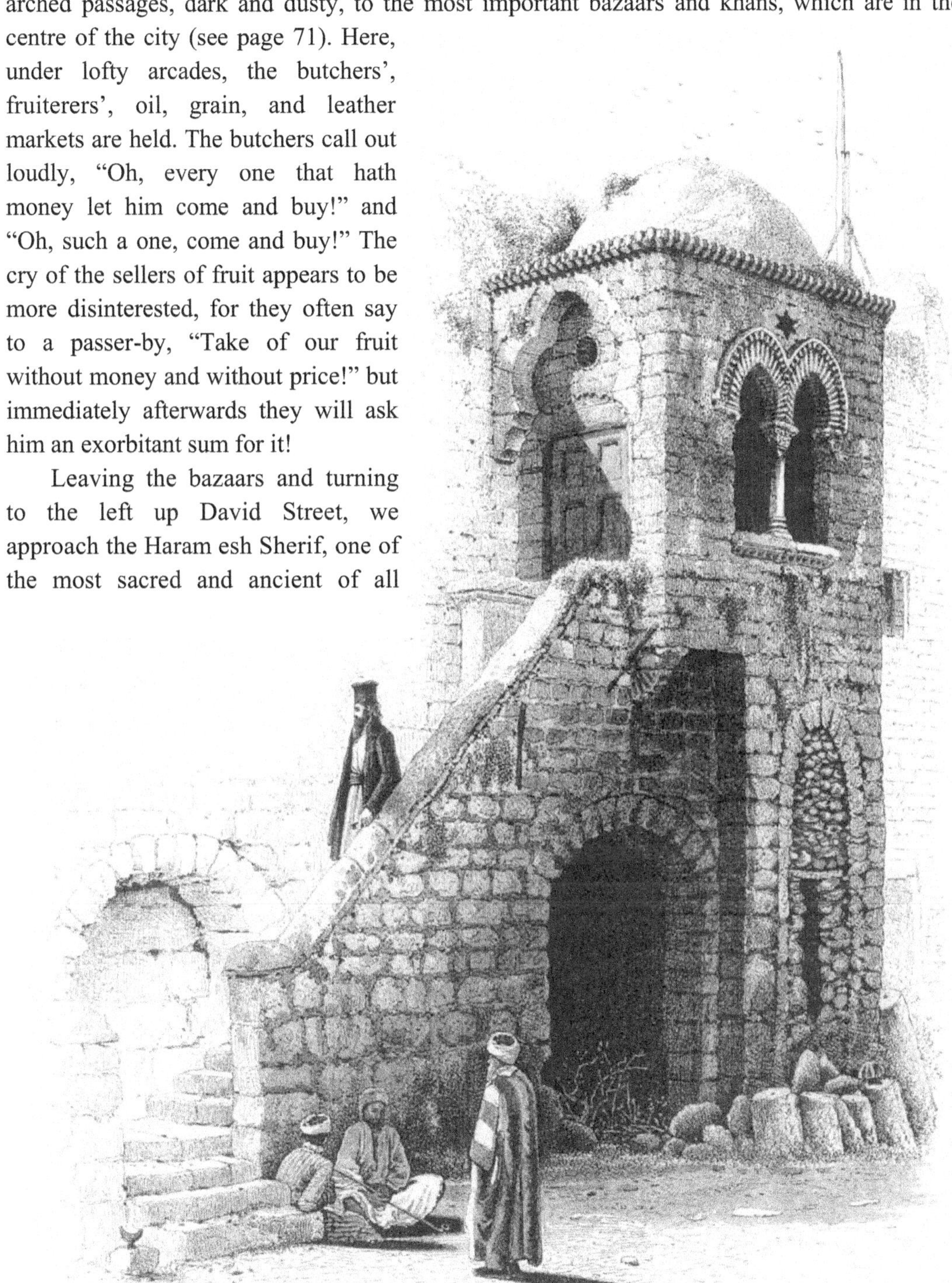

STAIRCASE LEADING TO THE CHURCH OF ST. JOHN.
A Greek priest descending the stairs.

holy places. Within its area was, according to tradition, the scene of Abraham's sacrifice (Gen. xxii. 3—14); and there was certainly the threshing floor which David bought from Araunah the Jebusite for fifty shekels of silver, and upon which he built an altar and offered burnt-offerings and peace-offerings. There, too, were the successive temples of Solomon, Zerubbabel, and Herod, the fortress of Antonia, and possibly the palace of Solomon; and there at the present day are the beautiful "Dome of the Rock" and the Mosque el Aksa, and the buildings which were once the home of the Knights Templars. All traces of the altar and of the temples of the Jews have long since disappeared, and their exact positions have for years been amongst the most fiercely contested points of Jerusalem topography. In the midst of all this ruin and desolation we can, however, feel that the hill is the same Mount Moriah round which cluster so many memories connected with Jewish history, with the earlier and later years of our Lord's life, and with the ministry of the Apostles, and that somewhere on its surface stood the building which excited the admiration and astonishment of the Queen of Sheba.

The sacred ground, or Temple Platform, was enclosed and supported by massive retaining walls which are described by the Jewish historian in glowing terms. The enormous height of these walls and the magnificence of the masonry, almost justifying the description of Josephus, have been fully brought to light by the excavations undertaken by Captain (now Lieut.-Col.) Warren, R. E., for the Palestine Exploration Fund. At one corner the solid masonry rises to a height of one hundred and eighty feet, at another to a height of one hundred and thirty-eight feet, above the ground; and at one point in the wall a great stone, thirty-eight feet nine inches long, four feet high, and ten feet deep, has been used at a height of eighty-five feet from the surface. Partially concealed as the walls are, here by ninety-five feet, there by sixty feet of rubbish, they still fill the traveller with admiration, and they must, when fresh from the builder's hands, have been the finest specimens of mural masonry in the world. It was with such walls before their eyes that the astonished Jews replied to our Lord, "Forty and six years was this Temple in building, and wilt thou rear it up in three days?" Above all this stood the Temple, of pure white glittering stone, covered in part with plates of gold, and surrounded by its courts and cloisters--a *tout ensemble* unsurpassed in magnificence by any temple of ancient times.

One of the finest fragments of the ancient masonry is that at the south-west angle of the Haram esh Sherif, but, unfortunately, only a comparatively small portion of the older work is visible above ground. No mortar has been used in building the wall, and the great blocks of stone are so beautifully fitted together that a penknife can hardly be introduced between the joints. The faces of the stones are also finely "dressed," and round the margin of each runs a chiselled draft from two to five inches wide and about a quarter of an inch deep. Thirty-nine feet north of the south-west angle is the fragment of an old arch known as "Robinson's Arch," from the fact that it was first brought to notice by the eminent American, Dr. Robinson, who may well be looked upon as the first and foremost pioneer in the systematic and scientific exploration of Palestine. The arch is fifty feet long, and it had a span of forty-two feet. Portions of the three lower courses, in which are stones from nineteen to twenty-five feet long, alone remain, and these, from the appearance and position of the stones, evidently formed part of the original wall. The remaining stones of the arch were found lying, just as they fell, on a pavement of polished stone, more than forty feet beneath the surface of the ground, and near them a portion of the pier was also discovered. Under the pavement were the remains of an older arch, and lower still a remarkable rockhewn channel for the conveyance of sweet water, which was in existence long before the Haram wall was built, and which may, perhaps, have been executed by order of King Hezekiah, who is known to have undertaken extensive works in connection with the water supply of Jerusalem. The position of "Robinson's Arch," and its dimensions, seem to indicate that it formed the first of a series of arches which supported a broad flight of steps leading from the Tyropoeon Valley to the centre aisle of the Royal Cloisters, "Stoa Basilica," which ran along the south wall of Herod's Temple. The arch may also mark the position of the fourth gate on the western side of the Temple, which Josephus says " led to the other city, where the road descended down into the valley by a great number of steps, and thence up again by the ascent." The "Stoa Basilica" was six hundred feet long and one hundred feet wide. It was divided into three aisles by one hundred and sixty-two Corinthian columns; and the centre aisle was one hundred feet, the side aisles each fifty feet, high. The roofs were adorned with deep sculptures in wood; the high part in the middle was of polished stone; and the whole was finished off with much magnificence. The dimensions of the cloisters, in plan and section, are almost identical with those which York Cathedral would present if the transepts were taken off the sides and added to the ends; and it would be difficult to imagine a finer effect than that which would be produced by a flight of steps fifty feet wide, carried on arches, and at one point raised fifty feet above the ground, leading up to such a noble pile of buildings.

At a distance of two hundred and seventy feet from the south-west angle there is a closed gateway in the wall called the Gate of Muhammed, but generally known as "Barclay's Gate," from its fortunate discoverer, Dr. Barclay, an American missionary to Palestine. The gateway, which is evidently one of those that Josephus describes as leading from the western cloisters of the Temple to the suburbs of the city, is partly concealed by rubbish; but excavations have shown that it was about eighteen feet ten inches wide and twenty-eight feet nine inches high. The lintel of the gate is one enormous stone, and its sill is no less than forty-nine feet nine inches above the rock. The approach was probably by a solid ramp of earth. Immediately behind the closed entrance there is now a mosque, in which is shown the ring to which Muhammed fastened his mysterious steed, el Burak, on the occasion of his famous night journey; but the gateway formerly gave access to a vaulted passage, one of the approaches to Herod's Temple, which ran for sixty-nine feet in a direction at right angles to the wall, to a domed chamber or vestibule, and then, turning at right angles to the south,

THE STREET OF THE DAMASCUS GATE.
With a characteristic group of Bedouins outside a cafe on the left, a party of Turkish soldiers breakfasting, and on the right a group of dealers in fruit and vegetables.

gained the Temple area by a ramp or flight of steps. North of "Barclay's Gate" is the well-known Wailing-place of the Jews, a small paved area in front of a portion of the retaining wall which is supposed by some writers to be the nearest point, without the enclosure, to the position of the "Holy of Holies." The pavement is at least seventy feet above the natural surface of the ground. Jews may often be seen sitting for hours at the Wailing-place bent in sorrowful meditation over the history of their race, and repeating oftentimes the words of the Seventy-ninth Psalm. On Fridays especially, Jews of both sexes, of all ages, and from all countries, assemble in large numbers to kiss the sacred stones and weep outside the precincts they may not enter (see page 43).

About six hundred feet from the south-west angle, and not far from the Wailing-place, is "Wilson's Arch," one of the finest and most perfect remains in Jerusalem, named

DAMASCUS GATE-BAB EL AMUD (GATE OF THE COLUMN).
The northern entrance to Jerusalem.

after the writer of these pages. The arch has the same span as "Robinson's Arch," and it formed part of the grand viaduct, of which other portions have been found, that connected Mount Moriah with the modern Mount Sion. West of the arch Captain Warren found a chamber, the "Masonic Hall," which may be a guard-house of the stormy period of the Maccabees, and a long subterranean gallery, which was apparently constructed to allow soldiers to pass freely and unnoticed from the Citadel, where Herod's palace was situated, to the Temple. This gallery appears to have been that which was used by Simon, son of Gioras, when, after the capture of Jerusalem by Titus, he passed from the

Upper City to the Temple area, and attempted to escape by appearing as a ghost to the Roman soldiers in the place where the Temple had stood. The principal approach to the Haram esh Sherif is by David Street, which passes over Wilson's Arch and enters the enclosure on a level, through a handsome double gate, of which the southern portal is called Bab es Silsileh (Gate of the Chain), and the northern Bab es Salam (Gate of Peace). At the bottom of the left jamb of the latter there is a massive stone with a marginal draft, the north end of which corresponds with the end of the great causeway arch beneath. The gate was built about 1492 A.D., and is ornamented with twisted columns, which were probably taken from some building erected by the Crusaders. In front of the gateway is a very beautiful fountain, which is supplied with water by the aqueduct from Solomon's Pools (see page 48).

Beyond the Gate of the Chain is "Warren's Gate," named after Captain Warren, R. E., whose excavations have thrown so much light on the topographical features of ancient Jerusalem. The gate, which is unfortunately concealed by rubbish, led into a passage eighteen feet wide, and was, perhaps, the second gate which gave access to the suburbs from the west side of the Temple enclosure. A short distance to the north is Bab el Kattanin (Gate of the Cotton Merchants), a handsome Saracenic portal at the end of the old Cotton Bazaar, said to have been repaired in A.D. 1336. A flight of steps leads up to the gate, which tradition asserts to be the "Beautiful Gate" of the Temple, where Peter healed the lame man. From Wilson's Arch northwards to the Gate of the Seraglio the retaining wall can nowhere be seen; but beneath the latter a portion has been found in a rock-hewn aqueduct, and near it Lieut. Conder, R. E., discovered the only masonry belonging to the original wall which is visible above the present surface of the Haram esh Sherif. This fragment is of great interest, as it has projecting pilasters and is similar in character to the masonry of the Haram wall, which encloses the last resting-place of the patriarchs at Hebron; it also shows that the outer walls of the Temple cloisters were built with pilasters, as represented in the restorations of Mr. Fergusson and the Count de Vogue. The north-west angle of the Haram esh Sherif has been cut out of the rock so as to leave escarpments from three to twenty-three feet high facing inwards on the north and west. There is here, in fact, a mass of rock, about one hundred feet thick, which is separated from the more northern hill of Bezetha by a ditch one hundred and sixty-five feet wide; and from twenty-six to thirty-three feet deep. Upon the rock stands a Turkish barrack, the successor, perhaps, of the Tower of Antonia, which Herod built to "secure and guard" the Temple. The tower, or castle, was of great extent, and played an important part during the siege of Jerusalem by Titus. It was on a rock fifty cubits high, which was covered from its foot with smooth stones, like the lower part of the Tower of David, so that "any one who would either try to get up or to go down it might not be able to hold his feet upon it." There were towers at each corner of the castle; that at the southeast was seventy cubits high, that it might overlook the Temple; and that at the south-west had passages to the Temple cloisters, by which the Temple guard went to its post, for, as Josephus adds, "the Temple was a fortress that guarded the city, as was the Tower of Antonia a guard to the Temple, and in that tower were the guards of those three." At the present day a pile of masonry in the street which runs westward along the north end of the Haram esh Sherif from St. Stephen's Gate is known as the "Tower of Antonia" (see page 30). This so-called tower appears to be part of an old mosque or church; it has attached to it a small court, in which several Moslem celebrities are buried; and the place is known to the native population of Jerusalem as the mosque and cemetery of those who fought against the Infidel, or, as we might call them, Knights of the Crescent. It was near this place that the distinguished French *savant,* M. Ganneau, was fortunate enough to find one of the tablets of Herod's Temple, which, as Josephus tells us, forbade strangers to enter the sacred enclosure. The tablet bears an inscription in Greek to the following effect: "No stranger is to enter within the balustrade round the Temple and enclosure. Whoever is caught will be responsible to himself for his death, which will ensue." The inscription throws light on the events described in Acts xxi. 26 *et seq.,* during which Paul nearly lost his life. The Jews of Asia supposed that Paul had brought Trophimus, an Ephesian, into the Temple, and thus polluted the Holy Place. A tumult

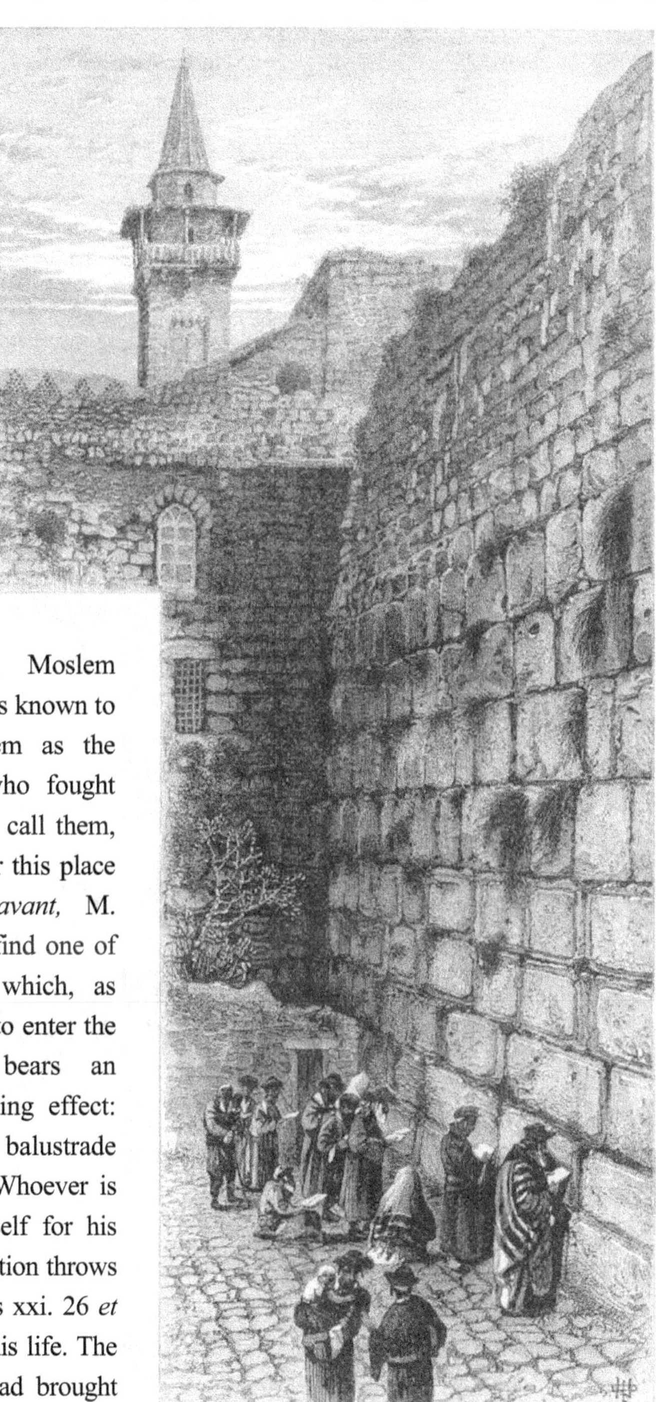

THE WAILING-PLACE OF THE JEWS.
The west wall of the Haram, or Sacred Enclosure. On Fridays, after four o'clock, Jews and Jewesses assemble here for prayer, and bewail the downfall of Jerusalem.

arose, and the people were about to put Paul to death, when the commandant of the fortress Antonia, gathering a number of soldiers together, ran down and rescued him. The minaret which stands on the rock at the north-west angle was built about 1207 A.D. (see page 52). Amongst the

A JEWISH COTTON-CLEANER.
Separating seeds from cotton by the ancient process of bowing it.

stones used in its construction is a marble capital with mutilated figures representing the "Presentation of Christ in the Temple," which was probably taken from the Chapel of the Presentation, situated during the Latin Kingdom in the "Dome of the Rock," then called the "Templum Domini." On the left Simeon receives the infant Jesus from the hands of the Virgin; on the right is a figure with a nimbus round its head, which seems to be intended for Joseph.

The ditch alluded to as separating the rock on which the Turkish barrack stands from the hill on the north has been traced for some distance along the line of the Via Dolorosa, and it can be seen in two vaulted passages or *souterrains* which lie beneath the street. At the end of one of the *souterrains* there is a rock-hewn aqueduct, from twenty to thirty feet high, which brought water from the north. It is an old and important work, but no one has yet been able to find the source from which it derived its supply of water. The eastern portion of the north side of the Haram esh Sherif is protected by the Birket Israil, known traditionally as the Pool of Bethesda. The reservoir is situated in a valley which takes its rise to the north of the city wall, and runs out into the Kedron valley about one hundred and forty-three feet south of the north-east angle of the Haram enclosure. The valley is now little more than a shallow depression, but excavations have shown that in the lower portions of its course it assumes the character of a deep ravine, and that its bed is no less than one hundred and forty feet below the surface of the Temple platform. The Birket Israil is three hundred and sixty feet long, one hundred and twenty-six feet wide, and eighty feet deep, but its great size can hardly be appreciated on account of the rubbish, which rises to a

STREET OF THE GATE OF THE CHAIN.
A narrow picturesque street, with projecting lattice-work windows of many kinds.

height of thirty-five feet above the floor. At the west end are two parallel passages running westwards along the Haram wall, whence a flight of irregular steps leads down to the pool; the east end is closed by a dam forty-five feet thick, which is also part of the city walls. No trace has yet been found of the system of conduits by which it was supplied with water. North of the Birket Israil (see page 66) is the street leading to St. Stephen's Gate, and immediately beyond it the Church of St. Anne, which was given by the Sultan Abdul Mejid to the French Emperor on the termination of the Crimean war. The church is built over the Grotto of St. Anne, an excavation in the rock remarkably like an old cistern, which is claimed by tradition as the home of St. Anne and the birthplace of the Virgin Mary. The building has been thoroughly repaired by the French, who have made no material alterations in the original edifice left by the Crusaders, and who have retained traces of the Moslem occupation in an Arabic inscription over the doorway and the *mihrab,* or prayer niche, which was cut in the south wall. The St. Stephen's Gate is called by the native Christians Bab Sitti Mariam (Gate of Our Lady Mary), from the circumstance that the road which passes through it leads to the tomb of the Virgin in the valley below. It dates from the restoration of the city walls by Sultan Suleiman. Above the doorway are two lions sculptured in stone in low relief.

The first point of interest in the east wall of the Haram esh Sherif is the Golden Gate, an entrance to the sacred enclosure which has long been closed, in consequence of a Moslem tradition that when the Christians capture Jerusalem they will make their triumphal entry by it. South of the Golden Gate is a postern, now closed with masonry, which is called by the Arab historian Mejr ed Din, the Gate of Burak. Beside it there are traces of an old fountain, once probably fed from the water in the cisterns of the Haram.

From St. Stephen's Gate to the postern, and even beyond it, the ground at the foot of the east wall is occupied by the Muhammedan cemetery, and closely covered with tombs—plain rectangular masses of masonry with rounded tops; they are generally badly built and soon fall to pieces, leaving nothing but a heap of ruins. Here and there may be seen a headstone with a roughly hewn turban, and in some cases the tombs are protected from the weather by a square building pierced with arches and surmounted by a dome (see pages 67 and 69). Moslem funerals pass into the Haram esh Sherif by the "Gate of the Tribes," and enter the Dome of the Rock by the "Gate of Paradise." After a few short prayers the procession passes out of the mosque by the gate that opens in the direction of Mecca, and leaves the Haram by the way it entered; it then proceeds to the grave. No coffin is used; the body is simply wrapped in a sheet and carried to the grave in a wooden box by six men. A man bearing a palm branch heads the procession, and the mourners follow the body in a confused crowd without any order or arrangement. At the grave a few verses of the Koran are recited, and if the deceased is rich alms are distributed to the poor.

The imposing mass of masonry at the south-east angle of the Haram esh Sherif, which overhangs the Kedron valley, has always excited the admiration of travellers. Its foundation-stones bear the Phoenician letters which at the time of their discovery attracted so much attention. The letters are either cut into or painted on the stones. The incised characters are cut to a depth of three-eighths of an inch; the painted characters, some of which are five inches high, were probably put on with a brush. They are in red paint, apparently vermilion, and easily rubbed off with a wetted finger. These *graphiti* were examined by the late Mr. Emanuel Deutsch, who says: "The signs cut or painted were on the stones when they were first laid in their present places. They do not represent any inscription. They are Phoenician. I consider them to be partly letters, partly numerals, and partly special quarry signs or masons' marks. Some of them were recognisable at once as well-known Phoenician characters, others, hitherto unknown in Phoenician epigraphy, I had the rare satisfaction of being able to identify on absolutely undoubted Phoenician structures in Syria." The pottery obtained during the excavations consisted of a small jar found in a hole cut out of the rock, "standing upright, as though it had been purposely placed there," and many fragments of lamps and other utensils. Dr. Birch, the keeper of oriental antiquities at the British Museum, states that it is just possible that this jar, which resembles Egyptian ware in shape, might be as old as the fourth or fifth century B.C. Mr. Greville Chester, the well-known antiquary, observes, in the "Recovery of Jerusalem," that the vase "is of pale red ware, and of a common Graeco-Phoenician type." Amongst the fragments were found several broken lamps of red or brownish ware, with one, two, or three lips, which "seem adapted for the burning of fat rather than oil." They are similar in design to lamps that have been found in Cyprus and Malta; and Mr. A. W. Franks, of the British Museum, considers them "to be of late date—not earlier than the second century before the Christian era." The south-east angle is by some writers believed to be one of the oldest portions of the wall and the work of Solomon; whilst others, from the peculiar character of the masonry, believe it to have been built by Herod Agrippa, or to be even as late as the reign of Justinian.

The most remarkable features of the south wall of the Haram esh Sherif are the large stones known as the "Great Course," and the Single, Double, and Triple Gates. The "Great Course" is a course of drafted stones about six feet high, which extends continuously for a distance of seventy feet west of the south-east angle, and can be traced thence at intervals to the Triple Gate. The stones have sometimes been supposed to be of great age, but in our opinion they are more probably connected with the great works which were undertaken at Jerusalem by order of Justinian. Procopius, in describing the Mary Church of Justinian, says that the fourth part of the ground required for the building was wanting towards the south and east; the builders, therefore, laid out their foundations at the extremity of the sloping ground, and raised up a wall until they reached the pitch of the hill. Above this they constructed a series of arched vaults, by means of which they raised the ground to the level of the rest of the enclosure. Procopius also speaks of the immense size of the stones and of the skill with which they were dressed. This describes exactly what is found at the southeast angle: solid masonry to the level of the top of the hill under the Triple Gate, then vaults to raise the level to that of the area, and the "Great Course" to mark the end of the solid

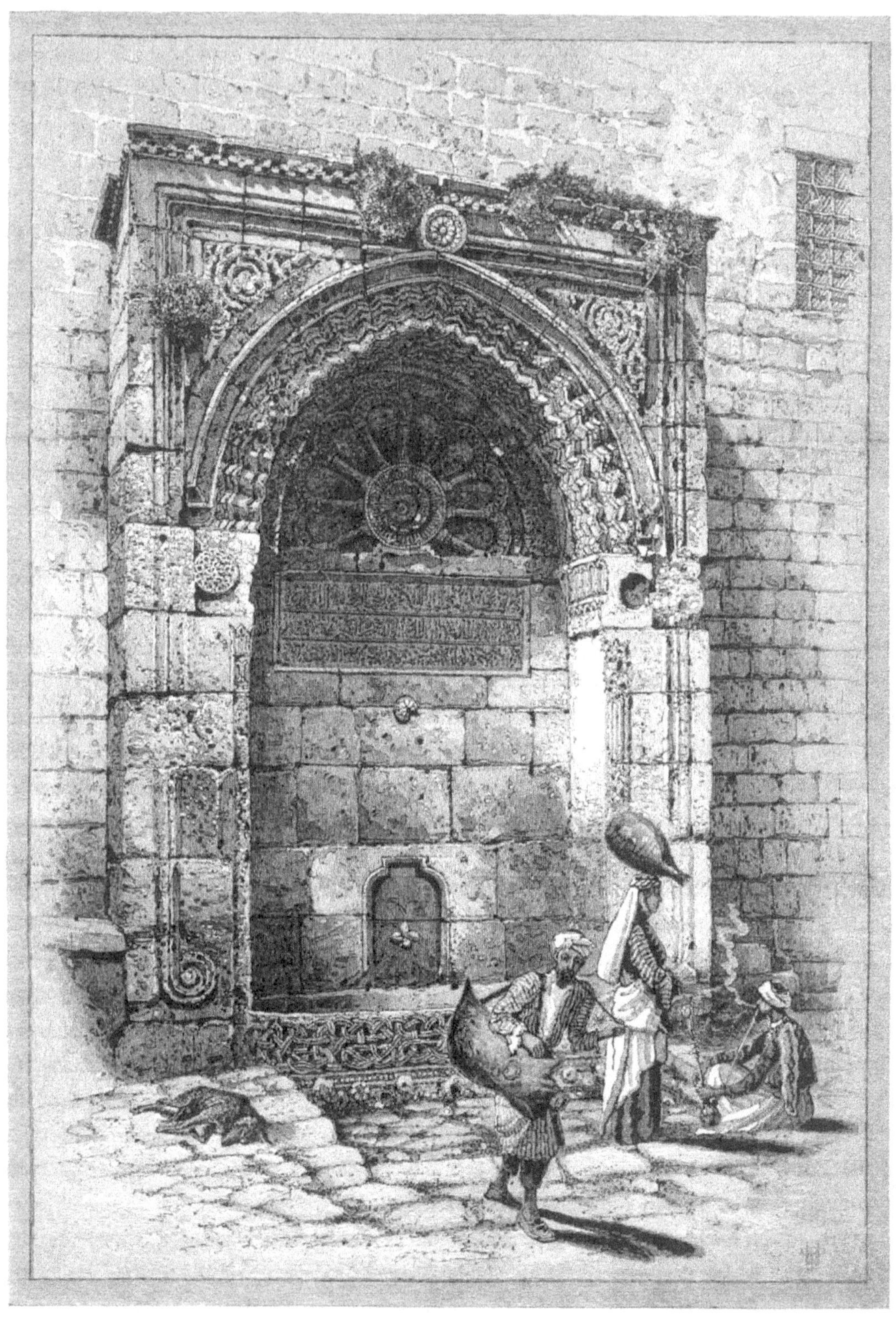

FOUNTAIN OF THE GATE OF THE CHAIN—BAB ES SILSILEH.
Supplied with water from Solomon's Pools.

masonry. The Single Gate, the nearest of the three gateways to the south-east angle, is a closed entrance of comparatively modern date, which at one time led directly into the vaults within the Haram, known as "Solomon's Stables." Beneath the gate Captain Warren found the "Great Passage," a narrow way from twelve to eighteen feet high and sixty-nine feet long, which lies beneath one of the aisles of Solomon's Stables. Next in order is the Triple Gate, which consists of three arched portals each thirteen feet wide. The openings are closed with small masonry, but they formerly gave access to three parallel passages, which, after running some distance beneath the surface of the Haram, are blocked with rubbish. The Double Gate consists of two entrances, now closed, which formerly opened into a vestibule, whence there was an ascent to the Haram area by a vaulted passage at right angles with the line of the wall. The gates are each

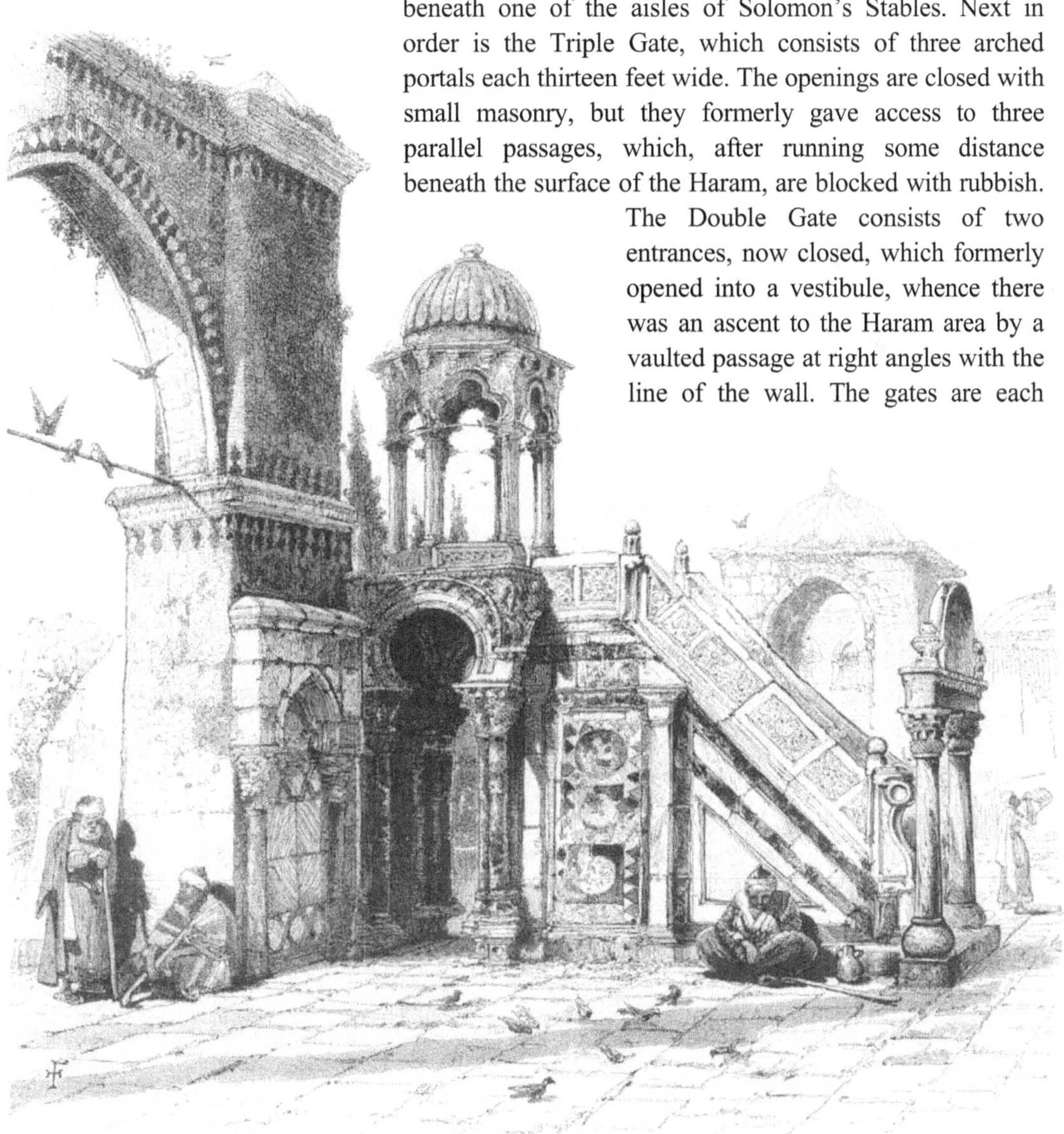

THE SUMMER PULPIT, PLATFORM OF THE DOME OF THE ROCK.
Showing a portion of the arcaded approach from the south. The pigeons in the foreground are characteristic of the place.

eighteen feet wide, and they are covered with large lintels, which have been cracked by the pressure of the masonry above, and are now columns. Immediately under the lintels are two ornamented arches, which form no part of the well, but are simply fastened on to it with metal cramps. The style of ornament is similar to that of the Golden Gate. The Double Gate is undoubtedly a relic of the Temple of Herod. Close to the eastern lintel is a dedicatory inscription to Hadrian, built into the wall upside down, which some writers suppose belonged to the statue erected to that emperor in the Temple area.

Allusion has frequently been made to Captain Warren's excavations for the Palestine Exploration Fund. Those excavations are, for their extent, for the boldness with which they were conceived, and for the skill with which they were carried out, without a parallel in the history of archaeological exploration. It will not be out of place to give here, in the explorer's own words, a description of one of the shafts by means of which he penetrated through the rubbish which conceals the foundations of the Temple platform.

"On Friday (October 11th, 1867), having arrived at a depth of seventy-nine feet, the men were breaking up a stone at the bottom of the shaft. Suddenly the ground gave way; down went the stone and the hammer, the men barely saving themselves. They at once rushed up, and told the sergeant they had found the bottomless pit. I went down to the spot and examined it, and, in order that you may have an idea of the extent of our work, I will give you a description of our descent.

"The shaft mouth is on the south side of the Sanctuary wall, near the south-west angle, among the prickly pears. Beside it, to the east, lying against the Sanctuary wall, is a large mass of rubbish that has been brought up; while over the mouth itself is a triangular gin with iron wheel attached, with guy for running up the excavated soil. Looking down the shaft one sees that it is lined for the first twenty feet with frames four feet six inches in the clear. Farther down, the Sanctuary wall and soil cut through is seen, and a man standing at what appears to be the bottom. An order is given to this man, who repeats it, and then, faintly, is heard a sepulchral voice answering as it were from another world. Reaching down to the man who is visible is a thirty-four feet rope ladder, and, on descending by it, one finds he is standing on a ledge which the ladder does not touch by four feet. This ledge is the top of a wall running north and south and abutting on the Sanctuary wall; its east face just cuts the centre of the shaft, which has to be canted off about two feet towards the east, just where some large loose stones jut out in the most disagreeable manner. Here five more frames have been fixed to keep these stones steady. On peering down from this ledge one sees the Sanctuary wall with its projecting courses until they are lost in the darkness below, observing also, at the same time, that two sides of the shaft are cut through the soil and are self-supporting. Now to descend this second drop the ladder is again required; accordingly, having told the man at the bottom to get under cover, it is lowered to the ledge; from whence it is found that it does not reach to the bottom by several feet. It is therefore lowered the required distance, and one has to reach it by climbing down hand over hand for about twelve feet. On passing along, one notes the marvelous joints of the Sanctuary wall stones, and also, probably, gets a few blows on skull and knuckles from falling pebbles. Just on reaching the bottom one recollects there is still a pit of unknown depth to be explored, and cautiously straddles across it. Then can be seen that one course in the Sanctuary wall, near the bottom, is quite smooth all over, the stone being finely dressed, all other courses being only well dressed round the drafts. One also sees two stout boards lying against the Sanctuary wall, under which the men retire whenever an accidental shower of stones renders their position dangerous. One is now at a depth of seventy-nine feet from the surface, and from here we commence the exploring of the 'bottomless pit.' After dropping a rope down we found that it was only six feet deep, though it looked black enough for anything. Climbing down we found ourselves in a passage running south from the Sanctuary, four feet high by two feet wide, and we explored this passage. It is of rough rubble masonry, with flat stones at top similar to the aqueduct from Triple Gate, but not so carefully constructed. The floor and sides are very muddy, as if water gathers there during the rainy season.

"It struck me that it might be an overflow aqueduct from the Temple, and that there might be a water-conduit underneath. We scrambled along for a long way on our feet, our skulls and spines coming in unhappy contact with the passage roof. After about two hundred feet we found that the mud reached higher up, and we had to crawl by means of elbows and toes. Gradually the passage got more and more filled up, and our bodies could barely squeeze through, and there did not appear sufficient air to support us for any length of time, so that, having advanced four hundred feet, we commenced a difficult retrograde movement, having to get back half-way before we could turn our heads round. . . . This passage is on a level with the foundations of the Haram wall, eighty-five feet below the surface of the ground. . . . We have sunk a shaft three hundred and fifty feet to the south of the Sanctuary wall, and have had the good fortune, at a depth of sixty feet, to drop directly upon our passage. . . . The passage was cleared out for a total distance of six hundred feet from the Sanctuary wall and was then abandoned. . . . This aqueduct appears to have existed before the south-west angle of the Sanctuary, and to have been cut across and rendered useless when the wall was built."

The Haram esh Sherif has a general elevation of two thousand four hundred and nineteen feet above the Mediterranean, and its surface is almost level, if we except the raised platform in the centre, a deep hollow in front of the Golden Gate, and a slight rise towards the northwest corner. It has been formed by cutting the rock away in some places, by building supporting vaults in others, and by filling in hollows with large stones and rubbish. The dimensions are—north side, one thousand and forty-two feet; east side, one thousand five hundred and thirty feet; south side, nine hundred and twenty-two feet; and west side, one thousand six hundred and one feet. The enclosure contains thirty-five acres, and is nearly one mile in circuit.

In the north-west corner the natural rock is either visible or but slightly covered with earth over some extent of ground, and the surface has been artificially formed by cutting down the rock under the Turkish barrack, and then entirely removing the upper strata as far as the north-west angle of the raised platform, where the rock is scarped, and rises nearly to the level of the pavement on which the Dome of the Rock stands. Between the corner and the platform the ridge of Moriah is in one place very narrow. Here the rock gives place to turf, and there are indications which point to the existence of a ditch cut in the solid rock.

The north-east corner has been formed by filling up the deep ravine, which has already

NORTH-WEST CORNER OF THE HARAM ESH SHERIF.
Showing the highest minaret of the Sanctuary, and the old Serai, which is now used as a state prison.

been alluded to as that in which the Birket Israil (Pool of Bethesda) is situated. The southwest corner, as far as we know at present, is, with the exception of the passage from Barclay's Gate, alluded to above, filled up in a solid manner with large stones and earth. On the south side of the Haram esh Sherif is the Mosque el Aksa, and in front of it is a level space shaded

ORATORIES ON THE WEST SIDE OF THE HARAM ESH SHERIF.

by fine trees. In the centre of the Haram is the raised platform on which stands the Kubbet es Sakhra (Dome of the Rock), erected over the sacred rock from which Mohammed is said to have ascended into heaven. The platform has four sides, but none of its sides are equal, nor are any of its angles right angles. Its general level is about sixteen feet above that of the Haram esh Sherif, and the top of the "Sakhra" is nearly five feet higher, or two thousand four hundred and forty feet above the Mediterranean. The platform is paved with flat slabs of stone. On the west and south-west it is partly supported by vaults. In other directions the rock rises up to, or nearly up to, the level of the pavement. The most interesting feature is the "Sakhra," or Rock, to which the beautiful building gives an air of mystery and a prominence that it would not possess if the pavement were removed and the ground were restored to its original form.

The platform is approached by several flights of steps, at the top of which are screens supported by light columns, called "mawazin," or balances. (See pages 49, 53, and 63.)

The Kubbet es Sakhra (Dome of the Rock) is an octagonal building, each side of which measures sixty-six feet. Internally it is one hundred and fifty-two feet in diameter. The great rock, the "Sakhra," which is in the centre, is encircled by four massive piers and twelve columns; three columns being placed between each pair of piers. They are united by arches and support the beautifully proportioned dome, which is sixty-six feet in diameter at its base. An octagonal screen, composed of eight piers and sixteen columns, divides the remaining space into two encircling aisles; the outer aisle being thirteen and the inner one thirty feet wide. (See page 59.) There is a door in each of the four faces fronting the cardinal points—on the north, Bab el Jenné (Gate of Paradise); Bab el Gharby (West Gate); Bab el Kiblé (South Gate); and the Bab en Neby Daúd (Gate of the Prophet David). Each of the doorways had in front of it an open porch of columns, but, with the exception of that before the Bab el Kiblé, they have been closed in and cased with marble. The chambers thus formed are made use of by the attendants of the mosque. The doors are covered with plates of bronze, and have very fine old locks.

The building consists of a basement sixteen feet high, pierced only by the four doors; then a story of plain masonry, twenty feet in height, with seven round arches on each side, thirty-eight of which are pierced for windows, and the remaining eighteen are blind panels. The basement is cased with slabs of various coloured marble, which are fastened to the masonry by metal clamps run in with lead.

The old round-headed arches are hidden by pointed arches probably dating from the sixteenth century. In course of time several of the pointed arches fell out, and the western faces became so ruinous that in 1873 the Turkish Government found it necessary to carry out extensive repairs. It was then that Mons. Ganneau discovered "that the parapet wall above the principal range of windows, which had always been believed to be solid, was in reality composed of a range of thirteen small arches on each face, each arch being adorned with a small dwarf pillar on each side. It may be assumed as certain that this arcade formed the front of a covered gallery, not only because no other view seems consistent with common sense, but because the description of it by John of Wurzburg, made in the time of the

Crusades, will bear no other interpretation." Some of these arcades were at one time formed into semicircular niches with semi-domical heads, and the upper parts at least were richly ornamented with mosaics in coloured and gilt glass. The presence of mosaics outside the Kubbet es Sakhra is a fact of much interest in the history of the building, because it has been often doubted, in spite of the formal affirmation of the ancient descriptions. From John of Wurzburg to Mejr ed Din, all writers agree in saying that the Dome of the Rock was adorned with mosaics inside and outside. The last trace of this system of decoration disappeared from the outside when the faience was applied in the sixteenth century. Mons. Ganneau considers the mosaics to be "the work of the Arabs, perhaps that of Saladin." On the other hand, Mr. Fergusson, from whose valuable works our description of the mosque is chiefly compiled, believes the mosaics to be late Roman or Byzantine, and thinks it not improbable that they may be part of the original design of the building, assuming it to have been erected in the fourth century. The external walls above the basement are entirely covered with tiles, which produce a very fine effect. Verses of the Koran, beautifully written in interwoven character, in blue and white, run round the parapet wall, and beneath are elaborately executed designs in various colours. The tiles are nine and a half inches square and firmly embedded in mortar. Three periods of workmanship can be traced: the tiles of the earliest period are far superior to the others in elegance of design and quality of workmanship; those of the second are also good; but the tiles of the third period are in bad taste and of inferior quality. They have been chiefly used in recent repairs.

The aisle screen is perhaps the most interesting part of the building, and it is that upon which the architectural arguments with reference to the age of the Dome of the Rock are chiefly founded. The bases of the columns are cased with slabs of marble, but they were uncovered during the repairs, and it was then found that, though classical in form, they differed in outline and height. This, however, is not an unusual occurrence in early Christian churches, for the builders made free use of columns, capitals, and bases taken from pagan temples. The shafts of the columns do not rest immediately on their bases, but on sheets of lead from three-quarters of an inch to one and a half inches thick. The capitals are of the Corinthian order, and they illustrate "one of the very first attempts to convert the hollow bowl of the Corinthian capital into a fuller form, to bear an arch or a longer entablature." The entablature, although of wood, would have looked crushingly heavy if maintaining its classical depth, across pillars spaced eight diameters apart. The architrave is consequently omitted and represented only by a square block of stone over each pillar, supporting the frieze and cornice, of fairly classical design; and over this comes a bold discharging arch, which again supports a cornice, originally apparently classical, but now hidden in more modern details of stone. The stone blocks are cased with marble slabs, which seem at one time to have been covered with bronze plates. The wood entablature is painted in bright colours, to bring out the details of the beautiful frieze and cornice, and its soffit and part of its side are covered with bronze *repousse* work of a very elaborate and beautiful class.

OLD CYPRESS TREES IN THE HARAM ESH SHERIF.
On the western side.

The piers of the screen are cased with marble, and the capitals are gilded. The arches are ornamented with fanciful designs in mosaic. Above the mosaics runs the remarkable inscription, written in letters of gold, which records the erection of the Dome of the Rock by El Mamun in the year 72 of the Hegira. As, however, El Mamun, who was a son of Harun al Reshid, died in 218 A.H., M. de Vogue and Professor Palmer believe that the name of Abd el Melik, who, according to their opinion, was the original founder, was purposely erased, and that of the Imam el Mamun fraudulently substituted; the short-sighted forger, however, omitted to erase the date. The inscription consists chiefly of verses from the Koran. The following are some of the most interesting passages of the inscription: "In the name of God, the Merciful, the Compassionate! The servant of God, Abdallah, the Imam el Mamun, Commander of the Faithful, built this dome in the year 72 (A.D. 691). May God accept it at his hands, and be content with him. Amen! There is no god but God alone; He hath no partner. Say He is the one God, the Eternal; He neither begetteth nor is begotten, and there is no one like Him. Mohammed is the Apostle of God; pray God for him. There is no god but God alone; to Him be praise, who taketh not unto Himself a son, and to whom none can be a partner in His kingdom,

THE GOLDEN GATE OF THE HARAM ESH SHERIF.
From the west. The Mount of Olives in the distance.

and whose patron no lower creature can be; magnify ye Him. Oh! ye who have received the Scriptures, exceed not the bounds in your religion, and speak not aught but truth concerning God. God is but One. There is no god but He, the Mighty, the Wise."

When the Crusaders reached Jerusalem it is said that they found the Dome of the Rock covered with inscriptions in the Cufic character, which stated that the building had been erected by Omar. These have disappeared, as well as the Latin inscriptions with which the mosque was adorned, inside and outside, during the Christian occupation of the Holy City. One of these inscriptions, which commenced "Domus mea domus orationis vocabitur, dicit Dominus," occupied, if our interpretation of the description of Theodoricus is correct, the place of the great Cufic inscription.

The aisles are covered by slightly sloping roofs with panelled wooden ceilings, and paved with mosaics formed of old material, amongst which there are many fragments of sculptured slabs. The bases and columns of the inner circle are similar to those of the octagonal screen; the capitals differ in size, in outline, and in details, and in their state of preservation; but in most cases the volutes and acanthus leaves have been much defaced, the projecting edges having been knocked off. The columns and piers are connected by a fine wrought-iron screen, which is said to be of French workmanship of the latter part of the twelfth century, and believed to be a relic of the Crusaders (see page 59). A fragment of the choir of the old Christian church (Templum Domini) also remains. The discharging arches, which spring directly from the capitals, are covered with a thin veneering of marble, black and white slabs arranged alternately. Above the arches is the drum upon which the dome rests, divided into what may be called the triforium and clerestory by a slight cornice. The former is ornamented by a band of scrollwork in glass mosaics, which in many of its features is late Roman. The clerestory is pierced by sixteen windows, between each of which the scroll of the triforium is repeated with some slight variations. Mons. Ganneau ascertained that on many of the vertical walls of the interior "the coloured and gilded little cubes of glass which produce together so marvellous an effect are not sunk in the walls so that their faces are vertical, but are placed obliquely, so that the faces make an angle with the walls. This ingenious inclination is evidently intended to present their many-coloured facets at the most effective angle of incidence to the eye below." This system of decoration produces a dazzling and magical effect, which must be seen to be perfectly realised. According to Mr. Fergusson, the history of the mosaic decoration is as follows: "When the building was first erected by Constantine he adorned it, internally at least, with mosaics, portions of which still remain. When the Saracens took possession of the Dome of the Rock they destroyed those parts of these mosaics representing emblems offensive to Moslem ideas, and replaced them by those others which we now see. When the Christians regained possession of the building in 1099 they obliterated the Saracenic inscriptions and replaced them by the Latin ones, copied and published by John of Wurzburg and Theodoricus. Lastly, when the Moslems recovered the Kubbet es Sakhra, Saladin, or some one about his time, obliterated the Christian inscriptions, remodelled entirely the mosaics of the side aisles at least, and inserted the Cufic inscriptions, which ascribe the erection of the building to Abd el Melik or El Mamun."

INTERIOR OF THE DOME OF THE ROCK.
Shewing a portion of the inner circle of piers and columns and the fine wrought-iron screen.

The dome of the building is of wood, covered externally with lead, and internally with stucco, richly gilt and painted; its height is about ninety-six feet. The windows of the external wall and clerestory are remarkable for the beauty of their tracery, no less than for the brilliancy of their colouring and for the admirable way in which the different colours are blended, producing perfect harmony in the whole. To be seen to advantage they should have the full blaze of a Syrian sun streaming through them. One window near the western door is of special

THE CAVE UNDER THE GREAT ROCK ON MOUNT MORIAH.

beauty. The light is admitted through three mediums. First, there is on the outside a thick perforated framework of cement covered with faience; this allows the light to pass to a second window of stone with white glass, and thence to the inner window, which gives the design and colouring. In this inner window the small pieces of coloured glass are inserted obliquely, and not vertically, so as to overhang and meet the eye of the spectator at right angles. Nothing can equal the exquisite taste with which the pieces of glass are arranged or the charming brightness of the colouring; and the combined effect is certainly not surpassed by that of any windows in Europe. Some of the windows bear the name of Suleiman, and the date 935 (1528 A.D.), the same period to which the finest specimens of the porcelain tiles are assigned.

The "Sakhra" Rock, which occupies the centre of the building, is overhung by a canopy and surrounded by a rude wooden railing. It rises four feet nine and a half inches

THE FACADE OF THE MOSQUE EL AKSA, JERUSALEM.
An old olive-tree in the foreground.

above the marble pavement of the mosque at its highest point, and one foot at its lowest; from north to south it measures fifty-six feet, and from east to west forty-two feet. Beneath the rock there is a small cave (see page 60), the entrance to which is at the south-east corner of the rock; a flight of steps passes under an archway and leads down to the chamber. The average height of the cave is six feet. In the roof is a circular opening which pierces the rock; the floor is paved with marble, and the sides are covered with plaster and whitewash. The floor, when stamped upon, gives out a hollow sound, indicating the presence of a lower chamber, possibly a well, the "Well of Spirits." The sides, too, when tapped give forth a hollow sound, which the Moslem guardian brings forward as a proof that the Sakhra is, in accordance with the legend, suspended in the air.

Many curious traditions are attached to the Dome of the Rock. Immediately within the "Gate of Paradise" is the "Sepulchre of Solomon." A small piece of marble, called the "Flagstone of Paradise," is let into the pavement above the tomb. Into this marble Mohammed drove nails, which at certain intervals drop through to the tomb below; when they have all disappeared the prophet will come to judge the faithful. Three nails now remain perfect, and one has sunk some depth. The place has a weird interest to the Moslem pilgrim, who approaches it with cautious step, mindful of the grave advice of the attendant sheikh, "Take heed to thy footsteps, O pilgrim! lest thou shake a nail through and hasten the day of judgment." Near the west side of the rock is preserved the shield of Hamzeh, the uncle of Omar. The shield is of very beautiful workmanship, and is, perhaps, of Persian manufacture. Its face is highly ornamented with figures of birds and animals in low relief, the peacock being most prominent; but it has been flattened in and turned towards the wall to conceal the forbidden figures from devout eyes. It is, however, round the mysterious rock that the legends gather most thickly. On the Sakhra, if we are to believe certain traditions, Melchizedek offered sacrifice; there Abraham was about to offer Isaac; there Jacob saw the ladder leading up into heaven; and there, too, was the threshing-floor of Araunah the Jebusite, by which the angel stood when he stretched out his hand upon Jerusalem to destroy it; the site of the "altar of the burnt offering for Israel," upon which David sacrificed; the altar of the Temples of Solomon, Zerubbabel, and Herod. Here Mohammed prayed, declaring that one prayer by the sacred rock was better than a thousand elsewhere, and hence he passed heavenward on his mysterious steed, El Burak. At the south-west corner of the rock may still be seen the "Footprint of Mohammed," covered by a rude shrine, which contains, carefully screened from vulgar eyes, an object of the deepest veneration, a single hair of the prophet's head. Here, too, are the banners of Omar, which were carried before him when he captured Jerusalem; they are now covered with cases which do not seem to have been removed for years.

When the Crusaders converted the Dome of the Rock into their Templum Domini they formed a choir in the centre, which was probably co-extensive with the inner circle of piers and columns, and placed the high altar on the Sakhra, which was covered with marble slabs and decorated with sculptured figures in marble. The principal entrance was at that time by the western door, on passing through which the visitor had in front of

THE PLATFORM OF THE DOME OF THE ROCK.
Showing one of the arcaded entrances on the north side. Mount Scopus in the distance.

him the choir, and on the left of the choir the Chapels of the "Presentation of Christ" and of "Jacob's Dream." Over the one was written the couplet—

> "Hic fuit oblatus rex regum virgine natus,
> Qua propter sanctus locus est hic jure vocatus."

and over the other—

> "Hic Jacob scalam vidit, construxit et aram,
> Hinc locus ornatur, quo sanctus jure vocatur."

The cave was at the same time converted into a chapel, ornamented with paintings and inscriptions commemorative of the appearance of the angel to Zacharias, and of the woman taken in adultery who was brought before Jesus. On the day of the Purification a solemn procession passed through the city from the Church of the Holy Sepulchre to the Templum Domini (Dome of the Rock); and on the occasion of the coronation of the Frank kings of Jerusalem a similar procession took place. According to the prescribed ceremonial the king was crowned in the Church of the Holy Sepulchre; he then proceeded to the Templum Domini to offer his crown on the altar of the Chapel of the Presentation of Christ, and afterwards passed to the Templum Salomonis (Mosque el Aksa), where the Knights Templars had their residence. Whilst the repairs were being executed in 1873, several fragments of figures and other memorials were found of the occupation of the Dome of the Rock by the Crusaders.

What is the origin of this beautiful building? To this question no decisive answer has yet been made. Mr. Fergusson, arguing chiefly on architectural grounds—and his arguments have never been answered by any one competent to deal with this side of the problem—maintains that the Dome of the Rock is in all essential particulars the identical Anastasis, or Church of the Resurrection, built by the Emperor Constantine over the cave which he believed to be the Sepulchre of Christ. He is also absolutely convinced that the "new sepulchre" was near this spot, probably in this very rock and under the very dome. Mr. Fergusson places the Basilica of Constantine on the north side of the platform of the mosque; and he considers a *souterrain* discovered by Captain Warren to be parts of one of the double aisles of that building, which Eusebius describes as partly above ground and partly beneath it. The conclusions arrived at by a committee of architects and engineers, who considered the question at Munich, seem to have been that the Dome of the Rock was not an old Arab building, and that it could not have been built by Constantine or later than the reign of Justinian. The view of the committee was that the evidence laid before them tended to show that the building could only belong to the first third of the sixth century. The Arab historians attribute the erection of the Dome of the Rock to Abd el Melik, and this is the view generally taken of its origin. The essentially Byzantine character of the building is explained by the supposition that Abd del Melik employed a Greek architect, the Arabs at that time having no style of their own. It is somewhat surprising, however, to find that, though the Arabs came in contact with Byzantine civilization in other places, there is no known instance of a similar style of building having been erected by them.

The platform on which the Dome of the Rock stands is paved with limestone slabs, and carries several minor buildings, of which the "Tribunal of the Prophet David," or "Dome of the Chain," in front of the east door of the mosque, is the most remarkable. This beautiful little building is an open pavilion of eleven sides, with six internal columns, which support an hexagonal drum and a domed roof. It has a "mihrab" on the south face. The bases, shafts, and capitals differ greatly from each other, and have been taken from an older building. The last are of a late Byzantine style, and have none of those classical features which are so characteristic of the capitals of the Dome of the Rock. The interior of the small dome is overlaid with faience, which produces a very pretty effect. According to tradition David's judgment-seat stood beneath the dome, and it was here that Mohammed caught a first glimpse of the houris of Paradise. In the twelfth century the building was looked upon as the tomb of St. James, the brother of our Lord, whose body is said to have been removed to this spot from the Valley of Jehoshaphat, where it was first buried. The remaining buildings are the " Dome of the Spirits," beneath which the natural rock may be seen; the "Dome of El Khydr" (Elias, or St. George); the "Dome of the Prophet Mohammed," and other structures of less importance. Near the flight of steps which leads down from the platform on the south is the "Summer Pulpit," a beautiful structure in marble, which affords a fine example of Arab art in the sixteenth century. The pulpit was built by Berhan ed Din Kadi, 798 A.H. (see page 49).

Passing from the "Dome of the Rock" to the Mosque el Aksa, at the south end of the Haram esh Sherif, the eye is at once struck by the difference in style, and by the inferior character of the material used in the construction of the latter (see page 61). The porch is Gothic, and appears to be the work of the Crusaders. The mosque is about one hundred and ninety feet wide and two hundred and seventy feet long, and is divided into seven aisles. The building lies north and south, and the centre of the transept at the south end is covered by a dome. The columns of the centre aisles are heavy and stunted, and have a circumference of nine feet three inches to a height of sixteen feet five inches; the remaining columns are better proportioned. The capitals of the columns are of four different kinds: those in the centre aisle are heavy and badly designed; those under the dome are of the Corinthian order, of white marble, and similar to those in the Dome of the Rock; those in the east aisle are of a heavy basket-shaped design; and those east and west of the dome are basket-shaped, but small and well proportioned. These last are made of plaster. The columns and piers are connected by a rude architectrave, which consists of beams of roughly-squared timber enclosed in a wooden casing which is poorly ornamented. Some of the windows are very good, one especially; of a delicate blue colour, which is situated in the tambour of the dome, and only seen immediately on entering the mosque. There is another fine window in the Mosque of Zechariah, but the colours are not so effectively blended as in the windows of the Dome of the Rock. A great portion of the mosque is covered with whitewash, but the drum of the dome and the walls immediately beneath it are richly decorated with mosaics and marble. The mosaics are of the same age as, but of different design from, those in the Dome of the Rock. Some wretched paintings by an Italian artist were introduced when the mosque was repaired at the commencement of the present century. Near the south end of the building is the Minbar Omar, a magnificent pulpit made at Damascus by Nureddin, and brought to Jerusalem by Saladin after he captured the city. It is entirely of wood, with exquisitely carved arabesques and raised panels, inlaid with ivory and mother-of-pearl. Close to the

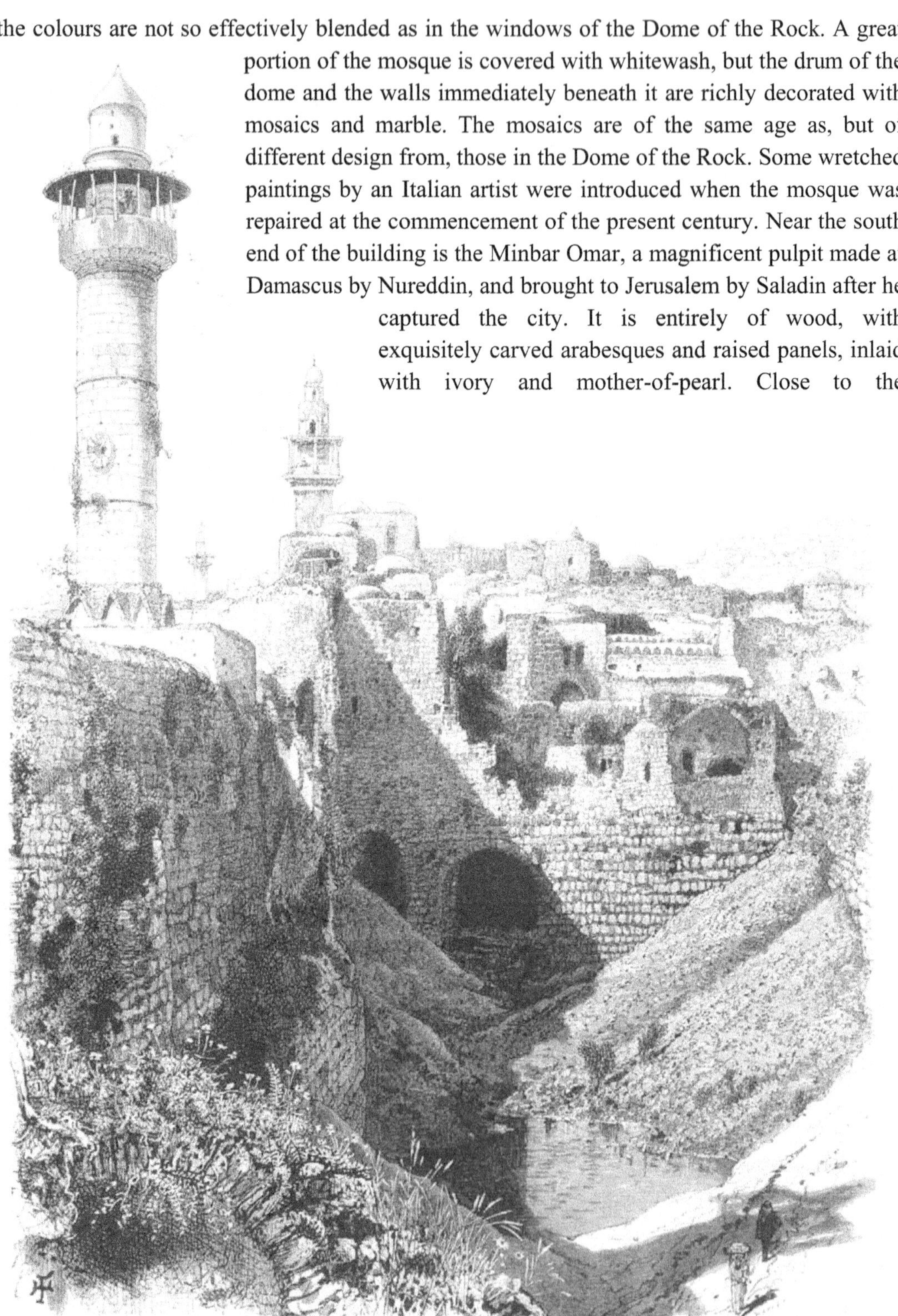

BIRKET ISRAIL-THE POOL OF BETHESDA.

pulpit, on the west, are the "Mihrab of Moses" and the "Footprint of Jesus;" and not far from them is a place where the faithful test their prospects of seeing the houris in Paradise by attempting to pass between two columns which stand close together. One of the columns is chipped, so that the ordeal is not a very difficult one. On the east side of the Aksa are the "Mosque of the Women," the "Mosque of the Forty" (Martyrs), the "Mihrab of John and Zechariah," and the "Gate of Elias." A black slab of stone let into the north wall of the mosque, beneath the porch, is connected with another proof of fitness for Paradise. Those

MOUNT SCOPUS FROM ST. STEPHEN'S GATE.
Mohammedan tombs in the foreground.

who wish to try their chance of finally reaching the desired goal place their backs against one of the pillars of the façade, shut their eyes, and walk with outstretched hands towards the slab; if they are fortunate enough to plant their hands in the centre they will be saved, if not they are doomed. Within the mosque is the entrance to the cistern known as the "Well of the Leaf," of which the following curious story is related. Mohammed said on a certain occasion, "One of my followers will enter Paradise walking, while yet alive." During the caliphate of Omar some Moslems came to Jerusalem to pray. "One of them went to this well to draw water, but while doing so his bucket fell to the bottom. He went down to get it, and to his great surprise found there a door opening into delicious gardens. Having walked through them for a time he plucked a leaf from one of the trees, placed it behind his ear, and hastened back to tell his companions. The matter was reported to the Governor, who sent his servants with the stranger to see these remarkable subterranean gardens; but no door could be found. Omar was written to, and he at once replied that the prophecy of Mohammed was now literally fulfilled, because a living man had walked into Paradise. To test the matter and settle all doubts he desired them to examine the leaf, and if it still remained green and fresh there could be no doubt that it came from Paradise. The leaf had, of course, preserved its verdure."

At the south-east corner of the Mosque el Aksa an open doorway leads to the "Mosque of Omar," a long low building with pointed arches. In its south wall is the Mihrab of Omar, which, according to the existing tradition, marks the place where Omar first prayed after he entered Jerusalem. On either side of the mihrab is a twisted column with a rich grotesquely carved capital. The capitals were exposed to view a few years ago, but have since been covered with plaster. They evidently belonged to some building or altar erected by the Crusaders. Much confusion has arisen from the transfer of the name of this mosque to the Dome of the Rock, for which there is no authority either in history or local tradition.

A flight of steps outside the principal entrance to the Mosque el Aksa leads down to the "Double Passage," which runs beneath the building to the "Double Gate," in the south wall of the Haram esh Sherif. The Double Gateway leads into a vestibule measuring thirty feet by forty feet, in the centre of which stands a fine monolithic column with a Corinthian capital of beautiful design. It consists of alternate leaves of the acanthus and water-lily, without any volutes or any of the accompaniments of the later Corinthian order. From its summit spring four flat arches, dividing the roof into four compartments, each of which is roofed by a low flat dome. The sides of the vestibule were originally built with stones ornamented by a marginal draft, but at some period of reconstruction the masonry was cut away to give relief to the pilasters opposite the monolith, and the drafts disappeared. The two entrances of the Double Gate are separated by a pier, upon which the ends of the great lintels which cover the openings rest. Above the lintels there are relieving arches, and over these a cornice.

The Double Passage is reached by a flight of steps at the end of the western vault. It is covered by well-built semicircular arches, and its walls, as far as the third pier, are of ancient masonry; beyond that point the masonry is of a mixed character. The ascent to the Haram esh Sherif is now easy, but it was at one time much more rapid, and the conduit connecting the "Well of the Leaf" with the aqueduct from Solomon's Pools was cut through when the passage was reconstructed in its present form. The vestibule is undoubtedly a portion of Herod's Temple, and the great monolithic column in its centre corresponds in position with one of the pillars in the Royal Cloisters, which ran along the south wall of the Temple. The direction of the passage, too, is of importance, as there seem some reasons for believing that the passage from the Huldah Gate led directly to the Altar of the Temple.

IN THE MOHAMMEDAN CEMETERY, JERUSALEM.

At the south-east angle of the Haram esh Sherif a flight of steps gives access to a small mosque, in which is shown the "Cradle, or Couch, of our Lord Jesus." The cradle is an old Roman niche for the reception of a statue, placed on its back and covered by a kind of shrine. A small window on the righthand side of the staircase looks into the extensive vaults which support the south-eastern portion of the Haram enclosure. These vaults are known to Franks as "Solomon's Stables," and to Moslems as "the Old Mosque."

In this south-east corner, according to Captain Warren and Mr. Fergusson, Solomon's Palace was situated, and, on the surface above, the latter places the group of buildings, churches, monastery, and hospital, which Justinian erected on the Temple mount. Some years ago Dr. Barclay, the American missionary, found a portion of the ground on which Justinian's buildings are supposed to have stood, paved with *tesseræ,* but all traces of the pavement have now disappeared.

On the east side of Haram esh Sherif is the "Golden Gate," called by Moslems the "Gate of Conversion or Penitence," and sometimes the "Gate of the Eternal" (see page 57).

The floor of the Golden Gate is much below the level of the Haram, and the door which gives access to the interior is at the foot of a steep slope of rubbish. The roof is of comparatively late construction, but the body of the work is in a good state of preservation, the finer parts of the sculpture having been protected by a coat of plaster, which was at some time put on to conceal it. A quasi-classical cornice runs along the wall on both sides of the interior. The style is identical with that of the decorated arch over the "Double Gate," and also with the portion of an old cornice which is built into the façade of the Church of the Holy Sepulchre. In the capital of the pilaster at the north-east corner a variation is produced by looping up the acanthus leaves with a cord. The two columns in the interior "are boldly and originally Byzantine, according neither with the corresponding pilasters in the wall, nor with anything else of that age." The arches spring directly from the architrave blocks and support flat domes with pendentives. Externally the entire entablature, architrave, frieze, and cornice are bent, as at Spalatro, and arching from pillar to pillar—a peculiarity which is said not to be found in any building after the fourth century. The two free-standing columns in the interior are said by Moslem tradition to have been brought on her shoulders by the Queen of Sheba as a present to King Solomon. Through the gateway itself, at the last day, the good will pass on their way to the houris of Paradise, after having safely crossed the Kedron on that bridge which is sharper than the sharpest sword; and through the same portal, according to a very generally received belief, the Christian prince who retakes Jerusalem will make his public entry. The belief that the Christians will recapture the city, and that their own tenure of the country is drawing to a close, is widely spread amongst the Moslems in Palestine. Mr. Fergusson believes the Golden Gate to be the "festal portal which Eusebius describes Constantine as erecting in front of his basilica." Count de Vogue, on the other hand, considers it to be a building of the fifth or sixth century, erected by the Christians, as the Beautiful Gate of the Temple—the Nicanor of the Talmud--to commemorate the miracle therein performed by St. Peter and St. John in curing the lame man, as narrated in the third chapter of the Acts of the Apostles.

North of the Golden Gate is a small modern building called "Solomon's Chair," which contains a sort of cenotaph covered with carpets and cloths. The Moslems attach peculiar sanctity to the place, and visit it every year at the Feast of Bairam. Tradition relates that Solomon died here, and supported himself on his staff to conceal his death from the demons. In course of time, however, the staff became worm-eaten and the body fell, much to the delight of the demons, who then for the first time became aware that they were freed from the king's authority. Many small buildings are scattered over the surface of the Haram esh Sherif (see page 53). One which merits especial notice is that called Saladin's Fountain, or, more properly, the Fountain of Kaït Bey, near the "Cotton Gate." According to the inscription, this beautiful little building was erected by Melek el Ashraf Abu Nasir Kait Bey in the year 849 of the Hegira (A.D. 1445). The dome is entirely covered with arabesques in

KHAN-EZ-ZAIT, THE GREAT BAZAAR OF THE OIL MERCHANTS.
From the south, looking towards the street of the Damascus Gate, which is in full sunlight.

relief. The western and northern sides of the Haram area are lined with cloisters, but there is nothing remarkable in their construction or appearance.

The ceremonies connected with the Temple service required at all times an abundant supply of water, and special arrangements had to be made for its storage. These arrangements consisted of a series of rock-hewn cisterns which were supplied with water by an aqueduct from Solomon's Pools, near Bethlehem, and were connected with each other by a network of conduits. There was also an overflow towards Siloam, possibly by the rock-hewn passages beneath the Triple Gate. The cisterns are amongst the most remarkable features of the Haram esh Sherif. They are from twenty-five to fifty feet in height, and vary considerably in capacity. One, in front of El Aksa, known as the "Great Sea," would hold two million gallons; and the total number of gallons which could be stored probably exceeded twelve millions. Some of the cisterns have been formed by making small openings in the hard stratum of limestone which forms the natural surface of the ground, and then excavating large chambers in the soft underlying stratum, the roof being supported in some places by pillars of rock left for the purpose. Other cisterns are made by forming an open tank, and

ROBINSON'S ARCH, JERUSALEM.
Part of a bridge which crossed the Tyropoeon Valley, named after its discoverer, Dr. Robinson.

then throwing a plain covering arch over the excavation. The former are certainly the most ancient, having apparently been made before the arch came into common use for covering large openings; and it is a remarkable fact that no large cisterns of this

THE HILL OF EVIL COUNSEL FROM THE SOUTH WALL, JERUSALEM.
The nearer hill-side is the eastern slope of Ophel; a good example of terrace cultivation.

description are found to the north of the Dome of the Rock. The form of some of the cisterns is so peculiar that it seems probable they were originally made for another purpose. One has a curious cruciform shape, with a flight of rock-hewn steps leading down to it; another has a long chamber raised nearly five feet above the floor-line; and a third, besides a raised chamber into which there are two entrances, has a small elevated platform with steps leading up to it, as it were to the altar of a church. One of the cisterns north of the Dome of the Rock is identified by Captain Warren with the passage which led from the Gate Nitsots to the Gate Tadi of the Temple, and by Mr. Fergusson with a passage connecting the Anastasis with the Basilica of Constantine; and another cistern is believed by the former gentleman to be part of the passage from the Temple gate Mokad.

The cisterns being covered in, they must always have kept the water cool and pleasant to the taste, and there could have been but slight loss from evaporation. The aqueduct which supplied the cisterns with water crosses the Tyropoeon Valley on the viaduct of which Wilson's Arch forms a part, and enters the Haram at the Gate of the Chain. Hence the principal branch runs to a fountain called El Kas (the Cup), nearly midway between the Dome of the Rock and El Aksa (see vignette), and close to the site assigned by Mr. Fergusson to the Jewish altar. From El Kas smaller conduits lead to the cisterns in the southern half of the Haram.

The description of the Haram esh Sherif which has been given above will, it is hoped, enable the reader to picture to himself the present state of Mount Moriah and the character of the buildings that now occupy its surface. A few notes on the Temple and the various theories with regard to its position may now be added. The altar of David was erected on the threshing-floor of Araunah the Jebusite, and the succeeding altars of the Jews were set up on the same spot until the capture and destruction of Jerusalem by the Romans. If, then, the site of the altar of Herod's Temple could be ascertained, the Temple questions would at once be solved. Of Herod's Temple there are detailed descriptions in Josephus and the Talmud, but unfortunately the question of its position is greatly complicated by the literal fulfilment of the prophecy that not one stone should be left upon another.

The Temple which Herod commenced to build in the sixteenth year of his reign was, according to Josephus, a square of six hundred feet. This is distinctly stated in three separate passages: in Ant. xv. 11, 3 the enclosure is said to be four stadii in circuit, each side measuring one stadium in length; in Ant. xv. 11, 5 the Stoa Basilica is described as extending "from the east valley to that on the west, for it was impossible it should reach any farther," and as being one stadium long; and again in Ant. xx. 9, 7 the length of the eastern cloister of the outer court is given as four hundred cubits, that is one stadium, or six hundred feet. If the dimensions had been mentioned once only it would be possible to suppose that an error had been made, but it is almost impossible to believe that the same mistake could occur in three different places, or that Josephus, who knew very well what a stadium was, should declare the Stoa Basilica to be one stadium long when it was one and a half, as it would have been had the cloisters extended the full length of the south wall of the Haram. The gates of the Temple enclosure were as follows: on the west there were four gates; the first "led to the King's palace and went to a passage over the intermediate valley," a description which agrees well with the gate at the end of Wilson's Arch, from which a street now runs in almost a direct line to the site occupied by Herod's Palace, over the old Tyropoeon viaduct. Two other gates led to the suburbs of the city; one of them is certainly that known now as "Barclay's Gate," and the other is probably "Warren's Gate," north of Wilson's Arch, which may have led

THE SOUTH WALL OF THE HARAM ESH SHERIF.
The Dome of the Mosque El Aksa and the Mount of Olives.

down from the cloisters which connected the Castle of Antonia with the Temple. The last gate on the west side "led to the other city where the road descended down into the valley by a great number of steps and thence up again by the ascent, for the city lay over against the Temple in the manner of a theatre." This corresponds with all that is known of the structural arrangement of the approach to the Stoa Basilica over "Robinson's Arch." On the north side of the enclosure there was one gate called in the Talmud "Tadi" (obscurity) "which served for no (ordinary) purpose; " and on the east also one gate, on which was portrayed the city Shushan.

"Through it one could see the high-priest who burned the heifer and all his assistants going out to the Mount of Olives." The south side had "gates in its middle"—the Huldah Gate, that served for going in and out which there is little difficulty in identifying with the "Double Gate" beneath the Mosque El Aksa.

The walls of the Temple enclosure were surmounted by cloisters of great magnificence. On the north, west, and east the cloisters were double, with monolithic columns of white marble and roofs of curiously carved cedar. On the south were the royal cloisters, Stoa Basilica, which consisted of one hundred and sixty-two columns with Corinthian capitals, arranged in four rows so as to form three aisles. The outer row of columns was attached to the wall; the remaining columns stood free; and the size of each was such "that three men might, with their arms extended, fathom it round and join their hands again." The centre aisle was forty-five feet, and each of the side aisles thirty feet wide, and the "roofs were adorned with deep sculptures in wood, representing many sorts of figures. The middle was much higher than the rest, and the wall of the front was adorned with beams, resting upon pillars that were interwoven into it, and that front was all of polished stone; insomuch that its fineness to such as had not seen it was incredible, and to such as had seen it was greatly amazing."

The cloisters were separated from the steps which led up to the Inner Temple by an open space which is supposed to have been from twenty-four to thirty cubits wide, the width varying on each side of the Temple. The cloisters and Court of the Gentiles formed the Outer Temple, and it was this portion of the building which our Lord characterized as a den of thieves. Here, as in a market-place, were assembled those who bought and sold, and here stood the tables of the money-changers and those who sold doves. Here the Jew who had come from some Gentile nation could change the foreign money he had brought with him into Jewish coin, which could alone be paid into the Temple treasury, and here turtle-doves and young pigeons could be purchased for sacrifice. The whole or a portion of the eastern cloister was called Solomon's Porch. Here Jesus was accustomed to walk; and it was here, too, that the people ran together and surrounded Peter and John after they had healed the lame man.

From the Court of the Gentiles a few steps led up to a flat terrace called the Chel, on the outer edge of which ran a stone screen or partition, three cubits high, of very elegant construction. Upon the screen "stood pillars, at equal distances from one another, declaring the law of purity, some in Greek and some in Roman letters, that no foreigner should go within that sanctuary" on pain of death. It was one of the inscriptions from these pillars which, as previously mentioned, was found by Mons. Ganneau. The Chel on the north, west, and south was ten cubits wide; but on the east, in front of the Temple, it was of greater width, and formed a rectangular space surrounded by a wall of its own, called the Court of the Women. Such as were pure were allowed to enter this court with their wives, but the women were not allowed to pass beyond.

From the Chel other steps led up through gates to the Inner Temple, which was square, each side probably about two hundred and ten cubits, and surrounded by a wall thirty-seven and a half feet high on the inside. In this wall there were seven gates: on the north the Gate Nitzus, the Gate of Offering, and the Gate Mokad; on the south the Gate of Flaming, the Gate of Offering, and the Water Gate, which opened directly on the altar, and appears to have been in continuation of the Huldah Gate; and on the east was the Beautiful Gate, or Gate Nicanor of the Talmud. In addition to the above, three gates led into the Court of the Women, one on the north, another on the south, and a third on the east. On each side of the gateways there were chambers which were used as stores, &c., in connection with the Temple service. Nine of these gates "were on every side covered over with gold and silver, as were the jambs of their doors and their lintels." The Beautiful Gate was of Corinthian brass, and ornamented in the most costly manner with richer and thicker plates of gold than the other gates. Within the wall of the Inner Temple enclosure were the Temple with its altar, the Court of the Men of Israel, and the Court of the Priests. In the Temple, as reconstructed by Herod, the Holy of Holies "remained a cube of twenty cubits, and occupied the same place as it had from Solomon's days. The Holy Place was forty cubits east and west by twenty cubits across, and thirty cubits high, as before." The porch was eleven cubits wide by "apparently fifty cubits north and south, bounded on the east by a wall five cubits thick, while one six cubits in thickness separated it from the Holy Place, making twenty-two cubits in all." The façade of the Temple was one hundred cubits long, and in front of it, at the top of a flight of steps leading down to the Court of the Priests, stood the Toran, or screen bearing the golden vine. The Temple was partly surrounded by thirty-eight little chambers, "fifteen in the north, fifteen in the south, and eight in the west. The northern and southern ones were (placed) five over five, and five over them; and in the west three over three and two over them. To each were three doors: one to the little chamber to the right, one to the little chamber to the left, and one to the little chamber over it." Internally the Temple was divided into the Holy Place—in which there were "three things that were very wonderful and famous among all mankind, the candlestick, the table (of shewbread), and the altar of incense"—and the Holy of Holies, inaccessible and inviolable, in which nothing was kept. The veil of the Temple is stated to have been a "Babylonian curtain, embroidered with blue, and fine linen, and scarlet, and purple," and of a very fine texture. The colours were symbolical of the universe: the scarlet and blue represented, by means of their colours, fire and air; the fine linen, earth, by the flax of which it was made; and the purple, the sea, from the circumstance that the dye was obtained from salt-water shell-fish. Upon the curtain was also embroidered "all that was mystical in the heavens, except the twelve signs of the zodiac representing living creatures."

There is much divergence in the views of the writers who have attempted to reconstruct the Temple and fix its position within the Haram enclosure. Mr. Fergusson supposes the Temple to have occupied a square of about six hundred feet at the south-west angle of the Haram esh Sherif, and he is followed in this by Messrs. Thrupp, Lewin, and others. xxxxxxxxxx

THE UPPER POOL OF SILOAM.
Its walls are covered with mosses and ferns, especially the maidenhair fern with which the picture is appropriately bordered.

THE LOWER POOL OF SILOAM.
The old mulberry-tree, supported by stones, is said to mark the spot where the Prophet Isaiah was sawn asunder, in the presence of King Manasseh.

Robinson's Arch, Barclay's Gate, and Wilson's Arch are identified with three of the west gates of the Temple, and the Double Gate with the Huldah Gate on the south. The altar is placed near the fountain El Kas, in front of the Mosque El Aksa (see vignette). Captain Warren, R.E., considers that the outer courts of the Temple of Herod are defined by the east, west, and south walls of the Haram esh Sherif, and by the northern edge of the raised platform of the Dome of the Rock. He places the altar over the west end of the curious cruciform cistern beneath the platform. Count de Vogue, Mons. de Saulcy, Sir Henry James, Dr. Sepp, and others, believe that the entire surface of the Haram enclosure was occupied by the Temple, its courts and cloisters. Drs. Robinson and Barclay, Professors Porter and Kiepert, maintain that the Temple enclosure was a square of about nine hundred and twenty-five feet, situated in the southern portion of the Haram. Drs. Tobler and Rosen believe that the Temple was a square of six hundred feet, nearly coincident with the platform of the Dome of the Rock. In these last cases the altar is placed on the Sakhra. With regard to the position of Antonia all differ. The questions are such as can only be settled definitely by excavation; but, so far as we can judge at present, Mr. Fergusson's theory of the Temple site most nearly accords with what is known of the features of the ground and with the written description of Josephus.

From the Haram esh Sherif we may pass out of the city by the "Gate of the Tribes" and "St. Stephen's Gate," and commence an examination of the modern walls of Jerusalem, which were built by Sultan Suleiman in the sixteenth century. From the gate of St. Stephen to Burj Laklak, "Stork Tower," at the north-east angle, the wall is partly protected by a ditch excavated in the rock, and the bases of the flanking towers, thirty-two feet wide, are also rock-hewn. Between Burj Laklak and the Damascus Gate in the north wall there is a similar ditch cut in the rock, and between these two points there is also a closed gateway known as the "Gate of Herod," but more properly called the "Gate of Splendour, or Blooming." Near the latter gate the ditch is of considerable depth, a feature which probably marks the original entrance to the quarries (see page 93). From the Damascus Gate to the north-west angle of the city, in which "Goliath's Castle" stands, the wall appears to have been built on the foundations of an older one; material of all kinds has been used in its construction, and at one point the Moslem builders have made a curious attempt to assimilate the older work to their masonry by cutting false joints in the stones of the former. The wall was protected by a ditch cut in the rock, but it is now almost filled with rubbish. The ruin known as "Goliath's Castle" is an old tower of rubble masonry, partly faced with stone having a marginal draft. Within the tower there is a modern chamber, and beneath it an older one with two piers, which are supposed by some writers to be Herodian; they are, however, more probably Crusading or Saracenic. The castle has been identified with the octagonal tower of Psephinus, mentioned by Josephus, but it is more probably the Tower of Tancred, mentioned in the histories of the Crusades. There seems evidence, too, that the castle is built on the foundations of one of the old walls of the city. From the north-west angle to the Jaffa Gate the wall is built on the remains of an older one; there is here a great accumulation of rubbish, and near the gate the original features of the ground are entirely concealed. South of the Jaffa Gate lies the Citadel (see page 3), protected by its ditch; thence to the south-west angle and onwards to the Zion Gate the wall has been reconstructed with old material; and from the Zion Gate to the Dung Gate in the Tyropoeon Valley, and thence to the Double Gate, the wall is of the same character (see page 75). From the Double Gate to the Castle of Antonia, near St. Stephen's Gate, the wall of the Haram esh Sherif is also the city wall. How far the existing walls follow the course of the old walls of Jerusalem is a question that has often been asked, and it is one that it is extremely difficult to answer, owing to the limited information we possess respecting the actual nature of the topographical features of the ground. There are, however, certain points which may now be looked upon as certain, and, taking these as a starting-point, future excavations may complete the good work commenced by Captain Warren. Josephus describes the walls as follows. The first or old wall commenced on the north at the Tower Hippicus, and extended as far as the Xystus, and then, joining to the council-house, ended at the west cloister of the Temple. Going the other way, it also commenced at Hippicus, and, facing west, extended through a place called Bethso to the Gate of the Essenes; after that it faced south, making a turn above the fountain of Siloam, where it also faced east at Solomon's Pool and reached as far as Ophlas, where it was joined to the eastern cloister of the Temple. In this wall there were sixty towers, each twenty cubits square. The first section of the wall, there can be little question, ran from the Jaffa Gate to the "Gate of the Chain" of the Haram esh Sherif, following a line a little to the south of, and nearly parallel to, David's Street. The second section of the wall is more difficult to trace. There is, however, in the Protestant cemetery, on the western slope of modern Zion, a remarkable excavation in the rock, which gives the line of the city wall thus far. The rock is here, for a distance of one hundred feet, scarped, or cut perpendicularly downwards, so as to have a cliff twenty-four feet high, on the top of which the old wall ran; and there would appear to have been a succession of these scarps, with rock-terraces in front of them, to the bottom of the valley. A flight of rock-hewn steps led down from the wall above, and the position of three flanking towers can be recognised. Beyond the steps the rock scarp turns to the east, and there are traces of either a ditch or an entrance to the city. This point appears to have been the corner of the wall at or near which was the Gate of the Essenes. The farther course of the old wall and the place at which it crossed the Tyropoeon are unknown. The word Bethso (Dung Place) gives a clue to the route followed by Nehemiah when he went out by night to view the walls. He apparently left Jerusalem by the Jaffa Gate, Valley Gate, and rode to the Dung Gate, or Bethso; he then went on to the Gate of the Fountain and to the King's Pool in the Tyropoeon Valley, but the deep narrow ravine was so encumbered with the rubbish of the fallen walls that there was no room for the beast that was under him to pass; he therefore went up by the brook, the more open Kedron valley, and "viewed the wall, and turned back, and entered by the Gate of the Valley and so returned." In the account of the rebuilding of the walls under Nehemiah, the Dung Gate is said to have been one thousand cubits from the Valley Gate, or near the south-west angle of the present city wall. The second wall, we are told, "took its beginning from that gate which they called Gennath, which belonged to the first wall; it only encompassed the northern quarter of the city, and reached as far as the tower Antonia." No distinct trace of this wall has yet been found, but the place at which it joined the Castle of Antonia seems to be defined by the rock-hewn ditch at the Convent of the Sisters of Zion, which Monsieur Ganneau was enabled to trace some distance towards the west. The position of the gate Gennath is uncertain Captain Warren's excavations showed that the old archway in the city now known by that name was a Roman portal built on made earth mixed with pottery, and that the roadway beneath it was twenty-five feet above the rock; the situation, moreover, is not such as would be suitable, having regard to the natural features of the ground, for

THE JEWISH CEMETERY IN THE VALLEY OF JEHOSHAPHAT.
Showing the tombs of Zechariah, St. James, and Jehoshaphat. Bridge over the rocky bed of the Kedron in the distance, and an Ashkenazi Jew in the foreground.

a city gateway. It appears to us that the straight street known as Christian Street may possibly mark the line of the second wall, and that the solid nature of the substructure upon

ABSALOM'S PILLAR, VALLEY OF JEHOSHAPHAT.
The village of Siloam in the distance partly concealed by olive-trees. Bridge over the bed of the Kedron.

which that street lies is indicated by the Pool of Hezekiah on the one side and the Church of St. John the Baptist on the other. In this case the gate Gennath must be looked for near the junction of David Street and Christian Street. The third or outer wall began "at the Tower Hippicus, whence it reached as far as the north quarter of the city and the Tower Psephinus, and then was so far extended till it came over against the monuments of Helena, which Helena was queen of Adiabene, the mother of Izates; it then extended farther to a great length, and passed by the sepulchral caverns of the kings, and bent again at the Tower of the Corner, at the monument which is called the Monument of the Fuller, and joined to the old wall at the valley called the Valley of Kedron." There were ninety towers, each twenty cubits wide, and for a height of twenty cubits built of solid masonry. From the remains of old foundations it is almost certain that the third wall followed the line of the present one.

The "Caverns of the Kings" have been sometimes identified with the great stone quarries near the Damascus Gate. These quarries are of great extent, and were worked with a view of mining or getting out stone from what is locally known as the "Malaki" bed of limestone. The quarries are thus entirely subterranean, and they formerly extended some distance on each side of the present city wall. When that wall was first built it was protected by a rock-hewn ditch, and the workmen in forming this cut through the upper strata, and so divided the quarries into two parts; that on the north is now known as Jeremiah's Grotto, that on the south as the "Quarries," or "Cotton Grotto" (see page 96). At the same period an aqueduct which conveyed water from the north to the Temple area was also cut through. The entrance to the quarries is by a small hole between the roof of the cavern and the rubbish with which the ditch is filled. The floor falls considerably towards the south, in which direction the quarry extends for about two hundred yards, and the roof is supported at uncertain intervals by pillars of rock.

The quarrymen appear to have worked in gangs of five or six; the height of the stone determined the distance of the workmen from each other, and each man carried in a vertical cut four inches wide till he reached the required depth; the blocks were then separated by wooden wedges driven in and wetted so as to cause them to swell. In many places the stones have been left half cut out, and the marks of the chisel and pick are as fresh as if the quarrymen had only just left their work; even the black patches made by the smoke of the lamps are still visible. In one part of the quarry, dropping water, derived probably from the leakage of cisterns above, has worn the rock away into the form of a basin. The water is impure and unpleasant to the taste. The floor of the quarry is covered with stone chippings, which seem to indicate that the blocks of stone were "dressed" before they were removed from the ground, and large flakes of the overlying strata have fallen from the roof, the spaces left between the pillars being much too wide. The portion of the quarry known as Jeremiah's Grotto (see page 97) is much smaller, but there are evident traces that it was worked in the same manner. Two Moslem tombs are shown within, and according to tradition Jeremiah here wrote the Book of Lamentations. In front of the grotto is an open court planted with fruit trees, beneath which there is a fine cistern.

One of the most pleasant excursions in the vicinity of Jerusalem is that to Bethany by the

THE VILLAGE OF SILOAM FROM THE TOMB OF ST. JAMES.
Shewing a portion of the great Jewish cemetery on the western slope of the Mount of Olives.

pathway over the Mount of Olives, returning by the lower road above Siloam. Passing out of the city by St. Stephen's Gate, a sharp descent leads to the bed of Kedron, which is spanned by

THE GARDEN OF GETHSEMANE.
Franciscan monks under the ancient olive-trees, and an Arab gardener at work.

a single arch; and a few paces now brings the traveller to the Chapel of the Tomb of the Virgin (see page 87), where according to tradition she lay after death until her "assumption."

The chapel is on the left of the road. A few steps lead down to an open court, in which there is a fine porch of the Crusading period, the only part of the church above ground. The chapel, which is about thirty-five feet below the court, is reached by a flight of marble steps. On

ENTRANCE TO THE CHAPEL OF THE TOMB OF THE VIRGIN.
In the valley of the Kedron. The lizards on the sunny wall are thoroughly characteristic of the place.

descending, a chapel on the right is said to contain the tombs of Joachim and Anna, the parents of the Virgin, and an altar in a chapel to the left marks the last resting-place of Joseph, the husband of Mary. The chapel, or subterranean church, is about ninety feet long from east to west, and twenty feet wide. In the east arm there is a small shrine containing the tomb of Mary, outside of which the Greeks and Armenians have each an altar. South of the tomb there is a Moslem "mihrab," and in the western arm of the chapel, close to a large cistern, the Abyssinians have erected an altar. The chapel is excavated in the rock, and in forming it advantage appears to have been taken of a natural cavern, or possibly of an old tomb chamber. In its present state the chapel has little in common with the tombs in the neighbourhood of Jerusalem. The Chapel of the Tomb of the Virgin was rebuilt by Millicent, the wife of Fulke, fourth king of Jerusalem, since which time it has apparently received little alteration.

On the right-hand side of the road is the Garden of Gethsemane (see page 86), a small enclosure surrounded by a high wall. The ground is laid out in flower beds, which are carefully tended by a Franciscan monk; but the most interesting objects are the venerable olive-trees, which are said to date from the time of Christ, and which may, in truth, be direct descendants of trees which grew in the same place at the time of the Crucifixion. A tradition, at least as old as the fourth century, identifies this plot of ground with the garden to which Jesus was wont to retire with His disciples.

The Church of the Ascension, on the Mount of Olives (see page 90), is a small octagonal chapel, surmounted by a circular drum and dome, standing in the centre of a paved court. The bases and capitals of the columns, taken from older buildings, are of white marble. At the east end of the open court the Greeks, Armenians, Syrians, and Copts, have altars. A tradition connecting the Mount of Olives with our Lord's Ascension existed at a very early period, though in direct contradiction to the words of St. Luke, who says, "He led them out as far as Bethany, and He lifted up his, hands and blessed them. And it came to pass, while He blessed them, He was parted from them and carried up into heaven." Eusebius mentions the large number of pilgrims who came from all parts of the world to worship on the Mount of Olives; and the Empress Helena, in erecting a basilica on the spot, about 333 A.D., only perpetuated the existing tradition.

The road from the Mount of Olives to Bethany for about five hundred yards follows the south side of the hill; it then turns abruptly to the south and crosses the narrow ridge which joins the Mount of Olives to the hill above Bethany. Upon the ridge the Crusaders placed Bethphage (see page 92), and here, in 1877, the ruins of a mediæval church, with its apse, were discovered, enclosing an isolated block of rock ornamented with paintings and inscriptions. The rock is about three feet high, and its position in the chapel, on the north side and probably between two columns of the nave, is remarkable. On the south side, facing Bethany, there is a fresco representing the raising of Lazarus; on the north side, facing Olivet, the disciples are represented as having just obtained permission to take the ass and the foal; on the east face the subject of the fresco appears to have been the consecration of the chapel; and on the west, figures are seen bearing palm-branches, perhaps part of a fresco representing our Lord's triumphal entry into Jerusalem. The inscriptions may be ascribed beyond doubt to the twelfth century, and the name Bernard Witard occurs on one of the faces. In the cartulary of the Church of the Holy Sepulchre the name of Johannes Guitard (Witard) is found, and Mons. Ganneau conjectures that Bernard belonged to the same family and defrayed the expenses of the monument. The paintings are sadly damaged, but they are said "to remind one of illuminations in a precious missal rather than an ordinary fresco drawn to hide the naked stone."

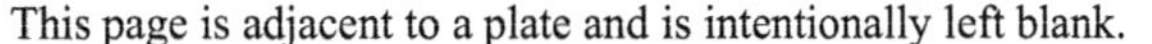
This page is adjacent to a plate and is intentionally left blank.

BETHANY.

Theodericus, 1172 A.D., in his account of the Holy Places, states that Bethphage lay between Bethany and the Mount of Olives, and that there was then a "fair chapel" in which was to be seen the stone on which our Lord stood before mounting the ass—evidently the monolith which was discovered in 1877. There is thus no doubt as to the site of the mediæval Bethphage, but it is doubtful whether the place is identical with the Bethphage of the gospel, of which no certain trace has yet been found.

GOLDEN GATE.
Moslem tombs in the foreground.

From the ruins of the little chapel the road descends to Bethany, now a small village of wretched hovels, surrounded by fig, olive, almond, and carob trees, which contrast pleasantly with the barren rocks of the adjoining hills. The Arabic name of this place is El Aziríyeh, from Lazarus, and the most prominent object is the Castle of Lazarus, erected during the period of the Latin Kingdom of Jerusalem. Near the castle is the tomb; a flight of steps leads down to a small square chamber, whence other steps give access to the vault in which the body of Lazarus is said to have been laid. The vault is lined with masonry, and has nothing in common with the rock-hewn tombs in which the Jews buried their dead. In Bethany are shown the houses of Mary and Martha and of Simon the Leper, and a short distance on the road to Jericho the place is pointed out at which Martha met Jesus. Though tradition may be at fault with regard to the tomb and the houses, there can be no doubt as to the correctness of the identification of El Azaríyeh with Bethany, the village in which Jesus lodged before the last Passover, and in the immediate vicinity of which He called Lazarus forth from the grave.

The Roman road from Jericho to Jerusalem, after leaving Bethany, winds round the southern slope of the Mount of Olives, and, passing above Siloam, ascends the Kedron Valley to the Garden of Gethsemane. Over this road Jesus must often have travelled with his disciples, and there is one place, where the road is partly hewn out of the rock, which has apparently undergone no change since the days of His earthly ministry.

MOSQUE AND CHURCH OF THE ASCENSION, MOUNT OF OLIVES.

It was by this road, too, that our Saviour made His triumphal entry into Jerusalem, an event which is so graphically described by the Dean of Westminster that we venture to borrow his words: "Two vast streams of people met that day. The one poured out from the city (John xii. 13); and as they came through the gardens whose clusters of palm-trees rose on the south-eastern corner of Olivet, they cut down the long branches, as was their wont at the Feast of Tabernacles, and moved upwards towards Bethany with loud shouts of welcome. From Bethany streamed forth the crowds who had assembled there on the previous night, and who came testifying to the great event at the sepulchre of Lazarus. In going towards Jerusalem the road soon loses sight of Bethany. It is now a rough but still broad and well-defined mountain track, winding over loose rock and stones, and here and there deeply excavated; a steep declivity blow on the left, the sloping shoulder of Olivet above it on the right;

NEBY SAMWIL, FROM THE MOUNT OF OLIVES.
The highest mountain near Jerusalem, 3,006 feet above the sea.

fig-trees below and above, growing out of the rocky soil. Along the road the multitudes threw down the branches which they cut as they went along, or spread out a rude matting formed of the palm-branches they had already cut as they came out. The larger portion—those perhaps who escorted Him from Bethany—unwrapped their loose cloaks from their shoulders and stretched them along the rough path to form a momentary carpet as he approached (Matt. xxi. 8). The two streams met. Half of the vast mass, turning round, preceded; the other half followed (Mark xi. 9). Gradually the long procession swept round the little valley that furrows the hill, and over the ridge on its western side, where first begins the descent of the Mount of Olives towards Jerusalem. At this point the first view is caught of the south-western corner of the city. The temple and the more northern portions are hid by the slope of Olivet on the right; what is seen is only Mount Zion, now for the most part a rough field, crowned with

TRADITIONAL SITE OF BETHPHAGE, THE HOUSE OF FIGS.
On the ridge which leads from the Mount of Olives to the hill above Bethany. Fig-trees grow by the wayside, and branches of the fig-tree border the picture.

the Mosque of David and the angle of the western walls, but then covered with houses to its base, surmounted by the Castle of Herod, on the supposed site of the Palace of David, from which that portion of Jerusalem, emphatically the 'City of David,' derived its name. It

was at this precise point, 'as he drew near, at the descent of the Mount of Olives'—(may it not have been from the sight thus opening upon them?)—that the shout of triumph burst forth from the multitude, 'Hosanna to the Son of David! Blessed is He that cometh in the name of the Lord.' (Matt. xxi. 9). There was a pause as the shout rang through the long defile; and as the Pharisees who stood by in the crowd complained, He pointed to the stones, which, strewn beneath their feet, would immediately cry out if 'these were to hold their

PART OF THE NORTH WALL OF JERUSALEM.
Formed of the native rock blended with masonry. A shepherd in the foreground is playing a double-reed pipe.

peace.' Again the procession advanced. The road descends a slight declivity, and the glimpse of the city is again withdrawn behind the intervening ridge of Olivet. A few moments and the path mounts again; it climbs a rugged ascent, it reaches a ledge of smooth rock, and in an instant the whole city bursts into view. As now the dome of the Mosque El Aksa rises like a ghost from the earth before the traveller who stands on the ledge, so then must have risen the Temple tower; as now the vast enclosure of the Mussulman sanctuary, so then must have spread the Temple courts; as now the gray town on its broken hills, so then the magnificent city, with its background—long since vanished away—of gardens and suburbs on the western plateau behind. Immediately below was the Valley of the Kedron, here seen in its greatest depths as it joins the Valley of Hinnom, and thus giving full effect to the great peculiarity of Jerusalem, seen only on its eastern side—its situation as of a city rising out of a deep abyss. It is hardly possible to doubt that this rise and turn of the road—this rocky ledge—was the exact point where the multitude paused again, and 'He, when He beheld the city, wept over it.'"

The road from Bethany to Jerusalem leaves Siloam (Silwan) on the left. This village (see pages 85, 115), which derives its name from the pool at the mouth of the Tyropoeon Valley, stretches north and south in a straggling, irregular manner along the lower slopes of the Mount of Offence. Entering the village at the northern end, the visitor has on his left hand a high cliff, which was evidently worked as a quarry at some early period. The houses and the streets of Siloam, if such they may be called, are filthy in the extreme, and the villagers are notorious thieves, sometimes not over-courteous to visitors. Their principal occupation is carrying water from "Job's Well" for sale in Jerusalem, and they have an ingenious way of blowing out the sheepskins in which the water is carried, so that they may appear filled when containing only half the proper quantity of water. About one hundred of the villagers form a group apart from the rest, called "men of Dhiban," the descendants apparently of a colony from the capital of King Mesha, which at some remote period crossed the Jordan and established itself on the borders of Kedron. Siloam, the village, is unmentioned in ancient times, but it may possibly mark the spot upon which Solomon built high places "for Ashtoreth the abomination of the Zidonians, and for Chemosh the abomination of the Moabites, and for Milcom (Molech) the abomination of the children of Ammon." The Mount of Offence (see page 107) behind the village would in this case be the "mount of corruption" of 2 Kings xxiii. 13, as it certainly is the "mons offensionis" of early travellers, the "opprobrious hill" of Milton.

Jerusalem is surrounded by cemeteries, ancient and modern. Without the Zion Gate, near the tomb of David, are those of the Latins, Greeks, and Armenians; and here may be seen the grave of the ill-fated Irishman, Costigan, who, after having successfully descended Jordan in a boat, and reached the southern end of the Dead Sea, died in the Latin convent at Jerusalem. Here, too, a little to the south of the Latin cemetery, two members of the American Mission, Dr. Dodge and Mrs. Thomson, were buried. The present Protestant cemetery is on the western slope of the same hill, above the Valley of Hinnom; it is the only burial place near Jerusalem which is efficiently closed and properly tended. Within its walls lie with remains of the two first Anglican bishops of Jerusalem—Dr. Alexander and Dr. Gobat and also those of Mr. Tyrwhitt Drake, who died of fever, due to exposure and over-exertion whilst engaged on the great work of the survey of Palestine. The Moslem cemeteries are—first, that extending along the eastern wall of the city, from a little north of St. Stephen's Gate to the vicinity of the south-east angle of the Haram esh Sherif, which, from its proximity to the sacred area, is most esteemed; second, the ground above Jeremiah's Grotto; and, third, the extensive cemetery round the Birket Mamilla, near the head of the Valley of Hinnom (see page 102). The great Jewish cemetery is on the western slope of the Mount of Olives; it extends northwards from Siloam, and runs up the hill almost to the Tombs of the Prophets. In places, especially near Absalom's Pillar and the Tomb of Zacharias, the ground is literally paved with tombstones (see pages 82 and 85). The simplest form of tomb is that in which a common grave is sunk in the rock, and a reveal cut round its mouth to receive a covering slab. In some cases the slab is flush with the surface of the rock; in others it is raised above it and ornamented like the lid of a sarcophagus. Another simple form of tomb, to which the name of "trough grave" has been given, is that in which an arched recess is cut in the face of the rock and a common grave sunk in its floor. A third simple form is that in which a rectangular space is cut into the vertical face of the rock, after the manner of an oven, extending six feet or more horizontally inwards, and sufficiently wide and high to admit of a corpse being pushed in. The opening is closed by a stone slab or by a rough unhewn mass of rock. Such a grave is called in the Talmud a "kok" (pl. "kokim"). A fourth kind of tomb is the "shelf grave"—a shelf or bench, six feet long, cut in the vertical face of the rock, upon which the corpse was laid even when it had first been placed in a sarcophagus. The most common description of tomb is that in which a number of kokim, shelf, or trough graves are grouped together in one or more chambers of the same excavation. These tombs may be divided into three classes. The first class is that in which a natural cavern in one of the softer strata of limestone is adapted to sepulchral purposes. Kokim are cut in the sides of the cave, with their beds on a level with the ground, and the openings are then closed with rough stone slabs resting against the face of the rock or fitting more closely into the excavation. In this class of tomb no arrangement was made for closing the entrance to the cavern. It seems not improbable that these tombs were used for the burial of the poor, and they were perhaps constructed at the public expense. In the second class of tomb a square or oblong chamber is carefully cut in the solid rock; the entrance is by a low square opening, closed either by a closely fitting stone slab or by a stone door turning on a socket hinge and secured by bolts on the inside. These tombs, remarkable for the care which has been bestowed on the excavation, were probably the family vaults of wealthy people. The third class of tomb is that in which one entrance leads to several tomb-chambers, each containing a large number of graves, and sometimes sarcophagi.

One of the best examples of this class is the Tombs of the Kings (see page 103), situated to the north of Jerusalem on the right-hand side of the road to Nablus. A large rectangular court, measuring about ninety-three feet by eighty-seven feet, and some twenty feet deep, is sunk in the solid rock, which here forms the natural surface of the ground. On the south side a broad trench was cut so as to leave a wall of rock seven feet thick between it and the court; a flight of steps leads to the bottom of the trench, whence an arched doorway, cut in the intervening rock, gives access to the court. In the west face of the court an open portico is excavated in the rock; the front was supported by two pillars, which are now broken away. The face of the portico is

THE QUARRIES NEAR TO THE DAMASCUS GATE.
Beneath the city of Jerusalem.

ornamented with a frieze and cornice of a debased Roman Doric order; the former is enriched with clusters of grapes, triglyphs, and paterae, and a continuous garland of fruit and foliage, which extends across the portico and is carried down the sides.

About half a mile from the Tombs of the Kings, on the road to Neby Samwil, is the extensive necropolis which includes the Tombs of the Judges (see page 103). Within an open vestibule facing west, ornamented with a simple architrave moulding, surmounted by a Greek-looking pediment of considerable beauty, there is a small doorway, also decorated with architrave and pediment, which leads from the vestibule to the principal tomb-chamber.

Returning to the Kedron Valley and following its course downwards, numbers of tombs of greater or less size are to be seen on either side. The most noteworthy is that of Simon the Just, to which the Jews resort the thirty-third day after the Passover to celebrate the memory of the son of Onias, who was high priest during the reign of Ptolemy Soter. We now come to the well-known group of tombs in the Valley of Jehoshaphat, the first being "Absalom's Tomb" (see page 83). The lower part of this monument is a mass of solid rock about twenty feet square, which has been completely detached from the cliff behind it by working away a passage ten feet in width at the sides and nine at the back, so as to leave the tomb standing in a square recess hewn out of the cliff. It contains a chamber eight feet

GROTTO OF JEREMIAH.
In the foreground is a goatherd playing on a double-reed pipe.

square, with shelf graves on two sides for the reception of sarcophagi. The original door was situated immediately above the cornice, and a few steps led down to the chamber. Another more modern door consisted of a horizontal passage on a level with the chamber, and opening to the exterior, at half the height of the monument. In the face of the rock behind the monolith is the entrance to the Tomb of Jehoshaphat, surmounted by a pediment in the same style as that of the Tombs of the Judges (see page 82). The door leads to an antechamber, whence three other chambers open out, one of which gives access to a small cell. The next tomb is that of St. James, which is excavated in the face of the rock (see page 85). A screen with two Doric pillars supports a frieze and cornice of the same order. Above the cornice there is an inscription in Hebrew, connecting the tomb with the family of Beni-Hezir, and the whole is supposed to date from the second or first century B.C. The Tomb of Zechariah is excavated in the same manner as the Tomb of Absalom. It is about eighteen feet six inches square, and has on each face two whole and two half engaged Ionic columns. The columns are surmounted by a cornice of purely Assyrian type, but the form of the volutes, and the egg and dart moulding beneath, show that it was ornamented after the influence of Roman art had been felt in Palestine. Above the cornice rises a pyramid also cut out of the rock. There is no visible entrance to the Tomb of Zechariah, but the base is hidden by rubbish, and the door may possibly be concealed.

Above these tombs, some distance up the slope of the Mount of Olives, is a curious sepulchral excavation in the soft chalk called the "Tombs of the Prophets." The entrance is by a hole in the ground, which gives access to a circular chamber having a round hole in the roof, probably intended to admit light. Three passages connected by two semicircular galleries run off from the chamber, and there are a few smaller passages which lead to chambers containing two or three kokim each. Mons. Ganneau, whilst examining this curious crypt, was fortunate enough to discover, under the stucco which covers the walls, a dozen or so Greek Christian inscriptions. The greater part is proper names. With the patronymic twice occurs the formula, "here lies," and "courage, no one is immortal." This crypt probably served as a cemetery to some one of the numerous monasteries founded quite early on the Mount of Olives. In the Kedron Valley, about half a mile below Bir Eyub, there is a remarkable tomb consisting of a vestibule, an antechamber, three tomb chambers with kokim, and a fourth apparently unfinished.

The next extensive group of tombs is that in the lower part of the Valley of Hinnom. Many of these are highly interesting from the fact that they have been made or modified at a later date than those on the north side of the city. Some of the roofs are dome-shaped and ornamented, and near the lower end of the series there are two recessed half domes cut in the rock, with stone benches running round them. Most of the entrances seem to have been closed by a stone door which turned on a socket hinge, and was fastened by bolts on the inside. Leaving the bed of the valley a little above Bir Eyub, and ascending by some rockhewn steps, the first tomb worthy of notice is that called the "Apostles' Cave," from the tradition that eight of the twelve Apostles concealed themselves in it after the betrayal in the Garden of Gethsemane (see page 114). Over the entrance is a frieze, ornamented with bunches of grapes, &c., in the same style as the façade of the Tombs of the Kings. A little further on is the building known as "Aceldama" (see page 110). It consists of a large pointed arch, covering a deep chamber, one side of which is composed of rock with masonry buttresses, the other of masonry. At the bottom are two caves or sepulchral chambers, with kokim and traces of steps which at one time must have led to the bottom. This is supposed to be the "potter's field," or "field of blood," which the chief priests bought with the "thirty pieces of silver," the price of our Lord's betrayal. It may not be without interest to note

THE MOUNT OF OLIVES, FROM MOUNT ZION.

that clay from this neighbourhood is still used by the potters of Jerusalem. From Aceldama a broad terrace runs along the side of the valley, with a sharp descent on the one hand and a cliff on the other. In this cliff most of the tombs are excavated (see page 111). Near the building itself there are seven kokim in the face of the rock, through one of which access is obtained to a tomb chamber containing several kokim; hence three other tomb chambers can be reached. The peculiar feature of this tomb is that the communications between the several tomb chambers are kokim. Thus when the graves of the innermost chamber were filled the entrance was closed and a body placed in the kok which led to it, and so on. A little higher up, the rock is chequered with a number of roughly cut crosses, and close beside them a small opening leads to a tomb possessing features not found elsewhere in the vicinity of Jerusalem. The antechamber has two ornamented doorways, one on the right and one on the left, each leading to a chamber containing two trough graves; near these there are two kokim, one on either side. In the antechamber there is a partly false door, at the foot of which is the real entrance. On either side, in the thickness of the jamb of the doorway, there is a gallery. The gallery on the right is closed; that on the left leads to a tomb chamber, and hence to a second chamber containing two trough graves; and from this last a gallery fourteen feet long,

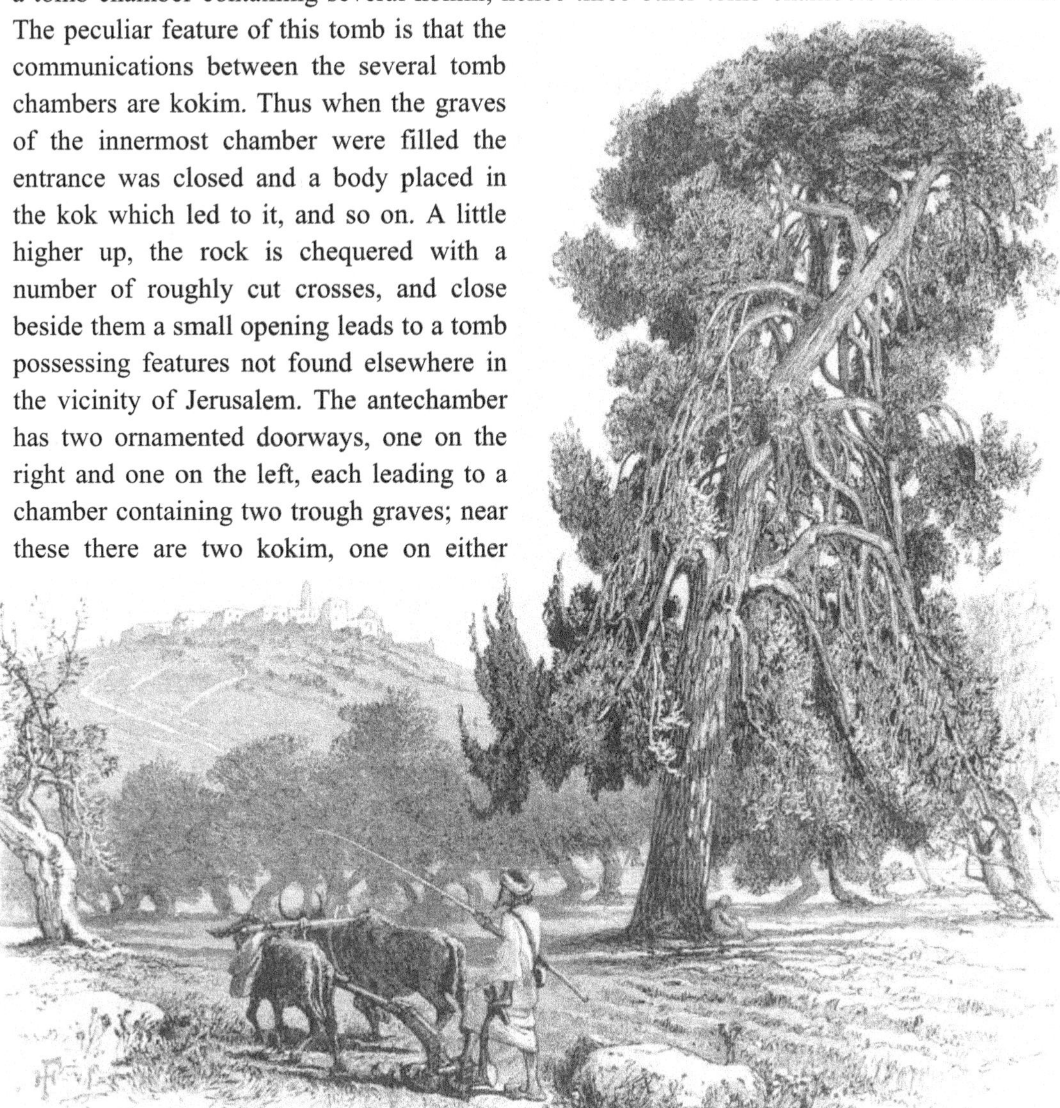

KEFR ET TUR, THE VILLAGE ON THE SUMMIT OF OLIVET.
From the so-called "Crusaders' Field," where an ox an ass yoked together are dragging a primitive plough.

with trough graves, gives access to a large chamber containing shelf graves. The roofs of all the chambers are cut into the shape of a flat, shallow dome.

Great numbers of sarcophagi have been found in the vicinity of Jerusalem, some of which bear inscriptions of high interest and Christian symbols. On a few the sign of the cross is found associated with names written in Hebrew. The names are such as are found in the Gospels, written in their popular and local Syro-Chaldaic forms. Amongst them are Salome, Judah, Simeon son of Jesus, Martha, and Eleazar (Lazarus).

There are a few tombs mentioned in the Bible and Josephus which cannot be passed unnoticed; and first in interest and sacred association is that in which for a brief while our Lord lay. It was a new tomb, "wherein never man before was laid," which had been prepared for himself, and possibly his family also, by Joseph of Arimathea, a rich man and "an honourable councillor," or member of the Sanhedrim. It was hewn out of the rock, and its mouth was closed by a "very great" stone that could be "rolled away," and upon which the angel could sit. It was, moreover, a tomb in which the place where the body lay could be seen from the outside by a person stooping down and looking in through the entrance. "And the other disciple did outrun Peter, and came first to the sepulchre; and he stooping down and looking in, saw the linen clothes lying, yet went he not in." Taking these things into consideration, we may almost be justified in assuming that Joseph's tomb was one of the second class, that is, a square, finely finished, rock-hewn chamber with kokim, a rock bench beneath the kokim for the anointment of the body, and a doorway closed by a circular stone similar to one which has been found at the Tombs of the Kings.

The next tombs of interest are those of David and of the Kings of Judah, which were probably large sepulchral chambers hewn in the rock. There would appear to have been several tombs, the chiefest of which was David's tomb or, as the catacomb seems to have been called, "the sepulchres of the kings." Many of the kings were buried "with their fathers," that is in David's Tomb, in the City of David; whilst of others, Joash and Jehoram for instance, we are told that they are buried in the City of David "but not in the sepulchres of the kings." Burial in the sepulchres of the kings was apparently considered a mark of honour. Josephus states that the high priest Jehoiada was buried in them "because he had recovered the kingdom to the family of David;" and that Joash was not buried in them on account of his impiety. According to the Jewish historian, David's Tomb, or at least one of the tomb chambers, was opened by Hyrcanus, who took from it three thousand talents; a second chamber was afterwards opened by Herod, who took out "furniture of gold and precious jewels," but two of the guards having been slain by fire, the tomb was closed and a propitiatory monument built at its mouth. St. Peter, speaking of David's death, says, "and his sepulchre is with us unto this day." There is thus no doubt that the position of David's Tomb was well known up to the date of the destruction of Jerusalem.

All the principal tombs at Jerusalem are cut in the thick bed of limestone called "malaki," which is extremely easy to quarry, and the natural inference is that David's Tomb was also excavated in this stratum. Captain Warren's excavations have shown us the deep rugged character of the Tyropoeon Valley in its normal state, and, judging from what is seen in the surrounding valleys, the malaki bed would appear on each side of the valley as a cliff; in the face of this cliff were, in all probability, the entrances to the tombs of David and the other kings who were buried in the City of David. David's Tomb appears to have been the lowest, or that nearest Siloam; the others were higher up the valley, and some at least, we may infer from Ezekiel xliii. 7, 8, were close to the Temple. There can be no reasonable doubt that excavations properly directed would recover these tombs.

The works connected with the water supply of Jerusalem are of very great interest. It is well known that in the many sieges which the Holy City has sustained the besiegers without the walls suffered from want of water, whilst the besieged within were amply supplied. The cisterns hewn out of the rock for the storage of water in the Haram esh Sherif have already been alluded to, but they only formed part of the general scheme for the supply of water to the whole city. The present supply is deficient in quantity and as a rule bad in quality; to this may be attributed the fact that the city which the Psalmist once described in loving terms as "the joy of the whole earth," has become one of the most unhealthy cities of the world.

The plateau on the edge of which the city is situated slopes uniformly to the south-east, and contains about one thousand acres; it is composed of white, yellow, and buff limestones of the age of the English chalk. The upper beds, from eighteen inches to four feet in thickness, provide an extremely hard compact stone, called by the Arabs "missae;" whilst the lower, some forty feet in thickness, consist of a soft white stone termed "malaki." In this latter bed most of the ancient tombs and cisterns at Jerusalem have been excavated. The strata are much broken and cracked, so that the rain readily sinks into the ground, and finds its way downwards through a thousand hidden channels, to be given out at a lower level. The general direction of this underground flow and of the surface drainage of the plateau is towards Bir Eyub ("Job's Well"), below the junction of the two main ravines, Kedron and Hinnom (see page 117).

It was at one time supposed that the quantity of rain which fell at Jerusalem each year was very large, from fifty to eighty inches, but the average annual rainfall is really not more than about nineteen inches, and the rainy season is spread over the winter months from November to March. During the remaining months even a slight shower is of the rarest occurrence, and the heavens become, to use the graphic language of the Bible, as "brass," and the earth as "iron." Every three or four years there is a fall of snow, which lies on the ground for a day or two; and, on the other hand, there is occasionally an almost total failure of rain. The number of cisterns and reservoirs which were excavated or built for the collection of the rainfall, and the skill exhibited in the construction of the conduits that brought water into the city, show pretty clearly that there has been no material change in the climate since the days of the Jewish monarchy.

The modern supply of water is derived from springs, wells, cisterns, pools, or reservoirs, and springs connected with the city by aqueducts.

The only true spring known to exist in Jerusalem at the present day is the "Fountain of

VALLEY OF HINNOM, FROM THE NORTH-WEST ANGLE OF THE CITY WALL.
On the right is the aqueduct from Solomon's Pools, which crosses the valley just above the Birket es Sultan, commonly called the Lower Pool of Gihon. The large building within the city walls surrounded with trees, is the Armenian Monastery.

the Virgin." This spring has a constant though small flow of water, and also an intermittent one, which appears to depend upon the rainfall, and which consists in a sudden increase of

THE BIRKET MAMILLA, COMMONLY CALLED THE UPPER POOL OF GIHON.
Surrounded by Moslem tombs. In the background the Jaffa Gate is shown, with the Citadel on the right and the Anglican Church on the left.

the ordinary flow. In winter there are from three to five flows per diem; in summer two; later on, in autumn, only one; but after a dry winter the flow takes place only

ROCK TOMBS NORTH OF JERUSALEM.
The Tombs of the Judges on the road to Neby Samwil, and the Tombs of the Kings on the road to Nablus.

once in three or four days. The water is conveyed from the spring to the Upper Pool of Siloam (see page 78) by a passage cut in the rock, and thence runs down to irrigate some gardens. Its taste is slightly salt and decidedly unpleasant, owing chiefly to the fact that the water has filtered through the mass of rubbish and filth on which the city stands. This peculiarity in the taste is intensified at Siloam, as the water passes over a slimy deposit, from two to three inches deep, which covers the bottom of the passage. The people make matters worse by bathing and washing their clothes in the same place from which they draw water for drinking purposes. The passage between the spring and the Upper Pool of Siloam is seventeen hundred feet long, about two feet wide, and from one foot ten inches to sixteen feet in height. The lower portion is not easy to pass through, especially if the spring commences to flow whilst the explorer is engaged in making the attempt. In connection with the passage Captain Warren opened out a rock-hewn canal, which ran for some distance due west, with a slight fall, so that the water from the spring could flow down to the western end, where a shallow basin had been excavated to receive it. From this point a circular shaft, more than forty feet high, led upwards to a great corridor excavated in the rock, whence a flight of steps gave access to the surface at a point, on that portion of Mount Moriah known as Ophel, which must have been well within the ancient walls of the city. It was thus possible for the Jews on the approach of an enemy to close or "seal" the well with blocks of stone, and at the same time procure a supply of water for their own use by means of the shaft or well within the walls. In the corridor three glass lamps of curious construction were found placed at intervals, as if to light up the passage to the shaft. A little pile of charcoal, as if for cooking, a dish glazed inside, jars of red pottery, and other lamps, were also found, as well as an iron ring overhanging the shaft, to which a rope might have been attached for drawing water. The Virgin's Fountain derives its name from the tradition that the Virgin drew water from the well and washed the swaddling clothes there.

The only real well at Jerusalem is Bir Eyub, Job's Well (see page 120), situated a little below the junction of the Kedron and Hinnom Valleys. It has a depth of one hundred and twenty-five feet, and the water, which is collected in a large rock-hewn chamber at the bottom, is derived from the drainage of the two valleys and their offshoots. The supply is directly dependent on the rainfall, and in winter the water occasionally rises above the shaft and flows down the valley in a stream. This generally occurs in January, after from three to five consecutive days' rain. At a depth of one hundred and thirteen feet there is a large chamber, from the bottom of which a shaft leads downwards to the present collector. This seems to indicate that the well was deepened at some period. There is much rubbish in this part of the valley, and the plan in constructing the well seems to have been to try and stop out the surface drainage, which might be charged with impurities from the city, and to depend entirely on the water which runs in freely between the lower beds of the limestone. The well, which is one of the principal sources of supply to the poorer classes, is inconveniently situated at the foot of a steep hill, and the water has to be carried to Jerusalem in goat skins. This traffic is almost entirely in the hands of the villagers of Silwan (Siloam), who charge from one penny to sixpence per skin for water delivered in the city, and are much given to cheating by partly filling the skins with air. The water of Bir Eyub has, though in a much less degree, the peculiar taste of that of Siloam. This probably arises from the fact that the surface drainage from the city is imperfectly stopped out.

In the Tyropoeon Valley there is a well that supplies water to the Turkish bath in the old Cotton Market. The shaft of the well, eighty feet deep, passes entirely through rubbish, and at its foot there is a rock-hewn conduit stretching in a southerly direction, in which the

THE CITADEL OF JERUSALEM FROM THE VALLEY OF HINNOM.

water lies. This conduit was probably connected with that discovered near Robinson's Arch, which was cut when the present south-west angle of the Haram esh Sherif was built, and it possibly formed part of the great system of water supply devised by King Hezekiah. The supply of water is due partly to infiltration, and partly, perhaps, to the flow of water from a concealed

SARACENIC FOUNTAIN ON THE AQUEDUCT FROM SOLOMON'S POOLS.
The causeway, to which the aqueduct forms a parapet on the north side, crosses the Valley of Hinnom just above the Birket es Sultan.

spring higher up the valley. In either case it passes through the foul mass of rubbish on which the city now stands, and acquires a nauseous taste.

There are four classes of cisterns in Jerusalem. First, those which have been formed by sinking deep shafts through the rock, and then making a bottle or retort-shaped excavation at the bottom to act as a collector. These cisterns appear to be of very great age. They derive their supply in part from surface drainage and in part from the water which finds its way in between the beds of limestone; even in the driest summer the percolation gives three or four buckets of water between sunset and sunrise. The second class, of which the "great sea" in front of the Mosque el Aksa is a good type, consists of great tanks, from forty to sixty feet deep, which have been formed by making small openings in the hard overlying beds of limestone ("missae"), and then excavating the softer "malaki" beneath. The roofs are of rock, generally strong enough to stand by themselves, but in the larger cisterns

MOUNT OF OFFENCE FROM THE VALLEY OF HINNOM.

supported by rough pillars left for the purpose. The labour expended in mining out the underlying rock and bringing it to the surface through small openings must have been very great, and it seems natural to suppose that these cisterns were made before the use of the arch for covering large openings became general. The third class comprises those in which the rock has been cut perpendicularly downwards and a plain covering arch thrown over the excavation. Such cisterns are found near the Golden Gate, beneath the platform of the Dome of the Rock, and in various places in the city. The cisterns of the second and third class were formerly supplied by aqueducts, now they have to depend on surface drainage. The fourth description of cistern is that which has been built in the rubbish of the city, and is of modern date. Cisterns of this class are entirely dependent on the rain which falls during the winter; those which have been constructed by Europeans in convents and dwelling-houses are good, and, being carefully cleaned out every year, furnish water that is always clean and sweet. Such, however, is not the case with those in the native house; when the rain commences, as much as possible is collected, even from the streets, which, being the common latrine of the city, are by the end of the rainy season in a very filthy state. Every duct is opened, and all the summer's accumulation of rubbish and refuse is carried from roof and courtyard to the cistern below. During the early part of summer little evil arises, but towards autumn the water gets low, the buckets in descending stir up the deposit, and the mixture which thousands then have to use as their daily beverage is almost too horrible to think of. At this time, too, a sort of miasma seems to rise up from the refuse and the fever season commences. The most remarkable cisterns are those in the Haram esh Sherif, and the cistern of Helena near the Church of the Holy Sepulchre; there are, however, a vast number both within and without the city, and some of them are of great size.

The pools or reservoirs of which remains exist at present are—the Birket Mamilla, the Birket es Sultan, the Birket Sitti Mariam, the two Pools of Siloam, and a pool near the Tombs of the Kings, without the walls; and the so-called Pools of Hezekiah and Bethesda within the city. There is also undoubted tradition of pools near the Jaffa Gate, the Gate of the Chain, and the Church of St. Anne; these are now concealed by rubbish. The Birket Mamilla collects the surface drainage of the upper part of the Valley of Hinnom, and transmits its water to the Pool of Hezekiah by a conduit which passes under the city wall a little to the north of the Jaffa Gate, and has a branch running down to the cisterns in the Citadel (see page 102). The average depth of the pool is nineteen feet; it is three hundred and fifteen feet long, and two hundred and eight feet wide; the estimated capacity is eight million gallons, but there is a large accumulation of rubbish at the bottom, and it now holds water imperfectly. The pool has not been well placed for collecting the drainage, as that from the western slope is lost, but the position was necessary to obtain a level high enough to supply the Pool of Hezekiah and the Citadel. A hole in the ground below the lower end of the pool gives access to a flight of steps leading down to a small chamber, where the conduit, which on leaving the pool is twenty-one inches square, narrows to nine inches, so as to allow of an arrangement for regulating the flow of water into the city. The Birket Mamilla has sometimes been identified with the Upper Pool of Gihon, but it is more probably the Serpent Pool mentioned by Josephus, a name which may have had its origin in the Dragon's Well of Nehemiah, which seems to have been situated to the west of Jerusalem. The Birket es Sultan (see page 102) lies in the Valley of Hinnom, but at so low a level that its only use could have been the irrigation of gardens lower down the valley. The pool does not now hold water; it is, however, of considerable extent, and would contain about nineteen million gallons. The reservoir has been formed by building a solid dam or causeway across the valley, and closing the upper end by a slight embankment; at the sides the rock is left for the most part in its natural state. Immediately above the pool the aqueduct from Solomon's Pools crosses the valley (see page 106), and a road, which may have existed at an early date, passes over the causeway. The Birket es Sultan was repaired by Sultan Suleiman, hence its name, but it appears to have existed at an early date, and was sometimes identified with the Lower Pool of Gihon; during the Latin kingdom of Jerusalem it was called Germanus. The Birket Sitti Miriam is a small pool near St. Stephen's Gate, which still holds water; it receives little or no surface drainage, and must always have been supplied by the conduit of which the mouth is still to be seen in the northeast corner of the reservoir. The two Pools of Siloam (see pages 78 and 79) are situated in the Tyropoeon Valley not far from its mouth. The upper and smaller pool receives its supply of water from the Fountain of the Virgin by means of the remarkable rock-hewn conduit which has already been noticed; the water runs off at the south-east corner, and after having been used by the washerwomen of the city passes on to irrigate the gardens below. From the centre of the pool rises the broken shaft of a column; at the south-west corner a rude flight of steps leads to the bottom; at one place there are some piers rapidly going to ruin; and all round the pool there is a large accumulation of rubbish. The remains which are seen now probably date from the twelfth century; but in the early part of the seventh century there was a round basilica, from under which the water rose, with two marble reservoirs, and enclosures with wooden railings.

The largest pool in the neighborhood of the city was probably that which lies to the left of the main road which leads northward from Jerusalem, a little beyond the Tombs of the Kings. It is now nearly filled with soil washed down by the winter rains, but at the upper end there is still a shallow excavation which holds water, and at the lower end the scarped rock is visible. The pool is admirably situated for collecting the surface drainage of the upper branches of the Kedron Valley, but all attempts to discover the conduit by which it transmitted its water to the city have hitherto been unsuccessful.

The Pool of Hezekiah (see page 13), within the city, is situated close to Christian Street; it receives its principal supply of water from the Birket Mamilla without the walls, and it is calculated to hold about four million gallons. The masonry does not appear to be very old, and but a small portion of the pool has been formed by actual excavation. The cement is bad and out of repair, and the bottom is covered with a thick deposit of vegetable mould, the accumulation of several years. When the pool is full in winter no inconvenience arises, but in autumn, when the water gets low, exhalations rise up which have a bad effect on the health of those who live in the neighbourhood. The water is chiefly used in the Turkish "Bath of the Patriarch," whence the pool derives its local name, "Pool of the Patriarch's Bath;" the Christian name, "Pool of Hezekiah," comes from the tradition that it was made by that king, as in 2 Kings xx. 20: "Hezekiah made a pool and a conduit and brought water into the city." There is perhaps, better reason for identifying the pool with that called by Josephus Amygdalon, where the celebrated tenth legion raised a bank against the city walls during the siege by Titus. The Pool of Bethesda, or Birket Israil, does not now hold water; it is filled with rubbish to a height of thirty-eight feet, and receives the drainage of the houses in the vicinity (see page 66). At the east end Captain Warren discovered an overflow

ACELDAMA.

arrangement by which the surplus waters could be discharged into the Kedron Valley. The source from which it originally derived its supply of water is not known, but at a later period

SUMMIT OF THE HILL OF EVIL COUNSEL.
This weird-looking solitary tree is a landmark for miles around.

it appears to have been connected with the aqueduct which brought water from Solomon's Pools. The Birket Israil has generally been called the Pool of Bethesda, or "Sheep Pool," by pilgrims and others who have identified it with the pool mentioned in John v. 2: "Now there is at Jerusalem by the sheep market a pool, which is called in the Hebrew tongue Bethesda,

THE VALLEY OF HINNOM.
Ancient tombs on the left and terraces planted with olive-trees on the right.

having five porches." Two arches at the west end of the pool are said to be two of the five porches. In the time of the Crusades there was a well or pool near the Church of St. Anne, over which a church was built; this well was said to be the place where the angel troubled the waters. Eusebius and Jerome say that the Pool of Bethesda was shown at the double pools, one of which was supplied by the periodical rains, whilst the other had reddish water, "as they say, from the sacrifices;" but they give no indication of its position. The Bourdeaux pilgrim says that the double pools were more within the city than the two large pools at the side of the Temple, and that the water was muddy and of a scarlet colour. This discoloration of the water no doubt arose from the quantity of rich red loamy earth which was carried into the pool after heavy rain. The actual position of the biblical Bethesda is uncertain; Dr. Robinson has suggested that it is identical with the Fountain of the Virgin, but the more general view is that the pool was to the north of the Temple, either in the position modern tradition assigns to it or farther to the west, where the souterrains connected with the Convent of the Sisters of Zion mark the position of a double pool in the old ditch. Near the Cotton Gate of the Haram there is said to have been a reservoir some years ago, and there was another close to the Jaffa Gate, which was called the Pool or Bath of Bathsheba on the supposition that David dwelt in the Tower of David opposite.

One of the aqueducts from Solomon's Pools is repaired occasionally and then delivers water to the cisterns of the Haram esh Sherif, and supplies some of the beautiful fountains in the city; but the repairs rarely last for any length of time, and the aqueducts may be considered as forming part of the ancient rather than of the modern system of water supply. The ancient supply was partly derived from the same sources as the modern one, but the inhabitants appear to have depended chiefly on water brought from a distance by aqueducts and stored in pools and cisterns.

Of the springs, wells, pools, &c., mentioned in the Bible and Josephus, Enrogel may almost certainly be identified with the Fountain of the Virgin, and the same spring is probably Gihon in the valley (2 Chron. xxxiii. 14), as *nachal,* the word rendered valley, is always employed for the Valley of the Kedron; the water running from the Fountain may also be identified with the waters of Shiloah (Isaiah viii. 6). So, too, the Fountain of Siloam of Josephus and the Pool of Siloam of the New Testament may be placed at the modern Pool of Siloam, which is fed from the Virgin's Fountain. There is, however, a passage in the Mishna which describes Siloam as being in the midst of the city, and Dr. Lightfoot asserts that there is a difference in the Hebrew between the Siloah of Nehemiah and the Shiloah of Isaiah; a distinction which seems, on one occasion at least, to be made by Josephus. The Septuagint, too, whilst rendering the latter Siloam, translates the former as "the Pool of the Sheep-skins." From this it may almost be inferred that there was another pool called Siloah higher up the Tyropoeon Valley, a position which would be more in accordance with the conditions required by the description of the rebuilding and dedication of the walls under Nehemiah. Gihon is mentioned in two other passages in the Bible: in I Kings i. 33, Solomon is said to have been anointed at Gihon; and in 2 Chron. xxxii. 30, Hezekiah is described as having stopped the upper source of Gihon, and as having brought the waters straight down to the west side of the city of David. The Targum of Jonathan, and the Syriac and Arabic versions, have Shiloha for Gihon in Kings, whilst in Chronicles they agree with the Hebrew text in having Gihon. Josephus, however, states that David ordered Zadok and Benaiah to carry Solomon "out of the city to the fountain called Gihon and to anoint him there." The spring stopped by Hezekiah appears to have been some distance up the Tyropoeon Valley. Its position has not yet been discovered, but the rock-hewn conduit which has been found running along the bed of the Tyropoeon Valley is believed to be the work of Hezekiah, and the water which sometimes finds its way through it may come from the spring.

No well has yet been discovered at Jerusalem except Bir Eyub (Job's Well), but others may possibly exist beneath the rubbish. Close to Bir Eyub there is a remarkable work which must have involved a great expenditure of time and labour. It consists of a drift or tunnel some six feet high and from two to three feet wide, cut in the solid rock. The tunnel is more than eighteen hundred feet long, and runs beneath the western side of the bed of the valley at a depth of from seventy to ninety feet from the surface. It is reached at certain intervals by flights of rock-hewn steps. The object of this tunnel seems to have been the collection of the water running in between the beds of limestone, and it is interesting to find that a work of such magnitude was considered necessary at a level so much lower than that of the city. It clearly shows that there must always have been some difficulty in providing Jerusalem with water.

The most important system of supply was, however, that by which water was brought into the city from the south by aqueducts. The supply was derived from three sources, and the conduits were apparently constructed at different periods. They were of considerable extent, and the remains exhibit a degree of engineering skill which could not well be surpassed at the present day. The first works, and perhaps the most ancient, are those connected with the Pools of Solomon. These pools, three in number, are cleverly and well constructed in the bed of a valley not far from Bethlehem, and they are so situated that the water from each of the upper pools can be run off into the one immediately below it as the supply is drawn upon.

The water was first carried to Bethlehem, and, passing under that town through a tunnel, was finally delivered in the Temple area at Jerusalem. From the pools to Bethlehem the fall of the conduit is about one in eight hundred, but from Bethlehem to Jerusalem it is only one in five thousand two hundred. The total length is seventy thousand feet, and the total fall thirty-two feet, which gives a mean fall of less than two and a half feet per mile. This conduit, to which the name "low-level aqueduct" has been given, crosses the Valley of Hinnom a little above the Birket es Sultan (see page 106) on several pointed arches, which just show their heads above ground, and, winding round the southern slope of the modern Sion, enters the city near the Jewish almshouses. It then passes along the eastern side of the same hill, partly supported by masonry and partly through a tunnel, until, taking a sudden turn eastward, it runs over the causeway and Wilson's Arch, and enters the Haram esh Sherif at the Gate of the Chain. The numerous Saracenic fountains in the lower part of the city were supplied by pipes branching off from the main aqueduct. The channels and conduits in the Haram esh Sherif are in such a bad state of repair and so choked with rubbish that it is impossible to trace them without excavation, but sufficient is known of them to show that there was at one time an elaborate system of waterworks, which provided for the delivery and overflow of the water brought by the low-level aqueduct. The waste overflow appears to have passed through one of the passages discovered by Mons. de Saulcy beneath the Triple Gate into the main drain of the eastern hill, which discharged itself into the Kedron Valley a little below the Fountain of the Virgin. As a large supply of water must have been necessary immediately upon the institution of the Temple services, and as there was not sufficient at Jerusalem itself, there seems no reason for doubting the current tradition that this aqueduct, and perhaps one or more of the pools, were the work of Solomon.

CAVES IN THE VALLEY OF HINNOM, EAST OF ACELDAMA.

The works connected with the second source of water supply are, perhaps, the most interesting, on account of the great skill shown in their construction. The conduit has been called the "high-level aqueduct," from the fact that it must have delivered water at a level more than one hundred feet above that of the low-level aqueduct, and sufficiently high to supply the western hill of Jerusalem. In a valley called Wady Byar, to the south of

Solomon's Pools, there is a place known as the "Well of the Steps," where a flight of steps gives access to a subterranean chamber from sixty to seventy feet below the surface of the valley. From this chamber a well-constructed channel cut in the rock, and varying from five to twenty-five feet in height, leads up the valley for some distance until it terminates in a natural cleft of the rock. A similar channel follows the bed of the valley downwards for more

TOPHET, THE LOWER PORTION OF THE VALLEY OF HINNOM.
The village of Silwan on the right, and the south-east corner of the Haram wall on the left.

than four miles, until it issues from the ground near a solid dam of masonry which extends right across the valley. This great tunnel, to facilitate the construction of which several shafts from sixty to seventy feet deep were sunk in the bed of the valley, was intended to catch the flood water of the valley, the dam being probably made to retain the water or prevent its running off before it had filtered down to the channel. There are a few small springs in the side valleys which contributed to the supply, but the principal source was the flood water. This mode of collecting water is very common in Persia and Afghanistan, where the underground conduit is called a kariz; but it is doubtful whether another instance could be found of a tunnel nearly five miles long cut in hard limestone. About six hundred yards below the dam the conduit enters another tunnel, seventeen hundred feet long, which at one point is one hundred and fifteen feet below the surface of the ground. Eleven shafts were sunk to aid the work of excavation, and the passage is in places fourteen feet high. After passing through the tunnel the conduit winds round the hill to the valley in which the Pools of Solomon lie. It then crosses that valley above the upper pool in an underground channel which tapped the Sealed Fountain, and formerly brought it, with its own waters, to the high level in Jerusalem. After leaving the pools the aqueduct at first runs along the side of the Valley of Urtas, but at a point not far from Bethlehem it enters a tank, and thence, when perfect, carried the water over the valley near Rachel's Tomb by means of an inverted syphon. This syphon was about two miles long, and consisted of perforated blocks of stone set in a mass of rubble masonry some three feet thick all round. The tube is fifteen inches in diameter, and the joints, which appear to have been ground or turned, are put together with an extremely hard cement. The whole work is a remarkable specimen of ancient engineering skill, and the labour bestowed on the details excites the admiration of all travellers. This portion is known amongst the native peasantry as the "Aqueduct of the Unbelievers." On approaching Jerusalem all trace of the conduit is lost. It has evidently been destroyed during one of the many sieges, and the point at which it entered the city is still uncertain. The most interesting feature, however, is that the supply was brought to Jerusalem at an elevation of twenty feet over the sill of the Jaffa Gate, and that the conduit would have been able to deliver water to the highest part of the city, and so provide an adequate supply for the whole population. Some persons have supposed that the high-level aqueduct supplied the Birket Mamilla and thence the Citadel; but it seems not improbable that the conduit wound round the head of the Valley of Hinnom and entered the city at the north-west angle, where the Tower Psephinus stood. This view is supported by the discovery some years ago of a conduit within the Russian consular enclosure, which was afterwards found in some ground belonging to M. Bergheim without the city, and beneath the house of the Latin Patriarch within the walls. The direction of this conduit was towards the tower which most nearly agrees with the Hippicus of Josephus, that at the Jaffa Gate; and thence the water was in all probability carried onward to the Temple enclosure by the conduit which was discovered far below the level of the present surface when the English church and vicarage were built. The date of the high-level aqueduct has been the subject of some discussion, without any very satisfactory result. There is, however, a passage in Josephus which seems to throw some light on the question. In describing Herod's Palace, which occupied the site of the present Citadel, the historian states that "there were, moreover, several groves of trees and long walks through them, with deep canals and cisterns, that in several parts were filled with brazen

JERUSALEM FROM THE SOUTH.
Showing the position of Bir Eyub (Job's Well) just below the junction of the Kedron and Hinnom Valleys.

statues, which the water ran out." This seems to imply the constant presence of running water; and as the palace with its gardens was distinctly the work of Herod the Great, it will perhaps not be very wrong to ascribe the constructions of the aqueduct, with its remarkable syphon, to that monarch. The only known instance of a similar syphon is at Patara, in Asia Minor, but it does not show such high constructive skill as that at Jerusalem.

The third source of supply was derived from several springs in a valley, Wady Arub, to the left of the road from Jerusalem to Hebron. One of the springs is estimated to yield as much as one hundred thousand gallons a day.

It will thus be seen that Jerusalem was during the brighter period of its history well supplied with water; and it may be inferred, from the numerous cisterns and conduits that have been found, that the supply was distributed throughout all quarters of the city. An English lady known throughout the world for her many kind actions, the Baroness Burdett Coutts, has on more than one occasion expressed a wish to construct at her own cost works which would give to every one in Jerusalem the most priceless of all gifts in the East, good water; but hitherto all efforts to overcome the difficulties thrown in the way by the local government have been unavailing.

The population of Jerusalem may be estimated at about twenty-one thousand, of which seven thousand are Moslems, nine thousand Jews, and five thousand Christians. The Moslems belong for the most part to the same race as the peasantry of Palestine, representatives it may be, though with a large intermixture of foreign blood, of the Jebusite that dwelt in the land. The higher classes, as a rule, pass most of their time in the bath, the mosque, or the bazaar, smoking, praying, or gossiping. The Turks, who for the most part belong to the official class, are very inferior to the Arabs in education and capacity; whilst the fellahin are chiefly remarkable for their fine physique, and that keenness in barter which seems to distinguish the descendants of the ancient races that peopled the eastern shores of the Mediterranean.

The Jews are divided into three principal divisions, the Sephardim, the Ashkenazim, and the Karaim. Nothing can be more striking than the marked difference in appearance and costume between the Sephardim and Ashkenazim. The former are far superior in culture and manners; they have generally dark complexions, black hair, and regular features; they are fairly industrious and honest; they dress in Oriental costume, and are not wanting in a certain dignity. The Ashkenazim, on the other hand, have pale complexions and flaxen hair, from which two long love-locks hang down, one on either side of the face; and they always wear the long Eastern robe (caftan), with a hat of felt or fur (see pages 40 and 82). The Sephardim speak Spanish, and trace their descent from the Jews who were driven from Spain by Ferdinand and Isabella at the end of the fifteenth century; hence their name from Sepharad, the Spain of the Rabbins. They are Ottoman subjects, and their chief rabbi, who bears the title of Hakim Bashi, is a recognised official and has a certain degree of civil authority. The Sephardim have a curious tradition that their ancestors were settled in Spain before the date of the Crucifixion, and they thus claim to be exempt from the consequences of the outcry of the Jews, "His blood be upon us and our children." The Ashkenazim are chiefly of Polish origin, they or their immediate ancestors having come from German, Austrian, or Russian Poland. They are subdivided into Peroshim (Pharisees) and Khasidim (Cabalists). The former accept the Talmud, whilst the latter believe also in oral tradition and the transmigration of souls, study the Cabala, and in their religious worship sometimes run into wild excess. The Karaim or Karaites, who do not acknowledge the authority of the Talmud, form a small community apart from the other sects.

Much has been done during the last twenty years to ameliorate the condition of the Jews at Jerusalem by Sir Moses Montefiore, Baron Rothschild, and other wealthy European Jews, and every year sums of money are sent for distribution amongst the poor.

The Christians are divided into a number of sects, of which the Orthodox Greek Church is the most influential. The Greek community consists of monks, nuns, shopkeepers, &c., very few of whom are natives of the country. The Patriarch of Jerusalem, who has several sees in Palestine subject to him, resides in the great monastery of St. Helena and Constantine.

The Armenians are few in number, but they form a thriving community, and occupy one of the pleasantest quarters of Jerusalem (see page 102). The Armenian Monastery, with its church dedicated to St. James, is the largest and richest in the city. The spiritual head of the Armenians is the Patriarch of Jerusalem, a well-educated man, who resides in the monastery.

The Georgians are now an insignificant body, but they had at one time eleven churches and monasteries in the Holy City, and even as late as the commencement of the sixteenth century had many rights and privileges not accorded to other Christians. All that now remains to them is the Convent of the Cross, about half an hour's ride from Jerusalem.

The Syrians or Jacobites, so called from Jacobus Baradaeus, a heretical monk who lived in the sixth century, are few in number, and have as their sole possession in Jerusalem the little monastery known as the House of St. Mark.

The Copts have a large monastery close to the eastern end of the Church of the Holy Sepulchre, which was repaired a few years ago with funds provided by wealthy Copts in Egypt; they have also a monastery near the Pool of Hezekiah.

The Abyssinians occupy a few cells in the ruins of a monastery above the Chapel of Helena. They are extremely poor, and are said to have had much of their revenue and some of their buildings taken from them by their powerful neighbours the Copts.

The Latins or Roman Catholics are the most numerous of the Western Christians. They possess the well-known Monastery of St. Salvator, the Church of the Scourging in the Via Dolorosa, the Convent of the Sisters of Sion, the Garden of Gethsemane, and other places. There is an excellent printing-press attached to the monastery, schools for both sexes, an industrial school, and a hospital. The monastery and other establishments are in the hands of the Franciscan monks, most of whom are Spaniards or Italians. Some of the monks are men of education and culture and the printing-press has produced useful works in different languages. In 1847 the Latin patriarchate, which had been in abeyance since the latter part of the thirteenth century, was revived, and Monsignor Valerga, who died in 1873, was appointed Patriarch. The Greek Catholic and Armenian Catholic Churches are affiliated to the Latin.

The Protestant community, though small, is active in good works, and there are several excellent Protestant establishments in the city and its vicinity. The schools especially have had a marked effect, not only in supplying a good education themselves, but in inciting other communities to improve their own schools, or to found schools when they had none. There are boys' and girls' schools for Jews, proselytes, and native Arabs, an industrial school for Jews, a church and parsonage, a hospital, a German girls' orphanage, a German boys' orphanage, a lepers' hospital, the hospital of the Kaiserswerth Deaconesses, a German Hospice of St. John, &c. The Protestant Bishop, under an agreement between England and Prussia, is nominated

BIR EYUB-JOB'S WELL.

alternately by either power; the first Bishop, Dr. Alexander, was nominated by England, the second, Dr. Gobat, by Prussia, and the present Bishop, Dr. Barclay, by England.

The full effect of the efforts which have been made to ameliorate the condition of the people of Jerusalem has, perhaps, hardly yet been felt, but gradually and surely education, with all its civilising influences, is forcing its way amongst all classes, and a time may be looked forward to, in the not far distant future, when the good seed sown in the Holy City will bear fruit throughout the length and breadth of the Holy Land.

BETHLEHEM AND THE NORTH OF JUDÆA.

OLIVE GROVE BELOW BIR EYUB—JOB'S WELL.
Watered by the Brook Kedron.

Few rides can compete in memories and associations with those six miles of uphill and downhill between Jerusalem and Bethlehem. By that track—for roads in the East are as unchangeable as springs—Abraham with his son must have come up and caught their first glimpse of Mount Moriah. Two generations later, and on it Jacob made his mournful halt and buried his best-loved wife. Across the valley did David muster the mighty men of Judah for the assault on the stronghold of the Jebusites. And in the peaceful days of his son, down this road, then smooth and paved, the chariot of Solomon must often have passed as he went to visit his favourite gardens at Etham. Here, too, after the lapse of a thousand years, the mother of David's greater Son wearily trod the last stage of her journey to be enrolled in her ancestral town, and there to give birth to the world's Saviour.

We leave Jerusalem by the western or Jaffa Gate. On the right, just above us, is the Birket Mamilla, or Upper Pool of Gihon, which still supplies the Pool of Hezekiah inside the walls with the drainage from the Moslem cemetery. Just below, on the left, at the head of the Valley of Hinnom, we pass the Birket es Sultan, or Lower Pool of Gihon. On their disputed identity we need not enter, though the lower pool, at least in its present form, appears to have been repaired, if not constructed, by the crusading besiegers of Jerusalem. In curious contrast with the antique surroundings, on the slope of the hill, opposite the lower pool, stand a modern windmill and rows of smart cottages, the gift of Sir Moses Montefiore—the Peabody of Jerusalem—for the benefit of his oppressed Hebrew brethren. And now we cross the valley, or rather plain, of Rephaim, the scene of two of David's encounters with the Philistine army, and for the identification of which we have at least the authority of Josephus. The road is rough and stony, for wheel carriages there are none. Nor less stony is the plain in winter, though in springtime all is clothed with a rich carpet of flowers, short and dense. Here and there we may trace on the slopes above us the broken aqueduct which by Solomon's care once conveyed the water supply of Jerusalem from the pools and springs of El Burâk. The first architectural feature on our road is the Convent of Mar Elyas, grey, grim, and unattractive, with a cold-looking wall almost concealing the inner buildings. The Greek monks will solemnly assure you that on this very spot Elijah lay down to rest when he fled from Jezebel, not under a juniper, but an olive, and that here angels miraculously supplied his needs. In proof of the truth of the tradition they will show, close to their gate, a shallow depression in the smooth rock, the mark of the prophet's body when he reposed here. The view, however, will repay the traveller who hesitates to accept the tradition. We catch a glimpse of Bethlehem climbing the shoulder of the ridge, and we can see a corner of Jerusalem, though the hill of Evil Counsel, with the tree on which a very modern tradition says Judas hanged himself, shuts out the minarets of Moriah. But the wild landscape eastward, with rugged hill and deep glen, wanting but forest to make it impressive, tells us how closely we are skirting the wilderness of Judaea, while a long ruddy line, the crest of the ridge, or rather the wall, of Moab, forms the distant horizon.

A sharp descent, and we halt by a modern "wely" or roadside chapel—a small square whitewashed piece of masonry surmounted by a central dome. It is Rachel's Tomb (see page 126). Here at least we have not our dreams and musings disturbed by the intrusion of the topographical sceptic. For once we have an undisputed site. Israelite, Christian, and Moslem have but one tradition respecting it, and all agree in recognising the spot where, when Jacob "journeyed from Bethel, and there was but a little way to come to Ephrath,.... Rachel died and was buried on the way to Ephrath, which is Bethlehem. And Jacob set a pillar upon her grave." The pillar has long since perished, though it existed there in the time of Moses, but other structures have preserved the memory of the spot. The present tomb, a Saracenic building, subsequent certainly to the Crusading times, is neither rich nor imposing, but no sumptuous mausoleum is needed to keep in memory the grave of Rachel—beautiful, beloved, untimely taken away. The Jews, who never accept a Christian or Moslem tradition, still pay visits of sympathy to this spot, which, as in the case of many other Old Testament worthies, the Moslem rulers open to Jew and Christian alike. It is mentioned by Jerome and in the Crusading chronicles, and was visited by Maundrell two hundred years ago. We may well recall how the prophet represents Rachel sitting weeping for her children as the long train of captive exiles passed from the south on their way to Babylon, and note how the tomb is close to the roadside; and then as we see Bethlehem not a mile distant we understand how aptly the Evangelist transfers the figure to the Massacre of the Innocents by Herod.

Crossing the shallow valley from Rachel's Tomb we rapidly wind up towards Bethlehem. There are various soil-covered heaps, the remains of ancient villages, here and there, and the modern guide will readily point out Ramah; but for this identification there is no good warranty, and the name Ramah, or some equivalent, is common all over the country applied to any ruin on a hill.

A steep ascent leads up to Beit-Lahm, "the house of flesh," a phonetic accommodation of the ancient name Bethlehem, "the house of bread." The hillsides are irregularly scarped with terraces sweeping round the eastern shoulder, on which are many gnarled and silver-grey olive-trees, while many a fig-tree occupies any spare corner, and vines are trained over the irregular walls of the terraces. Below them is a fine velvet turf, on which tethered goats are feeding. All bespeaks a care and cultivation uncommon in Palestine, for the inhabitants of the little town above are Christians, and till the soil with perseverance and patience unknown to their Moslem neighbours. The loosened earth under the olive-trees is carpeted in spring with brilliantly coloured annuals and bulbs, bewildering in their variety and dazzling in their brightness. Most conspicuous is the gorgeous scarlet anemone, pimpernels yellow and blue, hyacinths, and especially a lovely pink campion.

The town itself, no longer walled, is still confined within its ancient limits. There are no suburbs, and in fact, planted on the crest of a narrow spur that projects eastward from the central ridge and then abruptly breaks off, it has no room to expand. The white chalky ridge crowned with the long narrow street, with various alleys on either side of it, presents us with one of the few remaining specimens of an old Jewish city, for, excepting in the disappearance of the wall, it is probably unchanged in architecture and arrangement from what it was in the days of David.

We can ascend to the roof of one of the houses in the main street, for the owner will give the Western traveller a hearty welcome, and here we can take in at a glance the chief features of the landscape. Looking eastward, the great pile of buildings, without any definite architectural features outside, is the famous shrine of the Church of the Nativity, and the

CHURCH OF THE NATIVITY, BETHLEHEM.

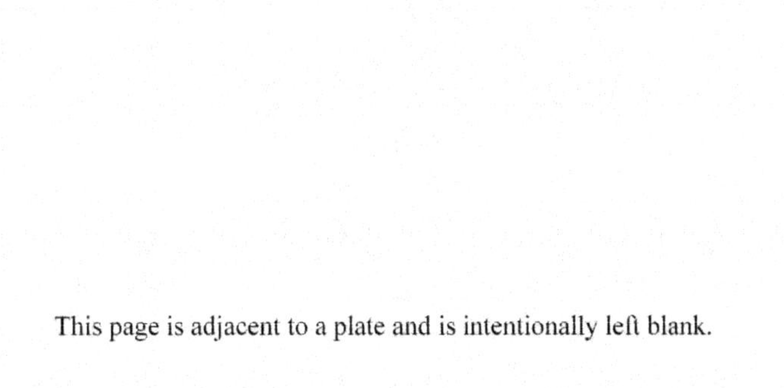

This page is adjacent to a plate and is intentionally left blank.

three convents—Latin, Greek, and Armenian—which surround it. The view is girt with Bible scenes. We see beyond the convents the bare wilderness of Judah creeping up almost to the very foot of the ridge. But a belt of rich green intervenes, the cornfields of Bethlehem. Here, probably, Ruth gleaned in the fields of her husband's kinsman. A little knoll of olive-trees surrounding a group of ruins marks the traditional site of the angels' appearance to the shepherds, Migdol Eder, "the tower of the flock." But the place where the first "Gloria in excelsis" was sung is probably farther east, where the bare hills of the wilderness begin, and a large tract is claimed by the Bethlehemites as a common pasturage. Here the sheep would be too far off to be led into the town at night; and exposed to the attacks of the wild beasts from the eastern ravines, where the wolf and the jackal still prowl, and where of old the yet more

VIEW OF THE SHEPHERDS' FIELD, FROM BETHLEHEM.
Looking towards the east, the mountains of Moab in the distance.

formidable lion and bear had their covert, they needed the shepherds' watchful care during the winter and spring months, when alone pasturage is to be found on these bleak uplands.

Looking a little to the north of the Shepherds' Tower we see the Well of David, a few minutes' walk from the town—not a spring, but a large, deep, rock-hewn cistern into which the water percolates (see page 134). There are narrow openings through which the supply can be reached. When David exclaimed, "O that one would give me to drink of the water of the well of Bethlehem that is at the gate," he was hiding in the Cave of Adullam. We can picture how, while the Philistines had but a small garrison in the town itself, and their main camp outside to the north, David's men broke through the garrison and drew water from the well without entering the Philistines' camp. All these and many another event in the story of the shepherd-king pale before the event which the pile of masonry in front of us records—the Saviour's birth. If it be not the exact spot, the error cannot be one of many hundred yards. The Church of the Nativity is supposed to cover the site of the inn or caravanserai in which our Lord was born. The Chapel of the Manger appears to have been a rude grotto hewn out of the side of the rock, and may once have been connected with a dwelling-house or a stable, or had some access for cattle, though the whole site has been so altered in shape by building that it is difficult to form any decided opinion. Very often in the ruined cities of the hill country we find several rooms hewn out of the side of the hill, and a large open cavern adjoining, evidently intended for the cattle. In

IN THE SHEPHERDS' FIELD, BETHLEHEM.
A shepherd watching a flock of the long-eared and long-tailed sheep common in Palestine.

some, as at Tekoa, and across Jordan, near Arak el Emir, the mangers still existing leave no doubt as to their use. The caravanserai which may have stood here was probably the very one founded by Chimham, son of Barzillai (Jer. xli. 17). It is pleasant to believe, when we reasonably may, in the identity of traditional sites, and for this one much may be said. It is at least far older than the time of Constantine, which cannot be affirmed of many of the holy sites. So far back as the days of Justin Martyr, in the earlier part of the second century, the place of our Lord's birth was pointed out in "a certain cave very close to the village;" and Constantine lost no time in destroying an idolatrous grove and shrine to Adonis, which Hadrian had impiously fixed here to pollute the spot. Under the direction of Helena a splendid basilica or Christian church was erected. This

RACHEL'S TOMB.
The terraced hills of Beit Jâla, the ancient Giloh, in the background.

still remains, having escaped destruction during the many convulsions which have ravaged the country for centuries. It has been added to, slightly altered, or, as modern architects would term it, "restored" occasionally, notably by the Emperor Justinian, but in its main features it is unchanged, the oldest existing Christian church not only in Palestine, but in the world. Justinian may have added to the central nave and its four side aisles. The three convents gradually rose as accretions after the time of Jerome. The Emperor Manuel Comnenus, about A. D. 1160, covered the walls with the glass Byzantine mosaics, a large portion of which, though sadly mutilated, still remain; but the central basilica (as shown in the frontispiece), with its noble monolith shafts of red and white marble, and the Corinthian capitals of a late style, with the cross sculptured on them, are agreed by the best architectural authorities to be veritable Constantinian work. The plan of the building is exactly the same as that which Eusebius gives of the Church of the Holy Sepulchre at Jerusalem as erected by Constantine. We have been struck, when examining the numberless ruined churches, of the plains of Moab and Gilead, by the miniature resemblance which most of them bear in design to this, pointing pretty clearly to their date. There is an outer court or western porch, now much dilapidated, then the wide nave with two rows of eleven columns each on either side, forming four aisles, and a shallow chancel of *three* apses. The double aisles and

EXTERNAL STAIRWAY OF A HOUSE AT BETHLEHEM.
Two women grinding corn on the stairs.

triple apse are frequently seen east of Jordan, as in the church on Mount Nebo, and in those of Ziza. Beneath the central apse is the Grotto of the Nativity.

The church escaped destruction when the Caliph Hakim laid waste the Church of the Holy Sepulchre and all the other sacred sites. It was protected by special efforts of the Crusaders in the First Crusade, in A.D. 1099, and again, in the Sixth Crusade, Frederick II. succeeded in preserving it; and within its walls Baldwin I., King of Jerusalem, was crowned. We are told that Baldwin refused to be crowned with a circlet of gold in the city where our Lord had worn His crown of thorns, and therefore selected Bethlehem as a holy site, but out

CHAPEL OF THE NATIVITY, IN THE CRYPT OF THE CHURCH OF ST. MARY, BETHLEHEM.
The star within the grotto on the left marks "the Place of the Nativity;" on the right is the Altar of the Adoration of the Magi.

of view from Jerusalem, the city of Christ's sufferings. His predecessor Godfrey, the first king, in the like spirit, had refused to assume the crown at all within the Holy City, and declined any higher title than Baron of the Holy Sepulchre. But the English visitor will not forget to notice its roof, no longer of cedar of Lebanon, but actually of English oak—huge beams provided by our own King Edward IV., A.D. 1482, in conjunction with Philip of Burgundy—and once covered with English lead, which the Moslems have stripped to provide themselves with ammunition. The roof is framed like one of a little earlier period which still exists intact on the dormitory of the Benedictine Priory of Durham, now the Chapter Library. Two winding sets of stone steps on the north and south lead us down to the Chapel of the Nativity below. After passing several rock-hewn chambers we reach the hallowed spot. Very little of the original can be seen, as almost all is cased in marble; but just enough appears to show by the glimmering lamps that it is really an old cave. A silver star let into the pavement marks the birthplace; a marble trough represents the

AN EXAMPLE OF A PEASANT'S HOME, WITH ITS MANGER, IN A VILLAGE OF PALESTINE.
The raised dais is occupied by the family. The steps over the arch lead to a store-place for grain, &c.; dried fruits hang from the rafters. The rude recess on the left contains mattresses, cushions, and coverlets.

manger—the original being said to be transferred to Sta. Maria Maggiore, in Rome; and the sides are hung with comparatively modern pictures. This grotto is common to all the sects. Adjacent is the Latin Chapel, with very old paintings, and passages lead to various caverns, the tombs of Eusebius, of Paula and Eustachia, the devout friends and companions of St. Jerome, but most interesting of all, the tomb of St. Jerome himself. From it is an opening to another rock-hewn chamber, which must ever have a fascination for the biblical student. Here for thirty-four years the aged and venerable father studied and wrote. Driven from Rome by the bitterness of theological partisanship, his fiery spirit found rest and employment in seclusion on the site of the cradle of the Christian faith. Here in his cavern-home he fasted and prayed. But here, above all, he carried out and completed what he had years before begun, the revision of the various versions of the Scriptures, and from this dark cave proceeded that precious heritage of the Christian Church for all time, the Latin version so well known as the Vulgate. Besides his great work he was ceaseless as a pamphleteer. Epistles, tractates, commentaries issued with marvellous rapidity from the Grotto of Bethlehem, till we possess one hundred and fifty epistles, sixteen treatises, thirteen volumes of commentaries, besides his Latin version and his translation and continuation of the History of Eusebius. Verily there were giants in those days. Nor can we forget that closing scene of all, which Domenichino has commemorated for all time in his immortal picture, when the aged saint, with his mortal frame worn and exhausted by years and labours, but rejoicing and triumphant in spirit, on the threshold of the next world receives the communion and yields up the ghost.

We shall see as we travel through Judaea how potent was the influence and example of St. Jerome in the caves and rock-hewn cells which fill the cliff sides of the Jordan Valley and stud the rest of the country, the homes of the anchorites and the small religious communities which sprang from Bethlehem, the faithful copyists of the austerities but not of the activities of the mighty Latin father.

Not content, however, with the historical, the traditional has been largely drawn upon for sacred localities. We leave the convent, and among the many little hillside caves, partly natural and partly artificial, is one which in popular estimation is second only to the Grotto of the Nativity. This is the Milk Grotto, of which an engraving is given (see page 135). It has no special feature beyond the unusual whiteness of the soft chalk out of which it is excavated. The story told is that here Joseph and the Virgin Mother concealed themselves and the Divine Infant before their flight into Egypt from the fury of Herod, and that some drops of the Virgin's milk gave the rock its peculiar whiteness. The place is consequently the resort of numbers of pilgrims, drawn especially by the belief that the application of a fragment of the rock will produce an abundant supply for any infant at the mother's breast. As the rock is very soft, there is no difficulty in breaking off fragments, which are carried as precious charms throughout all the Christian countries of the South and East.

As we descend into the valley, the corn-fields of Bethlehem, we are reminded by the peep we have just had of the Mountains of Moab how near we are actually to the home of Ruth. In the afternoon especially the western sun lights up the long distant line with a delicate pink, which gives an impression of nearness wanting in the morning, when they loom grey in front of the rising sun, or at noon, when there is generally a heat haze between us and them, caused by the evaporation from the Dead Sea. Most travellers visit Bethlehem in the early spring, long before the corn is ripe; but there are few parts of the country where the customs

BETHLEHEM, FROM THE SOUTHWEST.

of the people in harvest may be more freely studied than in Christian and peaceful Bethlehem. They are a practical commentary on the Book of Ruth. The corn-plain is, and always was, held in individual proprietorship, while the outlying and unfenced district beyond (*fores*), the "forest" of our ancestors in England, though strictly held by the townsmen as against all others, yet is pastured by all in common, according to regulations agreed on, exactly like the old common rights of many an English village before the days of Enclosure Acts. Fences there are none, but every here and there we see the stone set up, the landmark, a straight line from which to the next stone marks the boundary of each property. The stone is generally a rude undressed block partially sunk in the ground. We have seen an ancient Roman milestone thus used. When we note how very easy it would be for the dishonest to move the stone a few feet without detection, we can well understand the curse pronounced on the man who should remove his neighbour's landmarks. The harvest-field is a merry scene. The whole village turns out, and the children and aged are as busily employed in gleaning as the able-bodied of both sexes in reaping. But as the harvest is earlier on the plains than in the hills, commencing in April, and in the Jordan Valley sometimes in March, many labourers come down to work for hire, sleeping on the field by night, and bringing their families with them, who share with the residents the privilege of gleaning. Reaping is not made a toilsome labour, for weather is certain, and we have seen a whole row of reapers using their sickles as they sat, and working their bodies along after the corn without attempting to rise. This, however, is rather Moslem than Christian fashion. The farmer or proprietor still, as he walks up to the reapers, salutes them in the very words of Boaz, "The Lord be with you" (*Allah aleikum*), and the response is still the same, "The Lord bless thee." The threshingfloor is generally on the spot, so that it is not necessary to carry the crop in bulk far for threshing, and by the *baider* the owner and his family sleep, as did Boaz, generally under a tent, while the labourers from a distance lie on the ground around. The poor gleaners sit down by the roadside, as Ruth did, and beat out with a stick on their heavy veils the ears they have gleaned, to save the labour of carrying home the straw. Meantime the reapers prepare their simple evening meal. A small heap of stubble or straw is kindled, the ears cut off are tossed on the fire, and as soon as the straw is consumed, they are dexterously swept from the embers on to a cloak spread on the ground. They are then beaten out and winnowed by being tossed into the air, and eaten without further preparation. The green ears become half charred by the roasting, and there is a pleasant mingling of milky wheat and a fresh crust flavour as we chew the parched corn. Sometimes the corn is held in bunches over the fire till the chaff is burned off, instead of being tossed into the blaze. Of course the privilege of supplying themselves from the field by the labourers is never disputed. The boisterous mirth and rude practical joking which fill up the evening after the supper remind us that Boaz's caution to his young men to behave respectfully to the damsel was likely to be no less needful then than now. The barley harvest is finished sometimes before the wheat harvest begins; thus Ruth gleaned "unto the end of barley harvest and of wheat harvest."

We read that Boaz bid Ruth hold her veil, into which he put six measures of barley. The same veil, a large cotton or linen cloth, is still worn by the women of Bethlehem, and is still

MOTHER-OF-PEARL WORKERS OF BETHLEHEM.
Making beads for rosaries.

ample and strong enough to hold six measures of corn. The women of Bethlehem are now not only the best-looking, but the best-dressed women of Palestine. Perhaps they owe their beauty to the Norman blood in their veins, for there is little doubt the Christian population is descended from the knights of the Crusades and their followers. But their dress is certainly not Western, and was probably adopted by the settlers. Many of the towns and even villages of Palestine have peculiar female costumes, like the different cantons of Switzerland. The head-dress of the Bethlehemite lady is a stiff flat-crowned brimless hat, from three to five inches high in front, and longer at the back; it is generally almost covered with rows of gold or silver coins, and from each side of it a string of larger coins is suspended. This head-dress is sufficiently firm to support the large white

DAVID'S WELL.
Bethlehemite women filling goat-skins and water-jars.

linen veil, which should be folded neatly over it so as to hide all but the lower row of coins which rests on the forehead. The veil is generally about two yards long and not quite a yard wide, and is often embroidered at the ends with coloured silk. It falls in graceful folds upon the shoulders and down the back, and is drawn partly across the face in the presence of Moslems or strangers. The principal garment, and often the only one, is a long blue or striped gown, girdled at the waist, with very wide and long pointed sleeves. The front of this gown above the waist is always more or less ornamented with embroidery or appliqué work of red, yellow, and green cloth. Over the gown those who can afford it wear a bright red short-sleeved jacket, reaching to the waist or to the knees. When women are at work indoors they often fasten back the long sleeves of their gowns and wear small head-veils, as shown in the illustration page 133.

These Bethlehemite women lead no idle lives. The engraving on page 127 represents

THE MILK GROTTO, BETHLEHEM.

them grinding corn on an open stairway, and often, after having toiled in the fields through the day, and then just before sunset carried the water from the well, they will sit half the night at their monotonous labour. There are no water-mills in the south, though they are common enough in the watered mountainous region under Lebanon, and may be found in some places near the Jordan. The Crusaders were great benefactors to the country in the erection of water-mills wherever their construction was possible, and the ruins of their mills are more numerous than those of their castles. The first caliphs also understood their value, but all their works have long since been allowed to fall into decay and ruin. In all the south, hand-mills are the sole means of providing flour. Severe as is the labour, we fear that men never condescend to it. In the houses of the richer class several servant-maids or slave-girls are kept continually at the tedious task. "From Pharaoh to the maidservant that is behind the mill," shows the estimation in which grinding was held. As we pass through the streets at the evening hour we hear the low monotonous hum of the hand-mill—the "quern" of the Scottish Highlands. There is a hole in the centre of the upper millstone through which the grain is passed, a handful at a time, by one of the two women who sit facing each other. "Two women shall be grinding at the mill." Nearer the edge is another hole, in which an upright handle is fixed; both the women hold this together, and work it as two men would a crosscut saw. The flour falls out on to a cloth on which the nether millstone is placed. The stones are usually made of lava brought from the Hauran, harder and lighter than the sandstone of the country, which indeed is not very common, the whole formation of Central and Southern Palestine being soft, chalky, Eocene limestone.

But we cannot leave Bethlehem without recalling some of those picturesque ceremonies connected with the Church of the Nativity, which arouse in the thousands of pilgrims far more enthusiasm than any of the Scripture scenes and illustrations. Naturally the most remarkable and the most frequented are those of Christmastide. The ceremonial is very gorgeous, but few would care to undergo a second time the fatigue, crowding, and heat of a service held in these suffocating caves, which lasts for nine hours. The French Consul from Jerusalem is, next to the Patriarch, the most important personage on the occasion, representing "the eldest son of the Church." He sets out on the forenoon of Christmas eve from the city, in full state and with an imposing retinue. He is met by the Christians outside Bethlehem and conducted in procession to the Latin Chapel. The service continues without intermission until midnight, when there is a sudden pause, all the candles on the altar are lighted, and a little wax image appears above it, and the "Gloria in excelsis" bursts forth with the utmost power of organ, choir, and shepherds' pipes combined. Mass and other services follow without intermission for two hours, when the Patriarch carries the wax figure in a cradle from the chapel across the church and down to the Grotto of the Nativity, where he lays it on the slab that marks the supposed spot of the birth, and wraps it in strips of swaddling clothes, while the Gospel history of the wondrous event is being read. The procession, with the Patriarch and Consul, after a while return to the Latin Chapel, when high mass is again performed, and the services continue until after sunrise.

The Christmas festivals—for the Greek and Latin celebrations are on different days, O.S. and N.S. respectively—are to Bethlehem what the Easter ceremonies are to Jerusalem—the main support of the industry and manufactures of the place, which depend upon the production and sale of pilgrim wares. At Christmas the harvest is reaped for which ever since last Easter the Bethlehemite at home has been industriously preparing. Every one who has been down to the Jordan and there bathed is considered to have completed his pilgrimage, and is henceforth a palmer, entitled to wear the scallop-shell in his hat. The name "palmer" is derived from the palm-branch (*djereed*) which in former days each pilgrim cut in the Valley of the Jordan. But the palm has for ages been all but extinct round the "old city of palm-trees," and less poetic woods have to supply the modern staves. At Bethlehem everything can

HERODIUM, OR FRANK MOUNTAIN, FROM BETHLEHEM.

be supplied—relics, rosaries, palm-boughs, scallop-shells, crosses, and little images. Large quantities of the shell of the giant oyster of the Red Sea (*Meleagrina margaritifera*) are

VIEW FROM THE FRANK MOUNTAIN.
Looking towards the Dead Sea and the Mountains of Moab.

brought to Bethlehem from Suez, and there carved into the pearly scoops in which most English visitors invest. The articles most prized are the vases wrought out of the stinkstone brought from the Dead Sea. But by far the most popular wares to the pilgrims are the rosaries, of which piles may be seen heaped on the ground in front of the dealers. The cheapest are simply strings of olive-stones, with the round, hard seed of the "butm" inserted in each eleventh place. Others are turned beads of olive-wood, grown of course on the Mount of Olives; and some are really richly carved and elaborately ornamented in the lathe. To each rosary an additional value of about a piastre is imparted if it has been blessed by the Patriarch. It is remarkable that no unblessed rosaries or crosses are to be found, and unless they are consecrated wholesale this part of the Patriarch's labours can be no sinecure. The great mart for all such wares is about the Church of the Nativity and in its porticoes, where the dealers sit on the pavement, and no one who values peace and quiet will attempt to evade the not unreasonable tax which is laid on the stranger. Besides, a liberal purchaser is likely to give the opportunity for an invitation to visit the workshop, and consequently to see the interior of an Oriental home.

We have lingered long in and around hallowed Bethlehem. Thence our course lies towards the south-east if we would visit the spots of greatest historic and archaeological interest in the neighbourhood—the Pools of Solomon, Etham, and Herodium. As we descend southwards from Bethlehem the rich valley and fine olive-groves on the right give some idea of what the whole country was in the days when it was a land flowing with milk and honey. Here and there we see on the hillsides the broken aqueduct which once conveyed the supplies from Solomon's Pools to Bethlehem and Jerusalem. On our left we catch occasional glimpses of the wilderness of David's wanderings, and perched on a height are the mounds of Tekoa. We leave the Hebron road, and turning eastward we enter the little Valley of Urtas, near the head of which are the Pools of Solomon. A mound of ruins on the south side on the top of a hill is supposed to mark the site of the ancient Etham. The modern village of Urtas is below. The place is best known and visited as "the Gardens of Solomon." Etham must not be confounded with the rock Etam where Samson took refuge, and which is far to the westward near the Philistine plain, probably the modern 'Atab. From the upper valley of Etham Josephus tells us the gardens of Solomon were watered, and recent researches have corroborated the tradition which marks this as their site. We know that "Solomon made him a garden and orchards, and planted in them all kinds of fruits, and pools of water to water therewith the wood that bringeth forth trees," and Josephus amplifies the account by telling us that he made him a chariot of wood of Lebanon lined with gold, and a canopy of purple silk on silver pillars, in which he used, clothed in white, to drive to his gardens every morning; for he had laid causeways of black stone (basalt) along all the roads that led to Jerusalem, upon which he could drive his chariot with ease and swiftness. These smooth causeways have, alas! long since disappeared. When first we visited the valley, twenty-five years since, it was bleak and bare like the surrounding country; now on entering it we find ourselves suddenly in a bright contrast of cultivation and luxuriant verdure, with vegetables of every kind shaded by orchards that soon may recall Solomon's—apricots, mulberries, and peaches, with vines on the steeper slopes. This garden, which is now the important source of the supply of the Jerusalem market, owes its origin entirely to the efforts of friends of the Jews' Society, seeking to provide agricultural employment for the Christian Jews on their own land.

We now pass up the tiny glen to El Burâk (Solomon's Pools), by the side of the direct road from Bethlehem to Hebron (see page 145). Immediately on leaving the enclosed gardens barrenness resumes its sway. The valley was once full of oaks of large size, and stumps may here and there be seen, now sought for and dug up for firewood. The pools are marked at a distance by the great square castle at the north-west corner of the upper one—a late Saracenic structure serving the purposes of khan and barracks for a few soldiers. The pools are three in number and in steps, each at a considerably lower level than the one above it, and are formed by walls of massive masonry stretching across the valley. They are chiefly hewn out of the native rock, the upper one especially being considerably heightened by masonry strengthened by buttresses. There is a space of over fifty yards between each pool. We can see at once the reason for constructing three basins, for a single reservoir to hold so large a supply would have demanded an embankment of enormous strength. The tanks are all widest at the lower end, one hundred and twenty-seven, one hundred and forty-one, and one hundred and ninety-six yards in length respectively, and varying in width from fifty-three to eighty yards, and twenty-five, thirty-eight, and forty-eight feet deep respectively. To enable the pools to be cleaned and water to be drawn on the spot when not quite full, there are flights of stairs inside the lower end of each. Not only are the supplies from several springs, near and distant, carefully conducted by subterranean channels into the pools, but there are also channels for the collection and conveyance of rain-water, so that nothing shall be lost. The "sealed spring," as it is called, from the belief that it is identical with the "sealed fountain" of Solomon's Song, is the most important source of supply. It rises in a field a little to the west, is trapped in a vaulted chamber, and conveyed by a subterranean channel into the upper pool. Besides this there are at least three other fountains which by a similar contrivance feed the reservoir. From the lower end of the lower pool the great aqueduct, by a winding course along the hillsides, conveys the water to Jerusalem, to Mount Moriah, immediately under the Temple. There are, however, according to Mr. Drake, in reality six aqueducts connected with Urtas and Solomon's Pools. The first, coming from the south, proceeds to El Burâk, and is of a different and probably earlier style of masonry than the continuation to Jerusalem, which is the second, or low-level aqueduct; this is composed of earthen pipes set in masonry, with air-holes at intervals to relieve the pressure. The third is the high-level aqueduct which enters Jerusalem by the Birket Mamilla, near the Jaffa Gate. A fourth aqueduct in the same direction is entirely ruined, while the fifth and sixth supplied villages or towns to the eastward; one of them can be traced nearly to Jebel Fureidis. It is stated that several portions of these aqueducts prove that their builders were aware of the fact of water finding its level when confined. It is generally now believed that these are all of

VALLEY OF URTAS.

Roman work, and are the very aqueducts referred to by Josephus as being built by Pontius Pilate, who used for that purpose the moneys brought into the Temple treasury as "corban." But however this may be, the pools are undoubtedly of great antiquity, and the knowledge shown of the principle of the rise and fall of water when conveyed in pipes does not look like merely Roman engineering. It is difficult to understand how the Rabbis of the Mishna should have stated that Solomon made gardens at Etham, and conveyed the waters thence to Jerusalem, if there had been no such provision till the time of Pontius Pilate. It seems far more reasonable to suppose that during the many wars which desolated the land the original aqueducts were broken and were repaired at different times; and this at once accounts for the great difference in the style of the masonry in various parts. If it be objected that we find no mention anywhere of the pools being constructed by Solomon, it may be replied that neither do we have anywhere any record of the epoch of the erection of the Haram of Hebron, which is undoubtedly ancient, and neither have we any statement that Pilate made the pools. They are so much more remarkable a work than the aqueduct, that admitting he either repaired or made a new aqueduct, it is difficult to believe that the pools themselves should not have been recorded as his work; and if not here, where else could have been the aqueducts by which Solomon supplied the Temple with water? The roofing of portions of the work with half-developed arches and the style of much of the aqueduct near Jerusalem are far more antique than the Roman, and we prefer to believe, and to enjoy the belief as we sit under the shade of the Castle of El Burâk, that the huge cisterns before us are, at least in the portion hewn out of the rock, the work of the great king, and that though repaired and restored by Herodian and Roman hands from time to time, they are in their main features a veritable relic of the peaceful glories of the great Israelite kingdom. Broken aqueducts are throughout the whole of Palestine the most striking relics of departed wealth and fertility. They occur just in the most unexpected and now most desolate and barren tracts. We see how they spanned, again and again, the sublime gorges between Jerusalem and Quarantania, we find traces of them at Engedi; they still mark at intervals some of the most dreary spaces of the Judæan wilderness; and, strangest of all, in the wadies at the south-west corner of the Dead Sea, in the Wady Mahawat, Zuweirah, and others, we find traces of carefully cemented aqueducts which once supplied cisterns which still stand ready, waiting but for the return of peace and security to make that desolate land once more a land flowing with milk and honey.

To the east of the Pools of Solomon are several sites of interest. We pursue a track to the south-west, leaving on our left a conspicuous sugar-loaf hill which must be visited on our return, and after scrambling up a rugged little ravine without cultivation, on the brow of a long-backed hill about an hour and a half from El Burâk, come to a confused mass of crumbling walls, presiding over earth-covered mounds of rubbish—Tekûa, the ancient Tekoa.

Just north of Tekoa, intervening between it and the tall peak of Frank Mountain, is a rough ravine or valley, the Wady Khureitun, so named from a hermit, St. Chariton, in the fourth century, who, having been captured by robbers in this glen, after his escape founded a cell or *laura* of hermits on the spot, and himself died in the cavern which he had made his home. Before reaching the cave the open valley becomes a narrow fissure, several hundred feet deep, with rugged precipitous sides, and the bottom strewn with massive fragments of rock. Altogether there is a strange seclusion and wildness about the spot. The only access to the cavern is along a narrow ledge high up above the bottom of the ravine. A fragment of rock lodged on the edge almost bars the entrance. On climbing over this we enter a narrow low passage leading to a small cave, from which a winding gallery leads to the great cave, a natural grotto one hundred and twenty feet long by forty feet wide, probably the largest in Palestine. When candles are lighted the disturbed bats flutter out in myriads, dashing against the face of the intruders and soon extinguishing any unprotected light. Numbers of narrow passages branch out in all directions, often leading to chambers, some of which are partially artificial; one of the passages is one hundred feet long. Niches are frequently cut in the inner chambers, and fragments of urns and sarcophagi tell us that the dead as well as the living found shelter here. Through some of the caverns there are steep descents into a lower series of chambers, and a second cavern of considerable extent. Even in this land of caves, that of Khureitun is remarkable, if not unique. It seems to have been formed originally by water action eating away the soft limestone. It is now commonly but incorrectly spoken of as the Cave of Adullam. But this tradition only dates back to the time of the Crusades, and no doubt, as far as space for four hundred men and security of position are concerned, it would meet all the requisite conditions. But it will not meet the topographical necessities, and the early Christians had a far more accurate tradition that the cave was west of Bethlehem, on the frontier of Philistia, in the valley of Elah, in accordance with the statement of Josephus that it was near the royal city of Adullam, on the west side of the central range. This has been rescued from oblivion by Mons. Ganneau, corroborated by the officers of the Palestine Exploration Fund, at Ed el Miyé, in the low hills between Bethlehem and Gath, a strong natural position with good water supply and ancient tombs, and especially with a great number of habitable caves in the face of the hillside, amply sufficient for the accommodation of David and his men. Fond as the shepherds and inhabitants of Palestine are of dwellings in the rock, they always eschew the dark large caverns like those of Khureitun. The darkness, dampness, oppressive atmosphere, and the swarms of scorpions and bats are quite enough to prevent their use as ordinary dwellings. The marvels, then, of Khureitun can no longer be maintained to be historical as well as natural.

From Khureitun, half an hour's ride brings us to the foot of Jebel Fureidis, the Herodium of Josephus, the Frank Mountain of later history.

But what is the history of this lone fortress? Its earliest certain name, Herodium, was given it by the great Idumæan, who, after he had defeated the party of Antigonus on this spot, raised a great castle, as we are told by Josephus, with massive fortifications. Within was the royal palace, of great strength and splendour, combining luxury with security. At the foot of the hill he also built splendid edifices for himself and his friends, and conveyed the

VALLEY AND RUINS OF KHUREITUN, FROM THE CAVE OF ADULLAM.

water to it from a distance at a vast expense. Here, too, the tyrant was buried with great pomp, his corpse being brought hither from Jericho, where he died in frightful agony, after having in vain sought relief from the hot springs of Callirrhoe. The tradition in the locality is that Herod's unhonoured grave is in the reservoir at the foot of the hill, and is marked by a mound which still remains unsearched exactly in the centre of the dried-up pool. After the fall of Jerusalem, L. Bassus took Herodium without resistance, and with that event its history closes. The popular European name of Frank Mountain is an entire misnomer, not older than the close of the Crusades, and arising from a groundless tradition that the Crusaders here held out for forty years after the fall of Jerusalem. For this there is neither topographical nor historical warrant. There is no trace of their works, and after the destruction of the aqueduct of Herod, the place, with no natural water supply, must have been utterly untenable.

The view from the Frank Mountain at once suggests thoughts of David and his wanderings. We are looking on the scenes on one side where the youth of the shepherd-harpist was spent; on the other, the eye stretches over those naked and wild uplands and ravines where, in the hardships and struggles of his early manhood, the chief of four hundred outlaws learned the art of ruling men, and was gradually fitted to become the great warrior-king, as he wandered, hunted like one of its partridges, through those bleak wilds. In front of us is spread out for miles a rolling bare plain, with a gentle depression working towards the south-east—a plain, the desolation of which is much more conspicuous from the fact of its being neither level sand nor absolutely monotonous. Herbage there is but little, and then not green, but of a dark umber-brown hue. Trees there are none, and the general outlook is that of desolation mingled with ruin. There is a sort of impression that something is at fault—that there ought to be more trees and shrubs; and that those bare stones, scattered as from some Titan's hand over the waste, might have sheltered vegetation where their shadows powder the grim expanse under the sunlight with spots of darker hue. Beyond this dreary foreground rises one tier of low flat-topped marly hills after another, their flanks scarped and washed bare in their steeper portions, gleaming a pure white, but the bright colour only adding effect to the desolation of the landscape. Three or four of these parallel ranges can be distinguished, and then deep down the blue of the sea behind them, with a faint haze caused by the evaporation, and the straight line of Moab several hundred feet above. It was those nearer hills rather than the bare foreground which gave covert and protection to David and his followers, and where still the ibex takes the place of the gazelle, a herd of which latter we saw trotting down the wady in front, but which rarely venture into the arid hills, the refuge of the wild goat, or ibex. It must be admitted that when we enter on that labyrinth of the "south country" of Judah the scenery is neither grand nor wild. It is simply utter barrenness, not a tree nor a shrub, but scant and stunted herbage in occasional tufts, covered with myriads of white snails, which afford abundant sustenance to the thousands of larks and other desert birds which inhabit it. But when we enter on the hills eastward we are indeed in a labyrinth. What seemed from Frank Mountain to be continuous ranges, on closer acquaintance prove to be seamed on all sides diagonally with mountain torrent beds, leaving blocks rather than ridges standing between valleys of soft white marl sprinkled with flints, and the pebbly watershed (now, of course, dry) in the centre. Here trees never can have grown, and the expression "wood of Ziph" ought rather to be rendered "thickets." In tracing this theatre of some of the most eventful scenes of David's early life, we have still the Tell Zif to fix the locality. David's earliest refuge after his flight from the court of

POOLS OF SOLOMON.
Now called El Burâk-the tanks. The castle above them is occupied by a few soldiers for protection against the Bedouins.

Achish was the Cave of Adullam, which, as we have noted, was on the western slopes of the central mountain range, guarding the rich corn valley of Elah. Thence he moved south to Keilah on the same range, and then crossed to the neighbourhood of Ziph, where he had his interview with Jonathan. Close to Ziph, Lieut. Conder has discovered the ruins of Khoreisa and the valley of Hiresh, which exactly answer to the Hebrew word rendered "wood" in our Bible. Then again, by the treachery of the men of Ziph, David had to fly to the wilderness (Jashimon), *i.e.* the great desert plateau we have been describing above the shores of the Dead Sea. The hill Hachilah, his stronghold, is by Lieut. Conder placed at El Kolah, where the hilly desert and the southern wilderness meet; and it is curious to note that some caves on the north side of the hill retain the name of the "Caves of the

Dreamers," perhaps the very spot where David suddenly surprised the sleeping body-guard of Saul. From Hachilah he went to the wilderness of Maon, Nabal's home, which can easily be seen from Ziph, as can the great crusading town which marks the Carmel where Nabal had his flocks and herds. Lieut. Conder further suggests a deep gorge, "the valley of the rocks," between Maon and El Kolah, as the "cliff of division," as the scene of David's last interview with Saul, when he had taken his spear and cruse of water from beside his bolster. There is no other place in the neighbourhood which would meet the requirements of the history, and the chasm here is very narrow and absolutely impassable except by a detour of several miles. We have thus brought before us as in a panorama, which may be seen from the top of a single hill (Cain) east of Ziph, the whole scenery of David's flight and Saul's pursuit.

The traditional Cave of Adullam, or Khureitun, which has been already described (see page 147), is the most remarkable for its size, and the least changed from its original form of any of those caverns which are among the peculiar features of this country of limestone hills. The ancient Jews do not appear to have used the caves generally as dwellings, though in Palestine, as over all the rest of the world, we find traces of primitive man in the prehistoric period leading a troglodyte life. The predecessors of the Canaanites, the Horites, or "cave-men" (Deut. ii. 12), though in the Scripture texts specially spoken of as the aborigines of Edom—where still their excavated dwellings are to be found by hundreds—yet evidently extended to the south of Palestine. The Emim and Rephaim, who existed down to the time of Abraham east of Jordan, seem to have been of the same race. Their successors did not altogether abandon cave dwellings, for in the south of Judah, and even in the north, as at Endor in Galilee, we find many villages in which the caves in the hillsides have manifestly served for the store-rooms or inner chambers of the houses built out in front. But the principal use to which they were applied by the Israelites was that of tombs. The Jewish mode of sepulture was doubtless suggested by the vast number of caves, which, though common enough in all soft limestone formations, yet in this country, so universally hilly without being mountainous, seamed in every direction with little water-worn valleys, abound as in no other region. Land, too, was very precious. "God's acre" was unknown, yet nowhere were the resting-places of the dead held in greater respect. Poor indeed must have been that family which could not secure at least a portion of some rock-hewn chamber for a family burying-place. From Abraham to Joseph of Arimathea the custom remained unchanged. Rachel and Joseph are among the rare exceptions where the grave was not hewn out of the rock. So universal was the custom, that it is hardly possible to explore a cave in any part of this land without finding traces of its having once been a place of sepulture.

But after the second captivity we find the caves put to another use. When in the third and fourth centuries the fashion of a hermit life took root in Palestine, the disused sleeping-places of the dead became the homes of the living. A refuge adopted at first, perhaps, from necessity or for security, became an established type of dwelling; and he could hardly expect to be looked upon as an ascetic who adopted any other fashion than that of St. Jerome, or had any other shelter than the rock-hewn tomb afforded him. When the hermit life became more organized, and the ascetics began to associate themselves in communities, they still retained their attachment to rock-hewn dwellings, and many, though not all, of these "lauras" were

THE TRADITIONAL CAVE OF ADULLAM, AT KHUREITUN.
The above is the largest chamber of this labyrinthine grotto.

formed by a cluster of rock-hewn nests opening into each other. Such is the character of the one remaining unchanged monastery of this type, the famous establishment of Mar Saba, in the Kedron Valley, not far from the Dead Sea. The name "laura" is applied to a number of contiguous but separate cells, each inhabited by a single hermit or anchorite, in contradistinction to a monastery or "cœnobium," where the monks live together under the rule of one superior. The convent may be reached either from Jerusalem, across the wilderness, or from the Frank Mountain, skirting the Wady Nár (Valley of Fire), which is the channel of the Kedron to the Dead Sea, or from the north end of the Dead Sea up a pass by Ras Feshkhah. Whichever route is taken the country is bare, wild, and desolate. The most difficult, but certainly the finest, is that from the Dead Sea, where, soon after reaching the Wady, the whole of the buttresses and towers of the convent come suddenly into view, clustered upon the steep face of the precipitous cliffs, and covering them from top to bottom (see page 158). A strong wall clings to the side of the rocks the whole way down, effectually protecting the place from any sudden surprise of the Bedouin. From the dry torrent-bed of the ravine flights of steps are cut, leading some to a carefully protected postern, others to the plateau above. The entrance by which travellers are received is marked by a large tower with dilapidated battlements, commanding from its summit a wide prospect, and on which there is always kept a careful look-out. But the feature which at once strikes the eye is the cluster of massive buttresses, reaching by steps from the top of the lower wall far up the face of the valley, five of them parallel and close together, while patches of green and the tops of trees peep from behind them in bright contrast to the weird surroundings. These buttresses support the platform on which the greater part of the monastery stands. A little iron-barred door is the entrance, where travellers must present their credentials before admission, and where they are carefully scrutinised by the janitor. No Bedouin or ladies are admitted on any pretext, the former for fear of treachery—of which St. Saba's history affords many instances—the latter by the rules of the order. But for their reception a tower outside is provided, where they are supplied with simple fare and a night's lodging. From the iron gate a flight of steps descends to a second door, thence another to a courtyard with miniature garden, and a third stair leads to the guest chamber. The terraces are clustered one over another, or by the side of each other, much after the fashion of a colony of swallows' nests. In fact, the architecture of this bird seems to have supplied the type for their construction. Fig-trees peep from many a corner, and there is one solitary palm, watered and tended with great veneration, and said to have been planted by St. Saba, and to have borne fruit the day after he planted it (see page 153). The monks affirm that the dates have no stones, but we were not supplied with any proof of this phenomenon. In the largest court is the dome of the sanctuary, where the bones of St. Saba once rested till they were removed to Venice, and near it the Chapel of St. Nicholas, the church of the convent, with the area of the nave open, surrounded with stalls, and the walls, screen, and chancel gorgeous with gilding and paintings, chiefly gifts from the Russian Emperor, who not many years since renovated the buildings. Behind is a dark cave covered with pictures, whose silver casings gleam in the dim obscurity, and behind a grating we are shown the skulls and bones of the martyrs, said to have been fourteen thousand in number, massacred by Chosroes, the Persian invader, in the beginning of the seventh century. The grotto is also shown where St. Saba lived and died, consisting of two chambers, which tradition says he shared peaceably with a lion, who was the original tenant. Three times the lion ejected the saint, but he obstinately returned, and at length the lion

MAR SABA, VALLEY OF THE KEDRON

This page is adjacent to a plate and is intentionally left blank.

contented himself with a shelf in the little inner closet. The tomb is also shown of John of Damascus, and of other less celebrated saints. The library is reputed to contain rare manuscript treasures, but these are not kept to be read or examined; and, with the exception of Curzon and Tischendorf, very few travellers have been able to examine them. Curzon found several MSS. of great interest, among them a copy of the first eight books of the Old Testament, Homer's Iliad on paper, and one ancient Servian MS. All the others were in Greek, and he estimated the number at about one thousand. From the state of some we saw in the cell of the head of the

BALCONIES TO MONKS' CELLS, MAR SABA.
And a peep into the convent garden.

convent, we fear a librarian is much needed here. For better security the key of the library is kept by the Patriarch at Jerusalem. The history of this remarkable settlement begins with St. Euthymius, about A.D. 450. His favourite pupil, St. Saba, born in Cappadocia, A.D. 439, has eclipsed his master's fame. He gathered round him a vast number of anchorites, and formed them into a community under the rule of St. Basil. He was made Archimandrite by the Patriarch of Jerusalem, and in that capacity supported orthodoxy against the monophysitical heresy by driving his opponents, at the head of his armed monks, out of the sacred city. After his feats of arms and controversies he died here in peace, A.D. 532, at the age of ninety-four years. The convent-fortress has been often sacked, especially by Chosroes, the Persian devastator, about A.D. 604, and frequently during the stormy vicissitudes of the Crusading epoch. It was again pillaged during

ENTRANCE TO THE CAVE OF ST. SABA.

the Syrian troubles in 1834, and was subsequently repaired by Russia. The convent is considered by the Greeks almost a penal one, and scandal says that all its inmates except the superiors have been sent hither for heresy or other offences. Of heresy certainly they must be acquitted, so far as their knowledge goes, for they are profoundly ignorant, and whatever their other offences may have been, they are unwearied in their devotions. Every monk has to attend the services seven times in the twenty-four hours, from 4 A.M. to midnight. Only one-third of the sixty brethren are in holy orders, and many of the lay brethren are unable to read. They are from Turkey, Greece, the Archipelago, and a few Russians; but modern Greek is the language of daily intercourse, and few understand Arabic. All are under a vow never to taste fresh meat, and their diet is both meagre and stinted in quantity. Eggs are permitted on Sundays only. On other days the allowance is a small brown loaf, a dish of cabbage broth, a plate of olives, an onion, half an orange, a quarter of a lemon, six figs, and half-a-pint of wine apiece. A little raki or spirits is also permitted. There is all the difference between the monks of the Greek and Roman rites in Palestine that characterizes the political and religious position of the two churches, and nowhere is the contrast more clearly illustrated than at Mar Saba and Carmel. The one is always aggressive, the other on the defensive. In everything Greek there seems embodied a cold dead conservatism, tenacious it knows not why, and looking on every concession or relaxation of a rule as a confession of weakness. Thus, though the rule of the Carmelite may be as stringent as that of St. Saba, there is no fear of the former being enforced to the injury of health or the disadvantage of the order. "Reculer pour mieux sauter," is the motto of Rome in small things as well as in great. She has shown this in her management of the Maronites and the Greek Catholics, lost to Constantinople through obstinate mismanagement. The marriage of the priests, the use of the Syrian language, the liturgy of St. James, a different calendar of saints, all have been conceded, since union could be had on no other terms. The Greek never dreams of enlarging his fold, nor of concessions which might retain the waverers; in matters ecclesiastical all the proverbial astuteness of the Hellenic race seems to desert him. A monastic life is chosen, as one of the monks here told us, for the sake of peace and of eating the bread of idleness, and there is no training for their vow, nor any thought of applying this life of the religious to the advantage of the Church. Thus while every Latin monastery in Syria is the centre of an aggressive mission, the Eastern Church does not even adapt her battalions of celibates to man her defensive works. Ages of Moslem oppression and the dense ignorance of the local priesthood have done their work; and while the truth has been obscured and the written Word of God forgotten, she seems to have lost even the desire to discover or understand it.

These poor monks have but one amusement, and that is the feeding and cultivating the various wild birds and animals of the glen. In this they have been marvellously successful. I watched a pet wolf, which came every evening, as the bell tolled six, to the fort of the monastery for his ration of bread dipped in oil, which a friendly monk regularly dropped to him over the wall. The wolf was jealous of his privilege, and chased back several others

DEAD SEA AND MOUNTAINS OF MOAB, FROM MAR SABA

which attempted to accompany him. He might have been, from his manners, a lineal descendant of St. Saba's lion. There was a whole pack of jackals also which regularly came to be fed, and at another corner, by themselves, three foxes. But the most remarkable of their pets are the bronzewinged grakles (*Amydrus tristrami*), peculiar to the Dead Sea basin; elsewhere these birds are the most shy of the denizens of the rocks, but here they perch in flocks, and are fed from the hand, or catch berries as they are thrown up for them in the air, while their rich bell-like notes resound in sweet cadence from cliff to cliff.

ST. SABA'S PALM-TREE.

When we leave the hospitable convent—for hospitable it is to those who are reasonable enough to be content with what the monks can provide—we find ourselves in a region entirely distinct physically from either the plains or the hill country of Palestine. We have descended into the Dead Sea valley, and though over one thousand feet above its surface, yet the Wady Nâr, at the foot of Mar Saba, is on the level of the Mediterranean. The air here is hot and close; all the plants are new and strange; the entire flora has changed.

In the rocks of this Kedron valley the curious little Syrian *hyrax*, the coney of Scripture, abounds; and little miniature porcupines, true mice, but with the covering of a hedgehog instead of fur, may be seen nibbling among the brown brushwood. Everything is tawny. The Greek partridge gives place to the desert sand partridge; the hare is of the same russet hue; the foxes, the larks, everything that moves, are of the same uniform fawn colour, rarely with the least variation in shade. The only exceptions are a few chats, birds of bright black-and-white livery, which seek their safety not in flight or concealment, but in the fissures of the rocks. The foliage and the blossoms of most of the plants are alike, a brownish yellow or a yellowish white. The beetles alone of living things, apparently for the convenience of the birds which feed on them, retain their bright and conspicuously coloured liveries.

One of the most impressive views of the Dead Sea, at least of its northern part, is obtained by following the crest of this "Valley of Fire" to the edge of the precipitous wall where it enters the Dead Sea. From the top of the fissure a wide plain pushing out in several gracefully sweeping sandspits into the sea can be seen spread below, and at this distance does not reveal its barrenness. A strange conical hill, like a colossal cairn, stands isolated in the centre of the plain, a relic of the deposit which once filled the valley. The view of the coast-line is uninterrupted nearly to Engedi. A dark rich belt of tall cane brake fringes the plain twelve hundred feet beneath us, from headland to headland. The eye can trace the line of the eastern mountains, parallel to the hills of Judaea, almost from Mount Gilead to Kerak. The red ridge of Moab, with the sun casting purple shadows here and there, and patches of bright light on its level summits, is furrowed by the deep ravines of the Callirrhoe and the Arnon; while below the sea lies unruffled, blue and glossy, shining like oil, with here and there long streaks of what may be froth or ripple in narrow bands across it. Southward may be detected the Lisan (or tongue), a broad flat peninsula of barren marl, which stretches almost across the southern part of the lake. From these hills it looks like a narrow sandspit dovetailing with the wavy outlines of one low spit after another running out to meet it from the western shore. These white spits all sparkle and glitter in the sunlight like diamonds studded over a field of silver.

Perhaps it is by moonlight that that silent mysterious lake is most impressive. It is a long weary scramble from the ridge down to the shore, and horses must be carefully led down the passes, which are only fit for goats, *i.e.* if the route be taken from Mar Saba, for down to Jericho from Jerusalem the road is easy and good. When a full moon rises, the eastern hills, which gleamed so warm a glow before sunset, are shrouded in gloom, and the moon's radiance shoots over the burnished surface of the lake. There is a stillness that may be felt. Rarely does the wandering Bedouin visit these shores by day, and never by night. The Dead Sea has often been described and still more often been the subject of romance. But let us put aside all preconceived notions, and so long as we do not try to drink it or rub it into our eyes, we shall find a centre of landscape of rare beauty and endless variety. True there is no life, animal or vegetable, within its acrid waters; true that for the like reason its immediate shores are barren; but wherever fresh water approaches it there are nooks of surpassing loveliness and verdure. Such are Engedi, the Safieh, the mouths of the Callirrhoe and the Arnon, and other favoured spots where the fronds of the palm-tree almost lave its brine; and on all sides the cliffs and mountains between which it lies buried are rich in every hue save green. Dead Sea is a Greek and modern name. To the Jew it was the Salt Sea, to the Arab it is the Bahr Lût, "Sea of Lot." In one respect it is a lake without parallel in the world, the deepest depression on the earth's surface, being no less than one thousand three hundred feet below the level of the ocean. It is the lower extremity of a deep fissure or rent which runs down from the foot of Hermon, a sort of continuation of the Bukaa, or cleft, which at a higher altitude divides the Lebanon range from the Anti-Libanus, or Hermon. This deep chasm is drained by the Jordan, which leaps full grown at birth from one of the largest springs in the world, under Banias, the ancient Cæsarea Philippi. It makes a pause at Huleh, the old waters of Merom, feeding first an impenetrable papyrus swamp,

HERMITS' CAVES IN THE CLIFFS OF THE KEDRON.

and then the little lake four miles long. Its next halt is at the hallowed Lake of Galilee, six hundred and eighty-two feet below the Mediterranean, whence it pursues a tortuous course within narrow limits for a direct distance of sixty-five miles to the north end of the Dead Sea. It has no outlet, and the volume of water constantly poured into it from the Jordan and the rivers of Moab, as well as by the torrents on the west side and southern end, is carried off simply by evaporation. This alone in the case of a lake without exit would be sufficient to account for its saltness, for the saline particles carried down in solution are not evaporated, but remain, and by their continual additions add to the saltness of the stagnant water. Hence all such lakes are invariably salt. But in this case there is an additional cause in the vast salt deposit several miles long at the south end, Jebel Usdum, past which little streams flow into the sea, bringing fresh supplies of brine. Not only in the depression of its surface below the sea-level, but also in the enormous depth of its water the Dead Sea is unique among lakes. Its greatest depth near the north end is one thousand three hundred and eight feet, and close to the Moab shore it descends sheer for nine hundred feet. The southern portion, on the contrary, on the other side of the Lisan, is only about twelve feet deep. The extraordinary perpendicular depth on the east side is explained by the geological causes which have formed the whole fissure. Volcanic agency has only indirectly been at work, but at some recent geologic epoch, subsequent to the formation of the chalk, but before the eocene, there must have been a sudden and immense crack, dislocating the whole stratification. In fact, the bed of the valley must have fallen towards the centre of the earth, with line of dislocation along the eastern edge. This is shown by the entire change of the geological formation east and west of the Jordan. On the east side we have the new red sandstone, and hard limestone of the age of our greensand above it; while apparently on the top of the red sandstone at the south of the lake on its western side lies the great deposit of rock-salt, such as is found on our new red sandstone in England. These sandstone beds are but slightly inclined, and rise abruptly. On the west side, on the contrary, the red sandstone is never found, but we have soft strata of the chalk and eocene periods, dipping with many faults from west to east, and often strangely contorted. Hence they must have been deposited previous to the dislocation. But on the top of this chalk there remains on the tops of the hills an eocene deposit, very rich in fossils, and which, though washed out of the valleys, yet remains undisturbed elsewhere, and which has no eastward dip. At this period the sea must have rolled over the whole of Syria south of the Lebanon, and probably (though this is not clear) over the ridge of Akabah to the Red Sea. Subsequent to the formation of the Jordan valley appears to have been the great volcanic period, when streams of lava overflowed the whole of the Ledjah and Hauran (Trachonitis and Bashan), and covered a large portion of the country west of the Sea of Galilee, and as far south as Gilboa, with many eruptions in the east of Moab, none of which exhibit signs of being waterworn. Still there may have been many earlier epochs of volcanic activity, and the region has always been bituminous, as may be seen by the deposits and streaks of bitumen in the chalk rocks. These volcanic eruptions, draining out the molten rocks from beneath and pouring them forth in lava floods, may have caused the sudden subsidence along the axis of the valley.

But after it was formed it was long before the Dead Sea became reduced to its present level. The history of its gradual subsidence is written on the western slopes, not only of the sea itself, but on those of the valley as far as Kurn Surtabeh, nearly half-way to the Lake of Galilee. The eastern side is far too steep to allow any deposits to remain; but on the opposite side, and especially up the valleys which debouch on the plain, there are white deposits of chalky marl and gypsum strongly impregnated with salt, so that not the slightest vegetation can exist. These raised beaches have been left when the sea was double its present extent, and are four hundred feet above the present level. About two hundred feet lower down are the marks of a second coast-line, and a third former boundary of the lake is marked by another set of flat shelves of marl about a hundred feet above the present surface. Again, about seventy feet lower may be traced, especially at the south end, the register of another long pause in its subsidence before the lake became reduced to its present contracted limits. In historic times there is no evidence of the extent of the sea having varied much. True, it rises and falls a few feet—perhaps within the limits of four feet—at different seasons of the year; but taking one year with another its bulk appears to be almost stationary. Perhaps the supply scarcely keeps pace with the exhaustion by evaporation; but had it been much higher, for instance in the times of Joshua, the sites of Beth Hogla and Gilgal could scarcely have been habitable. At either end of the lake are wide level plains of several miles in extent, that at the south end being absolute desolation. For about seven or eight miles it is scarcely above the winter level of the water, and is sometimes overflowed, while both the soil and the waters of the several streams which drain the Arabah are so saturated with mineral salts that even marine vegetable life is impossible. But the moment we rise even three feet above this plain the vegetation, nourished by the abundant springs and rills from the eastern mountains, becomes dense and luxuriant, as in the Ghor Safieh, at the south-eastern corner of the lake. The northern plain, or Ghor, as it is called—the "Ciccar" of the Hebrews—though barren, is by no means so utterly lifeless, and on the east side the desert portion forms but a narrow fringe. The reason of this is the higher level of the northern plain.

When we return to the north end of the lake, we find the flat shores strewn for several hundred yards from the water's edge with the gaunt trunks and branches of palms, tamarisks, and smaller trees carried down by the winter floods, and then cast on shore denuded of their bark, bleached and incrusted with salt, and by their grim skeleton appearance most suggestive of the name Dead Sea.

It is on this northern plain of Ghor that it seems certain we must place the sites of the Cities of the Plain, "suffering the vengeance of eternal fire." Much labour and ingenuity has been exhausted on the question of their situation. Before arriving at a definite conclusion it may be as well to clear the ground by some general observations. In the first place, it has been frequently assumed that the destruction of Sodom and its sister cities was the result of some

CONVENT OF MAR SABA, FROM BROOK KEDRON,
Five hundred and ninety feet above the bottom of the ravine below.

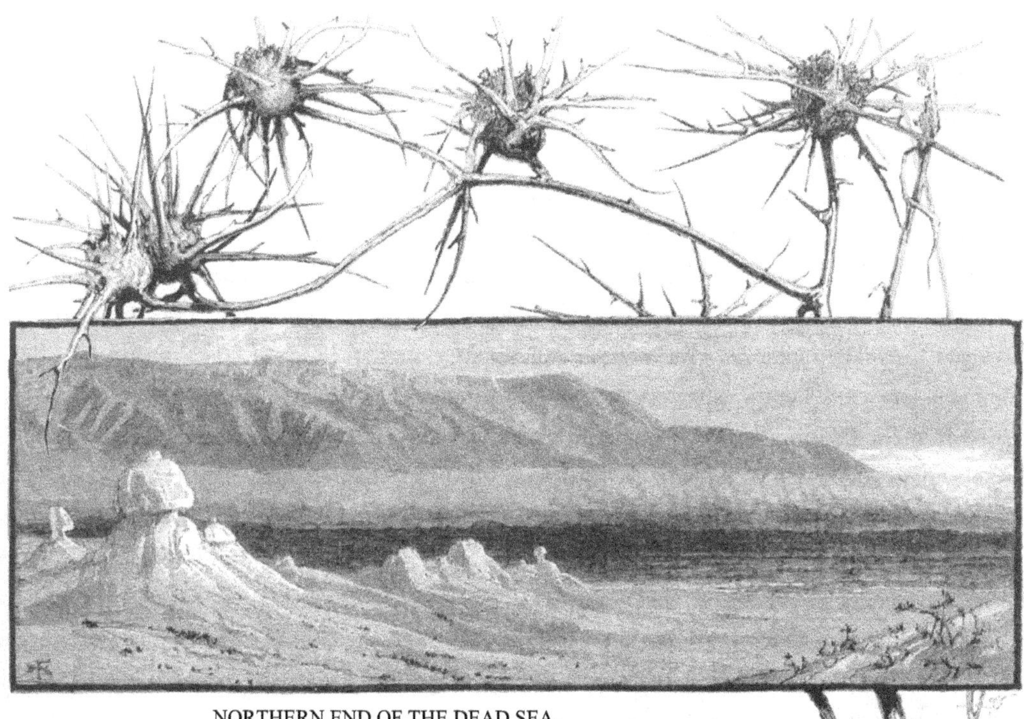

NORTHERN END OF THE DEAD SEA.

tremendous geological catastrophe which has left its record in existing phenomena of the region. Many writers have been misled by endeavouring to square the facts they observed with this preconceived opinion. Now careful examination by competent geologists, such as M. Lartet and others, has shown that the whole

KASR HAJLA, THE ANCIENT BETH HOGLA,
Known also as the Monastery of St. John, Hajla.

district has assumed its present shape slowly and gradually through a succession of ages, and that its peculiar phenomena are similar to those of other salt lakes of Africa, or referable to its unique and depressed position. In the second place, the simple narrative of Genesis states that "the Lord rained brimstone and fire out of heaven, and overthrew those cities . . . . and that which grew upon the ground." There is no authority whatever in the biblical record for the popular notion that the site of the cities was submerged. The simple and natural explanation seems, when stripped of all the wild tradition and strange horrors with which the mysterious sea has been invested, to be this—that during some earthquake, or without its direct agency, showers of sulphur and probably bitumen ejected from the lake or thrown up from its shores, and ignited perhaps by the lightning which would accompany such phenomena, fell upon the cities and destroyed them. The materials for such a catastrophe do exist. Sulphur springs stud the shore. Sulphur is strewn, whether in layers or in fragments, over the desolate plains, and bitumen is ejected in great floating masses from the bottom of the sea, oozes through the fissures of the rocks, is deposited with gravel on the beach, or in places appears to have been precipitated during some convulsion. During the great earthquake of January, 1837, whole islets of bitumen were suddenly detached and floated on the surface. The kindling by lightning of such a mass of combustible material, which in those times must have existed in at least as great abundance as at present, combined with an earthquake ejecting it from the lake, would soon spread devastation over the plain, so that the smoke of the country would go up as the smoke of a furnace. The history of the catastrophe has not only remained in the inspired record, but is inscribed in the memory of the surrounding tribes by many a local tradition and significant name. But as there is no warrant for imagining that the catastrophe was a geological one, so in any other case all traces of action must at this distance of time have vanished. The configuration of the sea-bottom shows that no cities can possibly have existed and been submerged except in the lagoon at the southern end. There are only two possible localities for the doomed cities, either near the southern or near the northern end of the lake. Modern writers have until recently assumed the neighbourhood of the lower end as a matter of course, from the tradition given by Josephus, from the similarity of some names, as *Usdum*, supposed to represent Sodom, and chiefly because Jerome identifies a Zoar at the south-eastern end of the Dead Sea with the Zoar of Genesis. But on the other hand they are called "the Cities of the *Plain*." "*Ciccar*" is the circle of Jordan, and used only of the district north of the lake. We read that Abraham and Lot stood together between Bethel and Ai and beheld all the plains of Jordan, and Lot chose the well-watered region of Sodom and Gomorrah. From the hill between Bethel and Ai it is utterly impossible to see the lower end of the sea, sixty miles distant, and shut out by intervening hills, while the plain of Jericho is spread almost at the beholder's feet, and the bright green oasis of Ain Sultan shines like an emerald on the dreary waste. What must it have been when the old region was well watered everywhere, "even as the garden of the Lord." Again, after the destruction of the cities, Abraham looked from Mamre "toward Sodom and Gomorrah, and, lo, the smoke of the country went up as the smoke of a furnace." From Mamre the plain itself is not visible, but the depression between the hills

THE PLAINS OF JERICHO, FROM THE WEST.

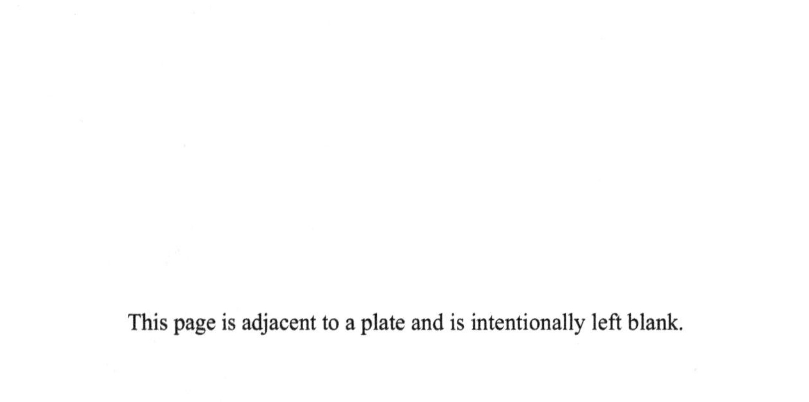

This page is adjacent to a plate and is intentionally left blank.

would enable a spectator to identify the region whence the smoke arose, which he could not do if it had been at the lower end. Again, in the account of the inroad of Chedorlaomer, we read that the invaders returning from Mount Seir smote the Amorites in Hazezon Tamar, and then were met by the King of Sodom and his confederates in the plains of Siddim, and were pursued by Abraham to the sources of the Jordan. This could not have been if Sodom and the other cities had been at the south end. Lastly, in the view granted to Moses from Pisgah, "he beheld the south and the plain of the valley of Jericho, the City of Palm-trees, unto Zoar." From Nebo it is utterly impossible to see the south-east of the Dead Sea, the modern Dra'a, supposed to be Zoar; but if Zoar were somewhere on the lower slopes below the Moabite range the description is perfectly natural. One very careful explorer (Lieut. Conder, R. E.), suggests Wady Amriyeh, near Ain Feshkhah, at the north-west shoulder of the Dead Sea, as radically identical in its name with Gomorrah, and near a great and plenteous spring. He suggests El Dâmieh, near Surtabeh, twenty-three miles higher up the valley, as pointing to the city Adam, which he identifies with Admah. Shaht ed Duba'a, *i.e.* the lair of the hyena, the cliff just above Roman Jericho, he suggests as answering to Zeboim, *i.e.* hyenas. We believe that the true topography is that which would place Sodom and Gomorrah in the wide eastern stretch of the plains of Jordan, in front of the wide plains of Shittim, and perhaps rather to the south of them, though possibly they may have been on the western side. But Zoar certainly was on the east side, and it seems more in accordance with the incidents of the narrative to place all the cities on the same side of Jordan, and probably at no great distance from each other. Of Admah we have no trace, though it has been conjecturally identified with the city "Adam," near Zarthan, in the plain of Succoth, some way higher up and too far to harmonize well with the narrative. Now one remarkable feature of this "Ciccar," or plain of Jordan, is the number of Tells, or barren artificial mounds, which stud it on both sides. They recall to the traveller the artificial mounds on which the villages of Egypt are planted to save them from inundation. They are unquestionably artificial, for in all which have been examined fragments of pottery and traces of sun-dried and frequently kiln-burnt bricks are found. In some, too, fragments of columns and dressed stones may be seen. Very probably some of these nameless heaps may mark the exact site of the doomed cities. Dr. Merrill has recently with much ingenuity suggested five sites on the Shittim plain, to all of which names are attached by the Arabs. Zoar he identifies with the southernmost mound, Tell Ektana (from the Hebrew *katan*, "little"?), and probably M'Shaggar, a spur in front of Nebo, sheltered the little city. Zeboim is placed about seven miles north-west of this at Tell Shaib, and the others at Tell Kefrein, opposite the upper ford (Abel-Shittim), at Tell Ramah, and Seweimeh, or Beth Jesimoth. But we can scarcely expect an unquestioned identification for any one excepting Zoar, which remained to after-times, and to which the allusions are so clear as to shut us up to the little corner close under the Moab Mountains for our investigation.

But we have lingered long enough over these faint traces of all but prehistoric cities.

When we come to places which still existed at the epoch of Joshua's conquest we are treading on firmer ground. At page 159 we have an illustration of one of the few remaining architectural ruins of the plain in the Convent of Kasr Hajla, the ancient Beth Hogla. Beth Hogla is only mentioned in Scripture as on the boundary line between Judah and Benjamin, and belonging to the latter. The only trace of the place, which must always have been insignificant, is the name which, with the tenacity of Oriental nomenclature, still clings to an isolated

BATHING-PLACE ON THE JORDAN.

spring, Ain Hajla. Leaving Er Riha, the modern Jericho, and crossing a stony plain, which might with very little care and irrigation be again made a fertile garden, at the distance of about five miles we come upon a patch of perennial verdure with a few inconspicuous shrubs. In the centre is a beautiful clear blue pool of tepid water surrounded by an old wall of solid masonry about five feet in circumference, which scarcely reaches above the ground, and over which the spring pours forth its stream of life. It is utterly neglected. No path leads to it,

VALLEY OF THE JORDAN, FROM THE CONVENT OF ST. JOHN THE BAPTIST.
Known also as Kasr-el-Yehûd, "the Jews' Tower."

no use is made of it by man; the wild boars alone frequent it, and paddle down the surrounding herbage. There is not a vestige of a ruin, but less than a mile distant is a pile of buildings of the Christian epoch, named from this spring, Kasr Hajla. It is one of the best-preserved of the curious group of monasteries founded in and around this district by Jerome and his followers. It is sometimes called also Deir Mar Yuhanna, or the monastery of St. John. Roofless and crumbling, its inner walls still retain not only traces of frescoes, but some very distinct figures of Greek saints, and inscriptions with the colours perfectly fresh. Many of the arches stand uninjured, and the walls and outlines of the chapel can be distinctly traced. Of the history of this most remarkable ruin very little is known. Jerome mentions a monastery at Gilgal, and it is said to have been two miles from the Jordan, which would sufficiently describe this site. It appears to have been occupied three hundred and fifty years ago by monks of the order of St. Basil, and was then called the monastery of St. Jerome. From that period we find no mention of it, nor any record of its being inhabited by a religious order, and it was a ruin pretty much in its present condition when visited by Seetzen at the beginning of this century. It was probably held by the monks during the Middle Ages as a place of refuge for the Jordan pilgrims, and became deserted when the caravans were placed under escort and protection.

From Kasr Hajla a ride of three-quarters of an hour brings us on a desolate expanse of grey salt mud, with occasional sand mounds burrowed by the jerboa, to the mouth of the Jordan, without a living tree to enliven it, but with many a bare bark-stripped trunk projecting out of the slime, on the naked boughs of which many kingfishers and an occasional cormorant perch to watch for their helpless prey, the fishes with which the river teems, and which incautiously swimming down the stream become stupified as soon as they enter the brine. In dry weather the grey mud is encrusted with salt and gypsum, and occasional layers of sulphur and oxide of iron. No wonder that Flora declines to display life on such a soil. But whenever a little sand-mound has collected, there a few desert shrubs plant their roots and relieve the monotony. The river itself lies completely out of sight. Never except from some commanding height can a glimpse be caught of the silvery bead which marks its course until within two or three miles of its end when its forest fringe ceases. But its course can everywhere be traced by the deep green ribbon of foliage just peering above the upper banks, the tops of the trees which guard its border. All along this lower plain there are three sets of terrace banks. The old bed of the river, or rather the upper end of the lake, where the mud deposits were laid against the slopes of the enclosing mountains, was about sixteen miles wide. This is the plain on which Jericho, Beth Hogla, and Gilgal stood. Then we have the higher plain, which even now on rare occasions is flooded. This is covered with shrubs and scant herbage. Then close to the river's bank we descend fifty-five feet into a dense thicket of tamarisk, silver poplar, willows, terebinth, and many other trees strange to European eyes, with a dense and impenetrable undergrowth of reed and all sorts of aquatic brushwood. This is perforated in all directions by the runs of wild boars, which literally swarm here, while the branches are vocal with myriads of birds—nightingales, bulbuls, and especially turtle-doves—which meet here and find abundant food in the herbage of the trefoil, astragalus, and other characteristic plants of the higher plain. In ancient times beasts more formidable than the wild boar had their lair in these coverts, and when driven out by the periodical swellings of Jordan the lion and the leopard sought their prey among the flocks of the villagers in the country above. The leopard still lingers in these thickets, and an observant traveller cannot explore far without coming on its traces, especially on the east bank. But the lion, though not extinct in the times of the Crusades, has long been exterminated from the region west of the

Euphrates. It is a startling contrast suddenly to descend into this narrow belt after seeing the black stork and the noble Houbara bustard running on the barren plain behind, and being startled by the whirring cry of the desert sandgrouse as it started in front, now to be greeted by the trill of European songster, and be soothed by the incessant coo of the turtle-dove in the glades. Beneath this shade the Jordan, generally not above fifty yards wide, hurries on in its tortuous but rapid course, the impetuous stream, muddy and dark, dashing from side to side and forming curling eddies at each sharp turn, generally most difficult to stem, and in most places too deep to ford, having generally ten feet of water. It is, however, easy enough for an expert swimmer to get across by choosing a spot just above one of these sharp turns, and steering himself with the stream till he strikes the opposite bank.

BANKS OF THE JORDAN ABOVE THE CONVENT OF ST. JOHN THE BAPTIST (THE KASR-EL-YEHUD).

The mouth of the Jordan is seldom visited except by European travellers; the crowds of pilgrims visit the river higher up, near what is called the Helu ford, though each sect of Christians has a special spot for the completion of the pilgrimage, which is maintained as an article of faith to be the place of our Saviour's baptism. Fortunately, as the Latin and Greek Easters do not fall on the same days, and as Easter is the prescribed time for the ceremony, there are no collisions on the banks of the sacred river. The Greek pilgrims bathe at a spot where there is a narrow clearing down to the water's edge; the Latin sacred place is higher up, near the ruins of an old convent. The ceremony is most interesting and picturesque from the start from Jerusalem to the return. In former times the crowd of pilgrims was said to number hundreds of thousands; and even now they amount to several thousands. The day fixed is Easter Monday, and the Turkish Government have for many ages guaranteed the safe conduct of the convoy. It starts from the neighbourhood of the Church of the Holy Sepulchre, in front of which the pilgrims generally assemble, preceded by a white flag and noisy instruments; the rearguard being composed of Turkish troops with the green flag of the Prophet. The number of pilgrims at the Greek Easter now rarely reaches five thousand, though it is said that formerly ten thousand joined the procession. A merry joyous crowd they seem, the roar of voices often drowning the incessant clatter of the tom-toms in front and rear. Few of them are on foot except the Russian peasants. Every kind of quadruped, camel, horse, mule, and ass, has been impressed for the occasion, and the hapless camels flounder down the steep descent to Jericho with huge baskets full of women and children on either side. The Bedouin of the neighbourhood hangs about the desert cliffs and dells ready to cut off any incautious straggler, and to send him to rejoin the convoy prematurely stripped for his bathe. Against these marauders was formed the company of nine knights who became the founders of the historic order of the Templars. Arrived long before sunset at Er Riha, the modern Jericho, but really near the ancient Gilgal, the motley crowd bivouacs for the night.

A stroll among the tented and untented groups will afford one of the most varied and picturesque scenes which even in that land of the picturesque the traveller can encounter. Every costume, from the sheepskin-clad and odoriferous Russian to the bright dresses of the Bulgarians, the quaint robes of the Georgians, the brilliant colours of the Greek, and the solid richness of the Armenian, is collected from all Eastern Europe and Western Asia. But soon all is hushed, and the camp fires are smouldering embers, and the long straggling camp, stretching some three miles across the plain, is buried in sleep, recalling the encampment of Israel first pitched at Gilgal, this very spot. Long before sunrise, about three o'clock, there is a sudden roll of kettledrums, and lights are struck all over the plain. There is none of the merriment of the preceding day, but by torchlight, in solemn silence, with the paschal moon hanging forward out of the deep black sky and dimming the glare of the torches, the mixed multitude presses on to the bank of the sacred river. Just after daybreak the head of the procession reaches the open space on the river's bank, and before the sun has well overtopped the hills of Moab the first-comers are plunging in the whirling eddies of the turbid stream. Some dash in naked and exhibit their prowess, acquired perhaps in the distant Nile or its Abyssinian feeders, as they strike or seem to strike across with their arms backwards and forwards. Most, however, of those who have come in families bathe in a long white garment, which after this Jordan baptism is carefully preserved till it serves as the winding-sheet of its owner. I have noticed devout families joining hand-in-hand in a circle in the water, the women having their babes slung round their neck, and reciting the creed, ducking at each sentence, while they hold on to the overhanging boughs. One remarkable feature is the number of little children and infants; but the age of the pilgrim matters not, and the Jordan baptism never needs to be repeated. Primitive and rude the scene may be called, but there is no indecorum or irreverence, and very little superstition—nothing like the ceremonies of the Church of the Holy Sepulchre. Who that has stood by the brink of that river could have turned back without having washed in Jordan? Who is so utterly devoid of sentiment as not to sympathize with that pilgrim multitude? and who can look on the Eastern baptism without feeling how he has reproduced before his own eyes the scenes and the surroundings that accompanied the preaching and the baptism on this river-bank of the great forerunner, St. John Baptist.

BIT ON THE PLAINS OF JERICHO.

The ceremony is not a long one. After it is over every one cuts a stick or bough to preserve in memory of the visit (a palmer's staff); and most come provided with a bottle, which is filled from the sacred stream. Silently the crowds remount and gradually depart; the last Turkish fez has closed the rear-guard two hours before noon. The camp of the previous night is reoccupied, and the pilgrims rest and sleep till sunset, when they eat their evening meal. At dead of night they set out, roused by the kettledrum, and in silence resume their march back to Jerusalem. The last act of the great pilgrimage has been completed, and every one of the caravan is now a true "palmer."

How long these pilgrimages have existed the ruins of the monasteries which stud the lower part of the Jordan valley bear witness. One of these, the Convent of St. John, from which the view on page 163 is taken, is close to the Latin bathing-place, and some little way above that held to by the Greeks, and where the scenes just described take place. The Moslems call this convent Kasr-el-Yehûd—"the Jews' tower." It was undoubtedly to the sacredness of the bathing-places that these monasteries owed their existence in the first instance. Gradually, as the pilgrimage became, under Moslem rule, a somewhat perilous journey, they were maintained as a sort of religious garrison for the reception and protection of pilgrims; but when the customary bathing became confined to Eastertide exclusively, and

ER RIHA, THE MODERN JERICHO.
On the Site of the "New Jericho" of the Crusaders.

the Turkish Government, from the mixed motives of gain and of conciliating the Christian powers, organized and protected the caravans, there was no longer any necessity for a permanent guard, and the excessive unhealthiness of the Ghor caused the monasteries to be speedily abandoned, and the monks were withdrawn to such healthier and safer retreats as Mar Saba and Mar Elyas. St. Jerome, to whom, directly or indirectly, it has been the fashion to ascribe

ONE OF THE ARCHES OF AN AQUEDUCT OVER THE WADY KELT, PLAINS OF JERICHO.
The stream is popularly known as the Brook Cherith.

every religious institution in Palestine, was certainly by his example the origin of the monasteries of the Jordan valley in their early form, when the ascetic hermits began to group themselves into "lauras." Yet Jerome himself was no devotee of unmeaning pilgrimages. He declared that Heaven may be reached from Britain as easily as from Jerusalem, that an innumerable throng of saints never saw the holy city, and that the sacred places themselves have been polluted by the images of idols. It may excite surprise that the buildings of the Christian period should be so numerous and so noble as are these monasteries. But this is explained when we remember how in the period that succeeded their foundation by Jerome and his immediate followers Palestine enjoyed an epoch of exceptional quiet amid the ravages of the northern barbarians in the rest of the Roman empire. Nor was the calm broken till the storm of Chosroes and his exterminating Persians burst upon the hapless East at the end of the sixth century. Then all these monasteries were sacked and fired, and their inmates butchered. Ere the country could recover itself, within fifty years, a yet more fatal though less cruel war of conquest swept over Palestine in the Caliph Omar and his Moslem Arabs. The Moslem did not exterminate the Christian or forbid his rites. Some of the monasteries were permitted to be repaired and reoccupied, but the cost was great and the Christian population utterly impoverished. Then came a transient burst of spasmodic prosperity, when the Crusaders erected their sugar-mills and cultivated this rich Jordan valley. When the Mohammedan sway was re-established the monasteries soon, as above stated, became useless.

As we pass across the narrow belt of open plain which intervenes between the Monastery of St. John and the oasis of Jericho, we step back from mediaeval remains to the mounds of primæval history. Jericho, "the City of Palm-trees," was the contemporary of the doomed Cities of the Plain, and whatever doubt may hang over their exact position, there is none whatever on the Jericho of the prophets. In speaking of Jericho we must bear in mind that the name is claimed by three distinct cities of different ages, succeeding one another. First, there is the old Canaanitish city, destroyed by Joshua and rebuilt by Hiel, the resort of Elijah and Elisha; secondly, the Jericho of the Herods and of the New Testament; and thirdly, Er Riha, the crusading and modern representative, the name, strangely different as it sounds is its English rendering, being the Arabic equivalent of the old Hebrew Jericho.

The first of these, and by far the most interesting, is that to which we will direct our steps on our return from the fords of Jordan at Helu. From the ruined monastery by the river, Kasr-el-Yehûd (see page 163), where the great cistern on which the colony depended for its water supply is still nearly perfect, we may trace the utterly ruined aqueduct by which it was supplied from the famous Prophet's Fountain. Of the seven monasteries recorded in history in the plain the ruins of five are known, but of these only three are identified. They are all a little to the south of our course. Looking at this barren plain, with its occasional copses of thorn-tree (*zukkûm*) and Spina Christi, we may wonder how a considerable population could ever have existed until we notice the remains of their aqueducts, no less than twelve of which have been traced and mapped by Lieut. Conder. When we leave the upper channel of the river not a tree or blade of grass, only a few shrubs with microscopic foliage, are visible till we reach the oasis of old Jericho, Ain-es-Sultân. Yet the plain is not level. It is studded with desert islands—flat-topped mounds of salt-encumbered marl without a particle of vegetation, and the crumbling sides of which are yearly being washed by the floods back into the Jordan, which once deposited them. At length we come upon a few scattered prickly jujube-bushes, then upon a rude fence of boughs thrown lightly on the ground, but impenetrable from the sharp recurved thorns with which every twig is studded. An artificial rill of water nurtures the crop, and we are within the slovenly farmed oasis of Jericho. We ride through a varied wilderness of indescribable luxuriance, the little plots of corn, melons, or tobacco interspersed among a dense tangle of false balsam-tree (*Balanitis Ægyptiaca*) or zukkûm, agnus casti, and dôm-tree, not to omit the apple of Sodom (*Solanum melongena*), with its potato-blossom and bright red or yellow fruit. Yet among all these where are the trees from which Jericho of old obtained its name, its fame, and its wealth—the palm? Not one remains. There are no stragglers in that wild and thorny tangle which have survived from the destruction of the gardens of Cleopatra; not one sorghum stem springs by the water-side as a relic of the plantations which yielded vast revenues to the Knights of Jerusalem; no balsam-tree lingers in the maze of shrubbery; and, above all, the last palm has gone, and its graceful feathery crown waves no more over the plain, which once gave to Jericho its name of the City of Palm-trees. Immediately in front towers the Quarantania, the Mount of Temptation, with its precipitous face pierced in every direction by ancient cells and chapels, and the ruined church on its topmost peak. We halt in front of the famous spring, the Prophet's Fountain, Ain-es-Sultân (see page 172), shaded by a fine fig-tree, where an immense volume of clear warm water, 84° Fahr., very pure, and swarming with fish, bursts from the shingle at the foot of a great mound, evidently artificial, and composed of the remains of ancient Jericho, full of fragments of pottery and frequent morsels of nacreous glass. Behind the spring, and partially enclosing it, is a ruined edifice, apparently a small Roman temple; and strewn about are fragments of shafts and Byzantine capitals. The copious stream is tapped within fifty yards of its exit by various artificial watercourses, through which the Arabs lead the life-giving liquid from time to time over their patches of cultivation, through jungles of cane and tamarisk. From the great "tell," or mound of ruins, the ground steadily rises till we reach the foot of Jebel Quarantania (see page 173). Old Jericho stood midway between the pass up to Jerusalem on the south and the passes of Benjamin towards Bethel on the north. There are three great springs which water it, and as we look towards the hills we can see how easily Joshua's spies could avoid observation as they stole up through the ravine choked with jungle and cane-brake to Ain-dûk, and thence to the mountain, amidst the caves and ravines of which they might be searched for in vain. In the oasis of Jericho, whose beauty was such that Wisdom compares herself with its rose-plants (Ecclus. xxiv. 14), Strabo tells us that for the space of a hundred stadia by twenty, opobalsamum, henna, myrrh, and all sorts of spices were grown.

From the Prophet's Fountain we may set out to search for the traces of Gilgal, the neighbour and contemporary of the older city. It had long passed away from history, and its name was almost lost to local memory, when a German traveller recovered it in a mound called Tell Jiljul, and an artificial pond, Birket Jiljulia. It is on the direct road to the upper ford at the Convent of St. John, about four and a half miles from it, outside the cultivation of the oasis, and not quite one and a half mile from the modern Jericho, or Er Riha. The situation exactly meets the requirements of the history of Joshua, and points to the place where the passage of the Jordan was made. It was here that the Israelites erected twelve stones in memory of their passage, and here the rite of circumcision

AIN-ES-SULTAN, THE SULTAN'S SPRING.
Commonly called the Fountain of Elisha, or the Prophet's Fountain.

was renewed. The pool is built of walls without mortar, about forty yards in diameter, and there are about a dozen small mounds, three or four feet high and evidently very ancient, scattered within a space of a mile. They are called generally "the city of brass," but also Jiljulieh, and it has been conjectured that they may be the remains of the Israelites' fortified

MOUNT QUARANTANIA, FROM THE SITE OF JERICHO.

camp. The water which flows through the pool is fed from the springs of Jericho. To this spot the natives, giving it a Mohammedan colouring, have transferred the miraculous fall of the walls of the besieged city and also the standing still of the sun over Quarantania.

But slight as are the vestiges of the Canaanitish cities, those of the great city of Herod are scarcely more distinct. An incurious traveller might wander over the whole site, and be scarcely conscious of any traces of antiquity. On each side of the pass from Jerusalem as it debouches into the plain is a ruined tower, marking probably the sites of the great castles which defended the pass, and which Pompey destroyed. Just below are the remains of a castle (El Kakûn), and running across the plain from the Wady Kelt is a magnificent aqueduct, under which the road passes, where eleven pointed arches span the dry river-bed. Near this is a large reservoir, Birket Mûsa, the Pool of Moses, one hundred and eighty-eight yards by one hundred and fifty-seven, long since ruined and neglected. There are traces of the Roman road, once the great thoroughfare from the East to Jerusalem, and two or three sycamore figs still linger by the roadside, lineal descendants perhaps of those trees up one of which Zacchæus climbed to see Jesus as He passed by on His way to Jerusalem.

After the destruction of the place by Pompey, Antony had it rebuilt, with the assistance of Herod, and gave it to Cleopatra, from whom Herod governed it for a time, and afterwards secured all its revenues for himself. Here he built palaces, forts, and amphitheatres, and often himself resided, and here, after vainly seeking a cure in the springs of Callirrhoe, he came to die. It was in the hippodrome here that the dying monster had all the chief Jews confined, that they might be massacred at his death and a general mourning insured; and in the amphitheatre of Jericho, Salome announced his death. Soon afterwards destroyed in a rebellion, Archelaus restored it in yet greater magnificence, and such it was when our Lord visited it. Vespasian again destroyed it; Hadrian rebuilt it, and garrisoned it with the tenth legion. It was the seat of a bishopric under the Byzantine empire and full of churches and convents, but appears to have been swept with the besom of destruction by Shahr Barz, the general of the ruthless Chosroes, A.D. 614. From that period to the time of the Crusades churches and monasteries arose again. The caliphs knew the value of the district and encouraged agriculture, but the city had gone for ever.

The present Er Riha, or New Jericho, sprung up in the times of the Crusades, when a few huts were clustered round the fort built for the protection of pilgrims (see page 168). A square tower is the only architectural feature of the wretched village, and is dignified by the name of the house of Zacchæus. It is occupied by a few Turkish soldiers. The huts round it are built of the remains of older buildings, and the inhabitants are a peculiar and most degraded race, very dark, and quite distinct from either Bedouin or the fellahin of the upper country. We feel inclined, as we look at them, to agree with the Jewish belief that they are the descendants of the old Canaanites, degenerated by the oppressive climate and the vices of the Ghor. They are the only people who reside during the whole year in the Jordan valley. The fellahin higher up only come down in autumn and winter to cultivate, and the Bedouin in spring to pasture. The chief resource of the population now is the

backsheesh obtained from travellers for the performance of their *zikkars*, or native dances. Near the gardens and plots round the villages may be noticed many of the tropical plants which are the most striking natural features of the district. Not only the two kinds of zizyphus-trees, the dôm and the nûbk, the false balsam, the oleaster, and the gum-arabic acacia, but the gorgeous *Loranthus indicus*, a scarlet parasite of striking beauty, is abundant on the trees, and the apple of Sodom abounds everywhere, while there are occasional plants of the curious Nubian asclepiad, the "osher," with its hollow puff balls filled with silky cotton fibre and used for their matchlocks by the Bedouin.

RUINED CONVENT OF ST. GEORGE.
In the Wady Kelt.

Leaving the sites of the deserted Cities of the Plain, we ascend from the Prophet's Fountain to Quarantania, following the course of an aqueduct still full of water, brought down from Ain Dûk, and passing the ruins of extensive mills. Besides the road to Jerusalem on the south bank of the Wady Kelt, no less than three mountain tracks leading into the hills of Benjamin all start from this point: one, the southernmost, along the edge of the crags between the Quarantania and Wady Kelt to Deir Diwân and Ai; a second turns north and, passing Ain Dûk, ascends to Taiyibeh, with a branch to Rummon, the ancient Rimmon; the third runs straight up from Ain Dûk to Deir Diwân, and thus joins the first. We can hardly doubt which of these was the route taken by Joshua and the army of Israel, when after the fall of Jericho they advanced into the interior highlands. It must have been by the first path, since they came to Ai before Bethel. By this track passed Samuel on his way to Gibeah of Benjamin; and down this mountain path Elijah and Elisha descended together for the last time. But Mount Quarantania derives its fame from later events, and from the not unnatural tradition that here was the wilderness, the scene of our Lord's temptation after His baptism. Certainly a spot more apparently remote from the haunts of men it would be difficult to find in any populous neighbourhood. Though by no means the highest point of the range, no other has so abrupt a face, nor one so admirably adapted for the construction of the hermits' dwellings which stud its front towards the Jordan, and also towards the Kelt. There are few more impressive views in Palestine than may be obtained in the clear bright atmosphere when pausing in the ascent of Quarantania. The debris, which rises some two hundred feet above Ain-es-Sultân, slopes from our feet to the oasis. Beyond it is the desert plain, then the Jordan belt, the plains of Shittim, and the bold headlands of Ajalon and of the Moabite range, Hesbon and Nebo rising straight from the north end of the sea. At our back rises the yellow cliff, the bluff of Quarantania, perhaps nine hundred or one thousand feet sheer. The great griffon vultures, singly or in parties, sail majestically past us backwards and forwards, spreading their wings ten feet across; the cliff swallows and swifts dash with their sharp scream within a few inches of our faces; and the clear ringing note of the orange-winged grakle from time to time seems to startle the caverns with its echo. In front of many of the cells seats have been scooped out of the rock, where the anchorites might sit and meditate. On this eastern face there are about forty habitable caves and chapels, and a very much larger number on the south side. Many of them communicate internally with each other. They have been approached by staircases and paths hewn out of the face of the rock, but time and water have worn many of them away, and left the upper caverns in some cases wholly inaccessible. The lowest tier is just above the top of the sloping debris, and the chambers are still tenanted by the Arabs for sheepfolds and stables, sometimes as granaries. The next tier, whither still a few Copts and Abyssinian pilgrims come every Lent and keep their forty-days' fast, on the spot where they believe our Lord to have fasted, is easily accessible by the sloping niche in the cliff side. The cells are a series of chambers, each having recesses hollowed out for sleeping-places, altar, and cupboard. Many of them communicate with a series of chambers above by a

RUINS IN THE GORGE OF THE WADY KELT, THE VALLEY OF ACHOR

hole in the roof, and we have found even three consecutive stories one above the other. Generally there is a chapel in the centre of each group, and hermits' cells running on either side of it. Frequently there is an inner dark chamber behind the cells. In these we found many skeletons lying east and west in undisturbed order, awaiting the resurrection, desiccated rather than decayed. Each anchorite thus dwelt almost in his grave, and many generations seemed to have succeeded each other. Higher up again are a third, and above these a fourth series of aerial human dwellings, some of them now, by the wearing away of the paths, quite inaccessible. One of the upper series can still with some difficulty be reached. In it we found beneath a slab in the flooring a dark dungeon, which had also been a burial vault, and was full of bones. The front of the inhabited chamber was vaulted with good masonry, and had an arched doorway into an adjacent chapel. The apse of the chapel was hewn out of the rock facing eastward, with a fresco of the Virgin in the concave, and a small pointed window below. On each side of the apse was a little arched niche, piscina or credence table. The walls of all the chapels and of many of the cells are covered with fresco figures of saints, the colours being still bright and fresh. We observed that all the lower stories in the mountains have been visited by iconoclast Moslems, for all the faces of the figures are mutilated and almost obliterated, while those in the upper stories have escaped. In all the chapels the figure of the angel Gabriel occupies the right side at the east end, and generally the figure of our Lord the centre. Nowhere is the Virgin and Child represented. St. Paul, St. Andrew, Gregory, Basil, Chrysostom occur, especially Athanasius, "the holy Athanasius, the witness for the truth" (Ὁ ἅγιος Αθανοσιος της αληθειας μαρτυς) being the legend. The mode in which the hermits were supplied with water was very ingenious. From the top of the mountain above and from the slopes below the crest, small carefully cemented channels are constructed in the face of the cliff, which collected and conveyed supplies of rain water to cisterns constructed inside the cells. The whole construction of this city of ascetic habitations, and especially the style and subjects of the frescoes, point to a period which is isolated from either the Roman, Crusading, or modern history of the land. When we observe the type of the frescoes, and the prominence given to the great fathers in the Arian controversy, all contemporaries at the beginning of the fourth century, and all owing their favour to the part they took in that controversy, may we not ascribe the date of these excavations to the period when that fierce struggle was at its height, and probably, too, to the hands of those who fled for safety and seclusion from the Arian persecution to these solitudes? It is remarkable, also, that we could not find any portraiture of St. Jerome among the frescoes. This leads to the conjecture that they were executed before his canonization. At least it is strange that one whose name and fame is so indissolubly interwoven with every part of this district should have been forgotten by orthodox Christian devotees. They were probably closely connected with the innumerable societies of ascetics on the banks of the Nile, which may explain why, whilst they are still resorted to with reverence by devotees from Egypt and which could scarcely have been the case had they been traditionally connected with the monasteries of the Jordan plain.

But let us now pass round the shoulder of Mount Quarantania to the entrance of the Wady Harith, down which Abraham and Lot descended to the fair plain of the Jordan, and in the gorges of which Joshua placed his ambuscade for his assault of Ai. Here, facing south, we find even more anchorite dwellings than on the eastward bluff, and provided with water by a like system, though here drawn directly from the aqueduct which collected and economized the supply of the upper part of the valley. Passing about a mile farther south we reach the opening of the Wady Kelt, by the edge of which, on the south, runs the road from Jerusalem, and which was the tribal boundary between Judah and Benjamin. No language can adequately describe the rugged wildness of this glen. It is the only one west of Jordan which in its depth and seclusion and its perennial verdure rivals the gorges of the Arnon and Callirrhoe on the opposite side Jordan. In many parts it is simply a fissure with a perennial stream at the bottom, to which the sun can never penetrate save for a few minutes, and which is shaded by a thick row of luxuriant oleanders. Its sides are unscalable save by the ibex and the coney, which are both found here, secure from the attacks of the hunter. This dell is their northernmost limit in Palestine. Yet this glen, like the face of Quarantania, was seized on and occupied by the anchorites. The Deir Wady Kelt, as it is now called, was one of the seven monasteries of the Jericho circle dedicated to St. John of Choseboth, and it has evidently been inhabited down to a much later period than the caves we have been describing. The old Greek frescoes have frequently been covered over with fresh paintings having Arabic writing. There is still an inscription in Greek and Arabic, or Coptic, over the doorway, but it gives no date, merely stating that the monastery was restored by one Abraham and his brothers, of the Christian village of Jufna. We may at least infer that it has been inhabited by monks since the Saracenic conquest. Wilder still, if possible, than the situation of the monastery of Wady Kelt is that of Deir-el-Mukellik, in a ravine a little farther south, not far from the road to Nebi Mûsa, the great point of Moslem pilgrimages just south of the road from Jerusalem. Its remains are insignificant, but there are many rock-hewn cells, and a visit to it gives a yet clearer conception of the vast amount of zeal, devotion, and energy that once peopled with a multitude of self-sacrificing devotees this now desolate wilderness. But the remains in the Wady Kelt are not confined to monastery and hermits' cells alone. On the extreme edge of the hills to the north are the remains of a Crusading fortress, and all down the ravine on both sides are noble aqueducts, in some parts remaining, at three different levels, and sometimes spanning the valley. One of the aqueducts on the north side was for the purpose of supplying the anchorites and monastery, and leads to an immense vaulted cistern in three compartments. The other aqueducts, far more ancient, were those by which Herod supplied his newly built Jericho. The Wady Kelt is popularly supposed to be the brook Cherith (see page 169), where Elijah was fed by ravens, and many ingenious arguments have been adduced in support of the theory. One is that the name 'Oreb, or raven, still clings to one of the overhanging peaks. But "The Raven's Crag" is a name naturally suggested for any cliff where the raven has taken up its permanent quarters. This gorge is the home of the raven as Quarantania is of the griffon vulture. But the raven is universally spread over the whole country wherever there are cliffs or ravines, and ravens'crags are not peculiar to the Kelt. However admirably suited for a hiding-place, it is difficult to see how Elijah should have fled to a place so out of the natural order of the narrative. It was a place opposite Jordan, and the other claimant, the Wady Yabis, on the other side, facing Bethshean, and in Elijah's native district, seems a more probable locality. But one other scriptural incident is undoubtedly connected with the Kelt. It is the valley of Achor in which Achan was stoned—not, of course, in the gorge or upper ravine, but on the open plain, where the brook runs south of Er Riha, past Jiljulieh, to the Jordan (see page 177). It would be in view of the Israelitish camp, and the valley is full of pebbles and boulders of every size, which would account for its being chosen as the place of execution, since there is hardly a stone to be found in the surrounding plain beyond the limits of this torrent bed.

Though the road by the south brink of the Kelt is by no means the most picturesque or interesting of the passes from the upper country to the Jordan Valley, yet it has been for over two thousand years almost the only route commonly used to reach the plains. It is only a short day's ride, but the descent is most rapid and continuous. It is but thirteen miles in a straight line to Jericho, yet the fall is three thousand six hundred and twenty feet, and four hundred feet more to the Dead Sea. The road is said to be still as dangerous as when it supplied our Lord with the scene for the parable of the Good Samaritan, and no doubt the wild ravines and gorges, labyrinthic in their plans and honeycombed with caverns, afford cover for freebooters which could nowhere be surpassed. But though to a Bedouin the temptation to pillage is generally irresistible, he is amenable to the laws for the regulation of robbery to which he has been an assenting party. Thus the traveller who has engaged a guard (and it need be only a nominal one, so long as the regulation fee has been paid) from the recognised authority—which is not the Turkish Government, but the Sheikh of Abou Dis, near Bethany, the representative of the Ghwarneh tribe—may roam in perfect safety so long as he abides within the limits of his jurisdiction, and no one will molest him. But should he, *e.g.*, incautiously cross the wady, which happens to be a frontier line, and be suddenly pounced upon and sent back in the costume of his birth, he has only himself to blame for his loss. The writer, when once he had placed himself under the protection of the tribes, and was spending several weeks in the Jordan Valley, was in the habit of frequently riding alone to and from Jerusalem, but, being known by sight or report to the robbers, though often reconnoitred, was never once molested, either by night or day. Recently the Turkish Government has undertaken the safe conduct of all travellers on this road, a proceeding not unnaturally resented by the Bedouin, as being an infringement of local self-government on the part of a centralizing authority. Any traveller who wishes to explore or to ramble at his leisure will do well to make his own terms in a friendly way with the resident tribes.

We have already rambled over the Jordan plain. We shall now, turning straight from the foot of the pass of the Kelt, proceed an hour's ride northwards to Ain Dûk, the great spring which divides with the Prophet's Fountain the honour of giving life and fertility to the great oasis. We cast a passing glance at Abou-el-'Aleik, two ruined forts which once held the entrance of the pass, the *Thrax* and *Taurus*, which were destroyed by Pompey, and below them a small Saracenic ruin (Kakôn), marking, perhaps, the site of the Castle of Cyprus, built by Herod to command Jericho, with the rocks steeply scarped in front of it, and we follow up by the side of ruined aqueducts past the mouth of Wady Harith and the cell-pierced front of Quarantania, and past the extensive works generally looked upon as ruined Crusading sugar-mills, till we reach the mighty fountain of Ain Dûk. The plenteous supply is evidently due to its situation at the foot of Quarantania to the north-east, where various wadys concentrate, and the underground drainage provides a perennial and inexhaustible supply. Two copious springs and several smaller ones burst close together from the southern part of the Wady Nuweimeh. The largest spring is overhung by the boughs of a dôm-tree, the largest existing tree on the plain. Only its overflow is allowed to go down the natural channel; the bulk of the supply is interrupted by the ancient aqueduct up the course of which we have been riding, and with the velocity of a mill-race is carried close above Ain-es-Sultan, watering the fields and plots on its way by little sluices, and still turning the wheel of a disused mill. Though no doubt mills were used for the manufacture of sugar, most of the so-called sugar-works are simply old corn-mills, erected by a people who looked upon water-power as more economical than the ceaseless toil of wives and slave-girls at the hand-mill. Not only is this fountain important as the greatest source of the fertility of the Jordan plain, it is also at the spot where three roads—and these the principal lines of communication from the centre of the country—converge; yet, unlike its rival, the Prophet's Fountain, it has barely a history and scarcely a ruin. The only historical incident connected with its name is that at the small fort which guarded it Simon Maccabæus and his two sons were treacherously murdered by his son-in-law Ptolemy. The Book of the Maccabees calls it "a little hold," and not more than such do the remains indicate. Two rock-hewn tombs above may not improbably be those of the Maccabæan family, buried where Hyrcanus endeavoured to avenge their murder.

Behind the ravines which open on the plain of Jordan at this point, and which run almost concentrically towards Jericho, lies that hill-country which was the very centre and heart of Israel, the hill-country of little Benjamin. No area in the whole land is more thickly studded with historical reminiscences. Its bare hills and rounded hollows, its deep glens and rugged passes, were the theatre of events which occupy the Bible narrative from Abraham to the Captivity. Here camped Abraham and Lot; here slept and dreamt Jacob; here were the first battles of the conqueror Joshua; here the struggles and the dark tragedies of the period of the Judges, the home of the great prophet Samuel, and the birthplace of the first king, the Benjamite Saul. Here was the ceaseless frontier warfare of Israel and Judah, and here was planted the great station and centre of the apostacy of the northern kingdom, the golden calf of Bethel. The passes of Benjamin naturally gave that little tribe a disproportionate influence in the land. It possessed strong fortresses for defence, conspicuous high places for national worship, and ravines by which it could command the Jordan Valley and the east on the one side, and the rich plains of Philistia on the other. Thus it earned its name of "little Benjamin, their ruler." Within its little territory are crowded the names of Bethel, Ai, Geba, Ramah, Mizpeh, Gibeon, Nob, Michmash, and many others, the scenes of historic events.

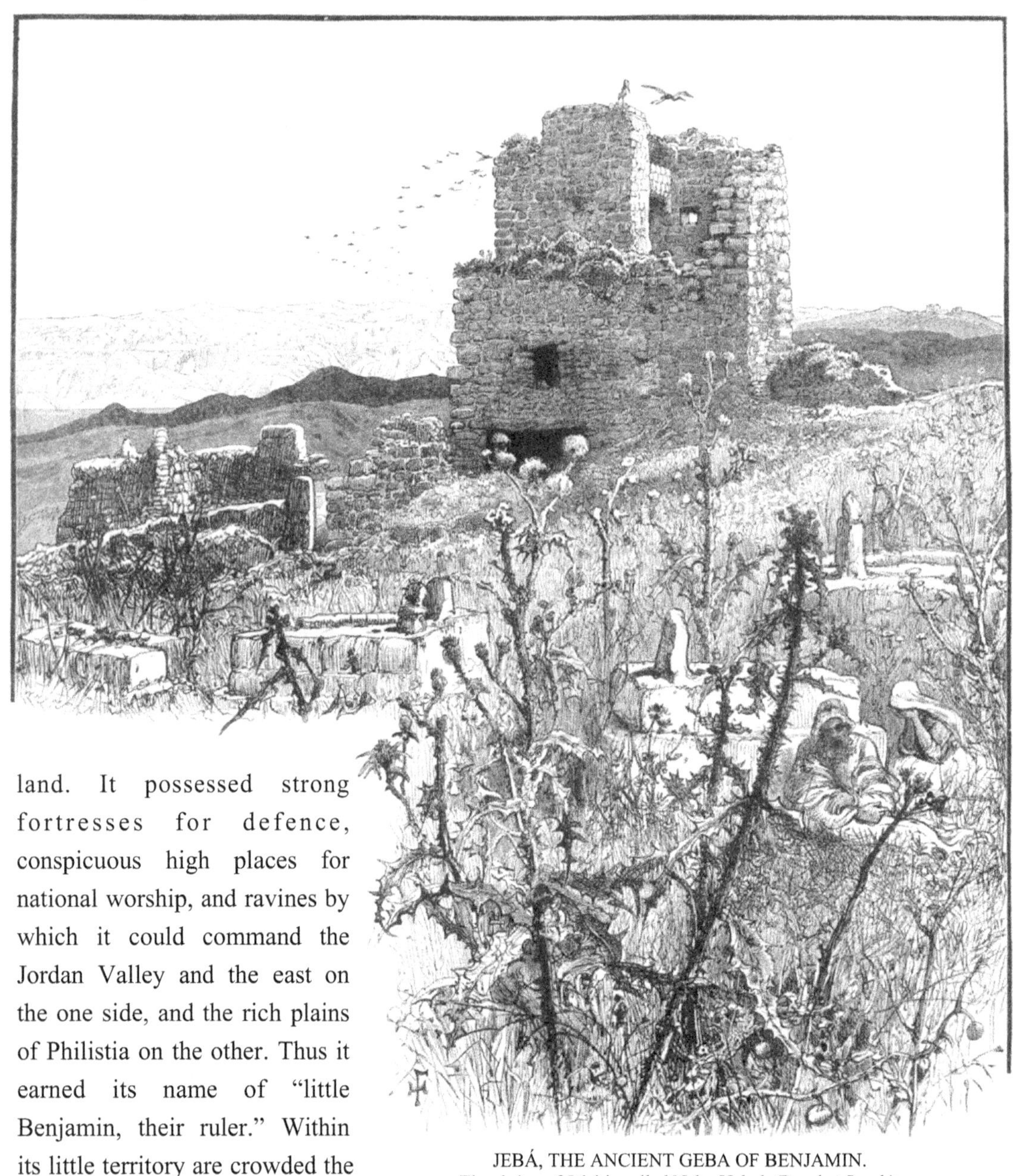

JEBÁ, THE ANCIENT GEBA OF BENJAMIN.
The shrine of Jebá is called Neby Yakub (Prophet Jacob).

Of these passes that of Michmash, here represented, is a typical example, and it is the theatre of one of the most romantic episodes in the history of Israel. Michmash, the modern

MUKMAS, THE ANCIENT MICHMASH, IN THE WADY SUWEINÎT.

Mukmâs, stands on the north side of a ravine, the Wady Suweinît, or Valley of the Thorn-tree, which takes its rise west of Ai, and soon becomes a narrow gorge with vertical sides eight hundred feet deep—a fissure across the country only detected when arrived on its actual brink. It is the true head of the Wady Kelt. There can be no doubt as to the identity of the present Jebá and Mukmâs with the position of the respective garrisons of the Philistines and Israelites. We read there was a sharp rock on the one side and a sharp rock on the other side; the name of the one was Bozez, *i.e.* "shining," and the other Seneh, "the acacia" (I Sam. xiv. 4). Josephus enters into more minute detail. Michmash, he says, was a precipice with three tops, ending in a long sharp tongue and protected by surrounding cliffs. Exactly such a natural fortress exists ending in a narrow tongue to the east, with cliffs below and an open valley behind it, and a saddle towards the west on which the village stands. Facing it on the south is an equally precipitous cliff, apparently as inaccessible from the ravine as the other, and still bearing the name of Seneh, from the acacia-trees which here and there are found in the nooks. Now the valley runs due east, and the southern cliff is consequently always in shade. As we have noted in going from Jerusalem to Jericho, there is a marked contrast in colour always between the slopes that face the north and the south, and here it is especially striking. The sun-dried chalk face of the northern side gleams brightly in the sunlight from the south, and has well earned its name of Bozez, or the "shining." To climb down from Geba must have been difficult enough, but the ascent on the other side, which Jonathan and his armour-bearer achieved "upon their hands and feet," would try an experienced mountaineer, and their apparition up such a cliff may explain the panic of the Philistines, as they would be taken for the advance guard of a numerous storming party. Across the narrow chasm the adventure could be easily watched, and the noise in the alarmed camp be heard. Saul's garrison would cross the valley higher up with ease by the path to the village behind, and thence naturally the pursuit was towards Bethel and down the Valley of Ajalon towards Ain Dûk, already the scene of the first great victory of Joshua. It is evident from the history compared with the topography that the Philistines had not secured any posts on the south of the ravine, but had spread their plundering parties east to Zeboim (Dûk), west to Beth-horon, and north towards Ophrah. On their panic the northern Israelites who had hid themselves in Ephraim, and also the numerous deserters in their camp, turned against them and pursued them down to the central valley.

With the identification of Michmash that of Geba is necessarily secured. There are few events of a circumstantial history three thousand years old more minutely identified in their every detail than this surprise of the garrison of Michmash. We see where Saul lay at bay. On the south side of the chasm stands Geba of Benjamin, on a rocky knoll, with cisterns beneath and corn-land to the eastward, still known as Jebá. There has been much confusion between this Geba and Gibeah of Saul, usually identified with the modern Taleil-el-Fûl; but the suggestion of Lieut. Conder that Gibeah of Saul applied to a district as well as a place seems to solve the difficulty. Once again in Old Testament history, after the period of Saul, Geba is mentioned. When Isaiah describes the advance of Sennacherib upon Jerusalem, we read, "At Michmash he hath laid up his carriages: they have gone over the passage: they have taken up their lodging at Geba" (ch. x. 28), *i.e.* "the carriages," or heavy

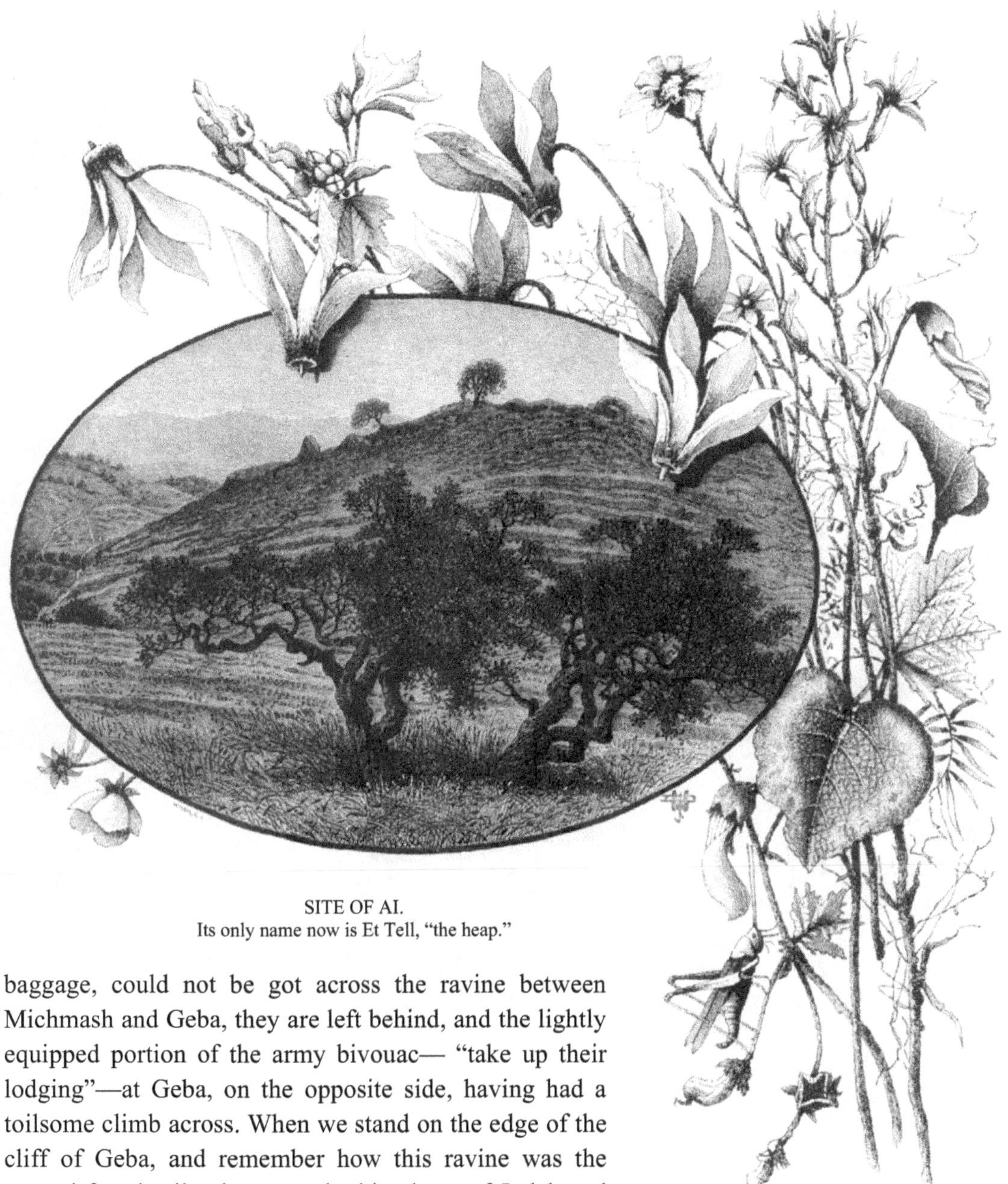

SITE OF AI.
Its only name now is Et Tell, "the heap."

baggage, could not be got across the ravine between Michmash and Geba, they are left behind, and the lightly equipped portion of the army bivouac— "take up their lodging"—at Geba, on the opposite side, having had a toilsome climb across. When we stand on the edge of the cliff of Geba, and remember how this ravine was the natural frontier-line between the kingdoms of Judah and Israel, we can well understand the care which King Asa took to dismantle Ramah, and to employ all the resources of his kingdom in the building and fortification of Geba. To what it has fallen to-day the illustration tells us (see page 182). There is indeed an old dilapidated castle, the fragment of a solid square tower, and a few

THE SUMMIT OF NEBY SAMWIL.
A woman carrying a goat-skin filled with water up the hill.

foundations. The hovels of the squalid village are formed of loose stones from old buildings and turf. But the view towards the east is wide and impressive. We are surrounded by the hills of Benjamin, each in shape and in the crumbling mound on its top a repetition of the last. In the immediate foreground we see the little village of Deir Diwân, one of the few remaining inhabited places in the district on its plateau, and beyond this slopes down tier after tier of the mountain chain, seamed and scarred in every direction, till it dips into the Jordan Valley. The huge thistles which fill the foreground of the sketch, in front of the Moslem burying-ground, where a family mourning their lost one, are but a sample of the herbage which covers all this neglected land when the first spring has passed. "Upon the land of my people shall come up thorns and briers." In fact, prickle, brier, quickthorn, and nettle are all combined in their formidable stems, whose only use is as fuel, and which are laboriously gathered by the women to heat their ovens. "As the crackling of thorns under a pot" is a simile which often recurs to the traveller as he watches his barley cake tossed on the quickly blazing thistles and then buried in their embers. And as the thorn has taken the place of the vine, so has the solitary stork on Jebá's crumbling tower supplanted the watchful sentinel of Israel's army. But beneath that cliff the ravine is still pierced with caves, and one large cavern just under the fort is surely the very cave out which rushed the liers-in-wait of the Israelitish army, who fell with such fearful slaughter on the hapless Benjamites in that dark epoch when the tribe was all but annihilated (Judges xx.).

From Geba and Michmash we turn four or five miles northward in search of a site yet more ancient and full of Patriarchal reflections, Bethel. But before reaching it we must find out Ai. We know it was to the east of Bethel, that there was a hill between them from which the plains of Jordan could be seen, and that it was the second city utterly destroyed by Joshua. We gather from the account of its capture by Joshua that there was a valley to the north of the town and low ground to the west, where an ambush could be set unseen from the city, while on the opposite side was a plain. The area, then, in which we must search is very limited. Colonel Wilson was, we believe, the first to point out the exact spot, in a knoll which bears the name of Et Tell, "the heap" (see page 185). The modern name is a remarkable incidental confirmation of sacred history. "Joshua burnt Ai, and made it an heap [*tell*] for ever, even a desolation unto this day." Now the place has no other name than "Et Tell," and it is to be noted that the word "tell" occurs only three or four times in the Hebrew Bible, while it is one of the most familiar words in Arabic, every place on a rising ground having this prefix. But nowhere else do we ever find it standing alone—*the* heap, the one made and cursed by the captains of Israel. We can follow all the military evolutions of Joshua. The ambush, following the ancient causeway, still to be traced, from Jordan to Bethel as far as Michmash, would ascend the valley west of Ai, and arrive within a quarter of a mile without coming in sight of it, and lie in wait unsuspected. The main body, keeping the road, would appear before the town on the open, east and south. From the knoll the figure of Joshua would be plainly visible to either party, with his spear stretched out towards the city. Lieut. Conder in his examination of the Tell has remarked, what had escaped former observers, that the débris which forms the mound is composed of masonry broken small, unlike other ruins—in fact, that it had been literally ground to powder.

Hither Abraham had returned with Lot to the same "place where his tent had been at the beginning, between Bethel and Hai, unto the place at the altar which he had made there at the first." This altar would naturally be on the hill, not in the plain below. From its top Lot lifted up his eyes and beheld all the plains of Jordan. This is the most westerly spot whence the plain can be seen. To the east there rises in the foreground the jagged range of hills above Jericho, in the distance the dark wall of Moab, and between them lies the Valley of the Jordan, its eastern side clearly visible. The view also south and west is wide and commanding as far as the hills round Hebron. Here it was that "the Lord said unto Abraham, Lift up, now thine eyes, and look from the place where thou art northward, and southward, and eastward, and westward: for all the land which thou seest, to thee will I give it, and to thy seed for ever" (Gen. xiii. 14, 15).

TALEIL-EL-FÛL, FROM NEBY SAMWIL.
Generally regarded as the Gibeah of Saul.

We proceed a little to the west, and we still find ourselves bewildered among that labyrinth of wadys which forms the hill country of Benjamin. They run in all directions, east, west, north, and south, and to the cursory observer there is little to mark off one from another. Yon tower, however, stands out conspicuous, and from its summit surely a commanding view may be obtained. It seems, if not modern, at least well preserved. We soon see that it is a minaret; it is, in fact, the minaret erected at the end of an old Crusading church, within which is the cenotaph which the Moslems reverence as the tomb of the prophet Samuel, the well-known Nebi Samwil, the Mount Joy of the Crusaders. But what was it in ancient times? Here the learned doctors

VIEW FROM NEBY SAMWIL.

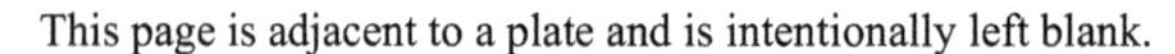

This page is adjacent to a plate and is intentionally left blank.

differ. One thing, however, is certain : a peak so conspicuous, a post so admirably adapted for defence, a knoll surrounded by a plain so exceptionally fertile, could not have been without its city in this once densely peopled region. We have now almost unconsciously crossed the watershed from El Jib, and are on the Mediterranean side of the great central ridge. It is three thousand and six feet above the sea, the highest point of the whole region, rising abruptly five or six hundred feet above the little plain of Gibeon; and the hillsides, however steep, are carefully cultivated, as shown in the illustration. The village of a dozen houses partly cut out of the rock is built of the materials of far grander buildings, and the great cisterns and a never-failing well plainly prove its antiquity. From the top of the minaret, which is a Saracenic addition to a Crusading cruciform church, now turned into a mosque, and covering the supposed tomb of Samuel, is the most

THE VILLAGE OF EL JIB, THE ANCIENT GIBEON OF BENJAMIN.

extensive view in Western Palestine. At our feet are deep rugged valleys, partially covered with scrub, and olive-groves contrasting with the white limestone ridges. Beyond are Beeroth and Ophrah, the rock Rimmon, and Ramah of Benjamin. Over the nearer ridges we look far away beyond the Jordan Valley, which lies far too deep to be seen, on to the dark outlines of the ranges of Gilead and Moab. With the glass we can detect the fortress of Kerak, Jebel Shihan (Sihon), the highest point in Moab, and the distant mountains of Jebal. Turning to the south, over the bare foreground of grey hills we see the mosques and domes of Jerusalem apparently sunk in a valley. Northwards we detect Mount Gerizim and the shoulder of Carmel; then westward push forth from beneath us the wide plains of Sharon and Philistia, sometimes green with corn, sometimes bare and red fallow, and dark patches which tell of olive-groves, while white spots gleam in the sunshine—the roofs of Lydda, of Ramleh, or some other olive and orange girt village.

Beyond these a ribbon of yellow sand marks the line between the green plain and the blue sea. That white green-encircled knoll at the edge of the sand is Jaffa, and the sail of a lateen-rigged vessel here and there dots the sea. If this be not Mizpeh, *i.e.* "the Watch-tower" of Benjamin, I know not where else we can find it, although the name be lost under a mediaeval tradition, and that again supplanted by a Moslem one.

At Mizpeh the people of Israel assembled to vow vengeance against the crime of Gibeah. Here, long after, Samuel gathered Israel to win back their freedom from their Philistine oppressors. Here, "between Mizpeh and Shen," he set up the stone Ebenezer in gratitude for their signal victory. Here

NEBY SAMWIL, THE ANCIENT MIZPEH, THE WATCHTOWER OF BENJAMIN.
From the village of El jib, the ancient Gibeon.

was chosen the first king of Israel, and the loyal acclaim, "God save the king!" for the first time ran through their ranks. Here Samuel judged Israel; and here the Chaldean governor during the Captivity oppressed them. Here the Crusaders caught their first sight of the Holy City, "and called it Mount Joy," says Sir John Maundeville, "because it gives joy to pilgrims' hearts, for from that place men first see Jerusalem." At this very spot King Richard of England fell on his knees, and, covering his face with his hands, refused to gaze on the hallowed but desecrated shrine, exclaiming, "Ah, Lord God! I pray that I may never see thy Holy City, if I may not rescue it from the hands of thine enemies."

Turning northward, and retracing the old road, and in ancient times the only road, between Jerusalem and the sea, the road by Beth-horon, down which Joshua drove the Amorites after his great victory over the five confederate kings, on an isolated hill stands the village of El Jib, once an important fortress, Gibeon of Benjamin (see page 189). The country round the little basin in which it rises is seamed with watercourses apparently running in every direction, but all ultimately find their way to the plain of Sharon, for we are here altogether west of the Jordan watershed. The ancient city has shrunk to a collection of a few scattered hovels, but the landmarks of old history are still here. Under a cliff where a cave has been hollowed out bursts forth a copious spring, which feeds not only a deep reservoir on the spot, but also a large open reservoir of very ancient masonry beneath the village on the east. Few spots can be more minutely identified than this Pool of Gibeon, where Abner, with the adherents of Ishbosheth,

BEIT-'UR-EL-FOKA, ON THE SITE OF UPPER BETH-HORON.
In the distance the sandy line of coast and the Mediterranean Sea.

Saul's son, met in the heart of Saul's own tribal district Joab and David's men, and the two bands sat down facing each other on opposite sides of the pool. When in the wager of battle, twelve against twelve, all the twenty-four fell, the plain was called "the Field of the Strong Men" (2 Sam. ii.). The tradition still lingers in the name Wady-el-Askur, "the Valley of the Soldiers." We may recall, too, the second tragedy on this spot, in which Joab took the leading part, when, "by the great stone that was in Gibeon," he basely assassinated his rival Amasa; and here, by a just retribution, he was slain on the horns of the altar by Solomon's sentence. By this tank, too, "the great waters," Johanan defeated the traitor Ishmael during the Captivity. But El Jib has more hallowed reminiscences than deeds of blood. Its Canaanite inhabitants, whose blood probably runs in the veins of the villagers of to-day, were the only Hivites spared by Joshua, lured by their wiles into a treaty with them; and here, for more than fifty years before the building of Solomon's Temple, stood the national altar of sacrifice, where King Solomon offered his one thousand burnt-offerings, and received in the visions of the night the promise of wealth, honour, and long life. Past glories, indeed, are these we feel, as we sit under one of the gnarled and contorted olive-trees which dot the slopes. Yet, bare and uninviting as the

VIEW FROM UPPER BETH-HORON,
Looking westward, to the Mediterranean Sea, at sunset.

land of Benjamin is to-day, every knoll, every hillside, ribbed and scarred with old terraces, bears testimony to what once it was. What it may be again, when life and property are secure from tyranny and oppression, when the olive-trees are planted again, the cisterns cemented, and the water-courses repaired, the gorges of the Lebanon, teeming with population and produce, unmistakably proclaim.

BEIT 'UR-ET-TAHTA, ON THE SITE OF LOWER BETH-HORON.
A Bedouin tent in the foreground. A woman preparing food, to be eaten at sunset.

THE MOUNTAINS OF JUDAH AND EPHRAIM.

A MOUNTAIN ridge, rising to about two thousand five hundred feet above the Mediterranean, runs unbroken from the pass north of Bethel to the neighbourhood of Hebron, a distance of about thirty miles in a straight line. The shed is extremely narrow, and the deep and rugged valleys which intersect the region, running down eastwards to the Jordan Valley and westwards to the plains of Sharon and Philistia, have their heads in some cases overlapping. The most peculiar feature of the mountain rampart is, however, the extraordinarily steep and sudden descent which occurs on the west at about ten miles from the watershed ridge or backbone of the country. The slopes here fall suddenly, leaving a mountain wall, which forms a conspicuous feature when viewed from the lower hills. Thus in the neighbourhood of Beth-horon there is a descent of more than five hundred feet in about half a mile, while from the hills round Adullam the traveller looks up at apparently inaccessible mountains rising east of the famous Valley of Elah. In the early morning, while the bright sunlight bathes the plains, the mountain wall formed by these steep western slopes is seen in the distance blue in the shadow, and it is only after midday, as the sun creeps round towards the south, that the white domes in the clustering villages begin to shine out, and the intricate network of ravines and torrent-beds is distinguishable by its light and shade.

The higher mountains consist of a hard crystalline limestone, generally dark grey in colour, but often stained with russet bands, and sometimes attaining to a dark purple hue, while thin streaks of soft white chalk are left by the action of immemorial rains on the summits of the chain. The ridge is a steep anticlinal—a great arch of hard rocks curving down east and west to valley and plain. The lower hills on the west belong to a distinct formation, and are indeed remains of the great chalk sea which once overflowed the hard limestone mountains. Hence it arises that the division between the higher mountains and the lower hills of the Judæan chain is so distinct; and the traveller looking down from the higher spurs sees the low hills gleaming with white chalk or dusky with long olive groves, forming an intermediate district between the grey mountains and the rich brown plains. In Scripture and in later Jewish writings the two regions receive distinct names, the low hills being called "Shephelah," and the higher range the "King's Mountain" in the Talmud.

Three main passes lead from the maritime plain to the King's Mountain or Chain of Judaea: one from the north-west, one from the west, and a third from the south-west. The first of these is the famous Pass of Beth-horon, the scene of so many Jewish victories; the second is the road by which the modern traveller approaches the Holy City, leading up from Ramleh and past the "Gate of the Valley," through Wâdy 'Aly, a gorge flanked by rugged mountains covered with mastic bushes and crowned by a belt of firs and other forest trees. The third pass leads through the broad corn vale of Elah and ascends to the neighbourhood of Halhûl, half-way between Jerusalem and Hebron. At the time of the great struggle for national existence Judas Maccabæus successfully resisted three Greek armies attempting to ascend by each of these three main approaches successively. The liberation of Judaea was the immediate result of the three victorious "Battles of the Passes" at Beth-horon, Emmaus, and Bethsura.

The three great valleys thus noticed—the main drains of the mountain system—are fed by innumerable torrent-beds, which form an intricate network of deep and narrow trenches, increasing in size as they recede farther from the watershed and plunge deeper towards the plain. Long and narrow spurs run out between these ravines, and a traveller who attempts to ride north and south instead of following the direction of the country will find his day wasted in tedious climbing and break-neck scrambles, and may consider himself fortunate if he makes a mile of way in an hour.

The western spurs of the King's Mountain present a far less bare and sun-scorched appearance than do the steep eastern spurs above the Jordan Valley. The mountains are full of springs of clear cool water gushing out between the slabs of shining limestone; and although the valleys and ravines never run water, except perhaps for a few hours in winter when filled by a sudden spate or thunderstorm, still there is no lack of "fountains and depths that spring out of valleys and hills." In the Shephelah, on the other hand, the water sinks through the porous chalk and finds its way beneath the surface, springing up again in great blue pools at the eastern border of the maritime plain. The inhabitants obtain water from wells and cisterns in the Shephelah, but almost every village has its spring in the King's Mountain.

The mountain spurs thus watered and exposed to the cool western sea-breeze, which in summer blows steadily throughout the day, are thickly covered with wild growth which has much encroached on the ancient cultivation. The lentisk or mastic—akin to the pistachio and to the terebinth—forms thickets of low brushwood, dark green in colour, with a gummy leaf, which gives it in Arabic the name *'Alaka*, or the "sticking" plant. One of the three

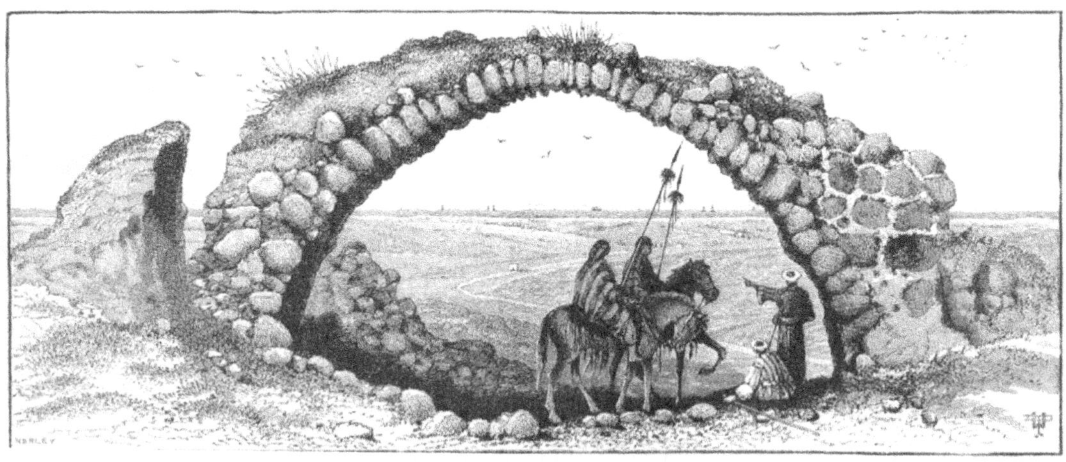

VIEW FROM THE RUINS OF THE MEDIEVAL FORTRESS AT LATRÔN,
Looking westward, towards the Mediterranean Sea; the watch-towers on the road to Jaffa are plainly shown.

species of Syrian oak also grows as a bush, and the hawthorn, the cornel, the arbutus, and the myrtle are found in the copse. Here and there a solitary oak of great size is seen hung with rags as votive offerings, and each of these trees has a well-known name. The Valley of Elah is still dotted with dark and heavy-looking terebinths, from which its ancient name was

VALLEY OF AJALON, FROM THE WEST,
Looking across the broad corn-fields to Mizpeh and the more distant mountains in the Valley of the Jordan.

derived. The Forest of Hareth is still represented by the thickets round the modern village of Kharas. The neighbourhood of Kirjath Jearim, the "town of woods," is still remarkable for its tangled thickets; and scattered pines along the higher ridges south of Halhûl represent the remains of the old pine forest, whence Arculphus describes Jerusalem as having been supplied with firewood in the seventh century of our era.

A remarkable feature of this mountain region is the manner in which the ancient inhabitants seized on the most conspicuous peaks and knolls as safe sites for their villages. As the eye glances along the rugged spurs the towers of the hamlets are seen standing up against the sky-line, while the flat roofs of the little cabins composing the village are crowded round the central house of two stories, which is occupied by the sheikh, and has the appearance of a keep or fortress, in the middle of the village climbing up the steep slopes of the knoll. Thus, in approaching Jerusalem, Soba on its high rocky ridge is visible from a great distance (see page 198), and Kastal dominates the broad Valley of Kolonia. Gibeon, Ramah, and Geba, north of the Holy City, stand in the same way on isolated knolls, and derive their names from the character of their sites; and, speaking generally, the villages, with hardly an exception, are built in situations of great natural strength, and are plainly visible from any of the more commanding points of view in the district, while the low-lying hamlets and scattered homesteads of our own country have no counterpart among the mountains of the Holy Land.

Unlike the rich corn-lands of Philistia and the pastures of Sharon, the King's Mountain is not a region possessed of a naturally fertile soil. The red earth scarcely covers the hard rock on the slopes, and only in the bottoms of the ravines and in the dells—called *khelâl* by the natives—is it possible to plough and sow corn. Patient labour and knowledge of the country overcame, however, these difficulties in ancient times, and even at the present day the cultivation is only curtailed by the scantiness of the population. The bright apple green of the vines may be seen trailing over the long ridges of stone, and yokes of diminutive oxen are found dragging the light hand-plough between the boles of the olive-trees which cover the hillsides round the villages.

The mountain region near Hebron and Jerusalem is specially fitted for the growth of the grape. A fierce summer sun, frosty nights in winter, a fat though scanty soil, hard rock reflecting the heat on to the ripening fruit, and in autumn damp mists to swell the juices of the vine—these are all requisites for vine-culture, and all occur in the Judæan mountains. Hence, in the vineyards of Bethlehem, Beit Jâla, and Hebron the grapes attain enormous size, and might be made into excellent wine; while the innumerable rock-cut presses which are found near the ancient ruins or hidden among the thick copses, near ancient towers rudely built of large unshapen blocks, attest the former widespread cultivation of the vine throughout the whole district.

The King's Mountain is a region full of famous places. Bethel, Michmash, Gibeon, Beth-horon, Emmaus, Bethlehem, Anathoth, and Mizpeh are names familiar to the English reader as household words; and there is no other part of Palestine which has witnessed so many important events of biblical history, or which is so thickly crowded with famous ancient sites. Not least interesting among these sites are the two little villages now called Beit

'Ur-el-Fôka (the Upper Beth-horon) and Beit 'Ur-et-Tahta (the Lower Beth-horon), situated less than a mile apart, and the one some five hundred feet above the other (see pages 192 and 193). Upper Beth-horon, a ruinous-looking hamlet with a great ruined reservoir, stands at the extremity of a narrow space of hard grey limestone, and is surrounded by a straggling olive grove. The ancient road, descending the hill by rock-cut steps through a narrow cutting, appears to be the work of the Romans, and leads from the plain near Lydda to the watershed east of Gibeon, being skilfully engineered along the crest of the long spur leading by the Beth-horon Pass.

The view from the village extends on the south-west across the open Vale of Ajalon to Gezer and the Philistine plain, while on the north the rugged range of Mount Ephraim is seen crowned with fortress villages. Beth-horon ("the House of Caverns") first appears in history as the site of the great battle when Joshua defeated the league of Hivite chiefs gathered to the assistance of the Gibeonites, and as the scene of the miracle when the "Sun stood still and the Moon stayed," until Israel was avenged of its enemies. The site has never been lost. It was known to the early fathers of the Church and to the Crusading pilgrims as well as it is to ourselves, and the village of Beth-horon is one of the few undisputed identifications in Palestine topography. Solomon fortified it as a frontier town; Shishak enumerates it in the list of the cities which he wrested from Rehoboam; Judas Maccabaeus twice saved the city and the Temple by victories over the Greek forces in the neighbourhood of this steep ascent. In the year 168 B.C. the patriotic son of Mattathias gathered a handful of zealous outlaws on the summit of the stony ridge and fell suddenly on the army of Seron, the Greek general, who was marching from Lydda on Jerusalem, and the victory which followed was the first blow struck for freedom by the national party. In the year 162 B.C. another Greek army attempted to advance by this route, supported by the sally of the garrison under Nicanor from Jerusalem, but the battle of Adasa was followed by a pursuit which drove the foreigners down the same steep slope which had witnessed the flight of the Amorites before Joshua, and that of the Philistines from Michmash before Saul and Jonathan. The little ruin called Il'asa, close to the Lower Beth-horon, also probably represents the site of Eleasa, where Judas arrayed his army before the fatal battle of Berzetho, in which he lost his life.

The Vale of Ajalon, named from the "village of deer" (Ajalon), now called Yâlo, which stands on a low hill to the south, is a broad corn valley below the mountains forming the mouth of the long narrow ravine which bounds the ridge of Beth-horon on the south, and which is now called Wâdy Suleimân (see page 195). Viewed from the neighbourhood of the village of Latrôn, three famous sites are seen grouped on the low hills south-east of this corn valley, namely, Ajalon itself; 'Amwâs, the Emmaus of the Book of Maccabees; and Beit Nûba, where King Richard fixed his camp when contemplating an advance on the Holy City, and which the early pilgrims erroneously supposed to represent the site of Nob, the city of the priests.

About a mile north of Latrôn the village of 'Amwâs clings to the side of a bare chalky hill. Its name preserves that of Emmaus, afterward called Nicopolis, a city famous in the annals of the Hasmoneans as the scene of the second great victory won by Judas Maccabæus in the year 166 B.C. The name Emmaus is explained by Josephus to mean a "healing bath," and is thus probably the Aramaic form of the old Hebrew Hammath, signifying a "hot" bath. There were three places in Palestine named Emmaus. One, originally called Hammath, was built over the thermal springs immediately south of Tiberias. The second, Emmaus Nicopolis, now under consideration, is said in the Talmud to have possessed springs often visited by sick persons as are the thermal springs near Tiberias at the present day.

SOBA, FROM THE JERUSALEM ROAD.
Two native ladies, mounted on asses and enveloped in large white cotton veils, called *izzars*, are ascending the hill.

In the Middle Ages a miraculous spring was shown at this second Emmaus, which was said to owe its powers to the touch of Christ while on earth, and the town was called Fontenoide by the Franks, from the fountain which still exists. The third Emmaus was that village mentioned by St. Luke, "which was from Jerusalem about threescore furlongs," and which was probably the same as the Emmaus assigned by Vespasian to eight hundred of his retired warriors, and described by Josephus as sixty stadia from Jerusalem.

From the fourth century down to the fifteenth the scene of the manifestation of the Master to the two disciples was fixed at Emmaus Nicopolis, which is distant about a hundred and sixty furlongs from Jerusalem; and the Sinaitic MS., with other ancient texts, reads a hundred and sixty instead of sixty as the distance noticed in the third gospel. The crumbling apse of a little chapel still remains in 'Amwâs, marking the supposed site of the spot where Christ was known by the breaking of bread; but it has been pointed out by many authorities that the distance from Jerusalem is too great to allow of the double journey undertaken by Cleopas and his fellow-disciple without any interval of repose, for the journey is considered sufficient for the ordinary traveller of the present day, even when mounted. Thus since the fifteenth century the site of the New Testament Emmaus has been sought anew.

KURYET-EL-'ANAB, THE VILLAGE OF GRAPES.
Probably the Kirjath of Benjamin. It is now commonly called Abu Ghosh. The large building on the right is the Church of St. Jeremiah.

Many identifications have been suggested by various authors. Kuryet-el-'Anab and Kolonia, on the road from Jaffa to Jerusalem, are among the most recent, and ecclesiastical tradition has fixed on Kubeibeh, a village on the spur immediately south of Wâdy Suleimân, at the required distance of about sixty stadia north-west from Jerusalem. There is, however, no circumstance beyond the modern tradition which tends to confirm the identity of Kubeibeh with the scriptural Emmaus.

Hidden from the sight of the traveller, in a deep valley among shady gardens of orange and lemon surrounding a group of beautiful springs, lies a little ruined site which may perhaps be considered to possess more claim to the honour of representing the scene of the first appearance of Christ after the Resurrection morning. The ancient Roman road from Jerusalem to Gath and Ashdod descends straight to the Valley of Elah, and runs along a plateau from which we look down on this secluded valley. Leaving the road, the explorer passes by ancient rock-cut sepulchres and by the village of Wâd Fûkin—probably the Pekiin of the Talmudic writers. Immediately opposite are the remains of a little chapel near a clear spring welling out beneath a low cliff, and here are ruins of an ancient site called Khamasa—a name which at once recalls the Hebrew Hammath and the late Emmaus. The distance of the ruin from Jerusalem is a little over sixty furlongs, and the beauty and fertility of the valley seem to render it a probable site for the little Roman colony established by Vespasian. The out-of-the-way situation of the place has probably caused the identification to escape notice, but the neighbourhood appears to have been once an important Christian centre, and the ruins of three other mediaeval churches lie within a radius of three or four miles from Khamasa.

Leaving the neighbourhood of Emmaus Nicopolis and Latrôn, the traveller advances into the mountains through the Pass of Bâb-el-Wâd, the "Gate of the Valley." Passing by the shady group of terebinths which surround the little shrine of Imâm 'Aly, who gives his name to the valley, the road climbs up between rough dark hills of limestone rising in natural steps formed by the regular stratification of the rock, and reaches the ridge on which stands the flourishing stone village called Kuryet-el-'Anab, better known as Abu Ghosh, the name of a celebrated family of bandit chiefs once the terror of the neighbourhood, but now reduced to insignificance (see page 199). Abu Ghosh is another of the places which has offered an irresistible temptation to the antiquary anxious to recover its scriptural name. In the fourth century it was regarded as the site of Kirjath Jearim, the "City of Forests," where the Ark found refuge for nearly half a century, and the identification has in modern times been supported by the authority of the famous Dr. Robinson. Nevertheless there are weighty objections to the view, for Kirjath Jearim was close to Bethshemesh, as Josephus tells us, and the whole line of the border of Judah is thrown into confusion by fixing the site at Abu Ghosh, while the "forests" which gave their name to the ancient city have no counterpart at Kuryet-el-'Anab, although east of Bethshemesh the thickets are still wild and tangled, covering the steep ridges with luxuriant natural growth. The Crusading topographers, with the recklessness and disregard both of older tradition and of probability which seem generally to characterize their fanciful distribution of ancient sites, arrived at the conclusion that Kuryet-el-'Anab was the ancient Anathoth, the home of the prophet Jeremiah. A

THRESHING CORN.

This page is adjacent to a plate and is intentionally left blank.

splendid church was built in the flat dell north-east of the village, and a convent was founded not far off beside a stream of clear water running over the rocky bed of a ravine. The church is still standing, and is one of the most perfect buildings of its period left in the Holy Land. The dim shadows of the frescoes which once adorned its walls are still traceable, though the colours and outlines are obliterated by age. The west window is remarkable for the intricacy of its mouldings, and the vaults below contain a fresh spring reached by steps, and to which no doubt some tradition now lost was formerly attached. The names of the early pilgrims are still visible scratched on the stucco of the internal walls. Kuryet-el-'Anab, as before noticed, is one of the claimants for the name Emmaus, though its only pretension is its distance from Jerusalem; but perhaps the most satisfactory suggestion which has been made, as to the Hebrew name of this village, is that it is the ancient Kirjath of Benjamin.

Leaving the open valley with its green vineyards, above which the white houses of the village rise west of the church and its solitary palm, the road to Jerusalem ascends by a zigzag to another long ridge, from which the picturesque village of Soba becomes visible on the right, separated from the road by an extremely deep and almost impassable gorge. Soba is one of the most picturesquely situated places in Palestine. The village crowns a conical knoll rising from a dark ridge clothed in thick copse of mastic and oak, and the topmost tower forms a conspicuous landmark from all sides. The modern name is exactly descriptive of the site, the word "sobah" indicating one of the conical heaps of grain which may be seen in the centre of a Syrian threshing-floor in August. The site is so conspicuous that almost every writer has offered his conjecture as to the identity of the place with some ancient town, and Soba has been supposed at various periods to represent Kirjath Jearim, Zuph, Ramathaim Zophim, and even Modin. There can be no doubt that Soba is an ancient place. Rock-cut tombs of the most ancient form used by the Jews are to be found among the vineyards south of the village, and rock-cut wine-presses exist near them. In the twelfth century the place was called Belmont by the Franks, and the traces of a Crusading fortress are still visible on the hill. Its claim to represent Modin is more ancient than that of Latrôn, although equally unsatisfactory. In the fourteenth century the Jewish pilgrims were quite at a loss to decide between the rival sites, and Isaac Chelo even suggests that Ramleh may have been Modin; but in the fourth century the true site of the home of the Maccabees, the present village of El Medyeh, seems still to have been recognised on the low hills east of Lydda.

Following the ridge north of Soba, the traveller arrives at the descent which leads across the Wâdy Beit Hanîna, and sees before him the bleak grey range capped with white chalk which hides the Holy City from view. Beneath him is the small village of Kolonia, with its white shrine perched on the slope above the gardens of orange and pomegranate which surround a little hostelry beside a bridge of several arches spanning the shingly bed of the torrent (see page 202). The descent to Kolonia is more than a thousand feet, and an equally steep ascent leads up on the east to the barren plateau of the watershed on which Jerusalem stands. As the eye travels round southward, following the course of the great valley, another long and stony spur becomes visible, while on a shelf of rock between this ridge and the torrent bed the village of 'Ain Kârim is picturesquely perched (see page 205). The stern and rugged beauty of this view is especially striking in early morning, when the walls of rock and the rugged slopes on the east are still dark in the shadow; and in winter the

KOLONIA, AND WADY BEIT HANÎNA.
A favourite place of resort of the people of Jerusalem; it is famous for its well-kept vineyards and vegetable gardens.

long lines of vapour rising from the valley leave the white convent wall floating as it were in the air, backed by dark cypresses and the grey rocks stained with rusty bands. The valley itself is, however, a striking contrast to the barren hills which enclose it. The springs which ooze out of the mountain sides drip over the precipices and fertilise the good soil beneath. The open ground is covered with olive yards and vineyards rising in terraces on either side of the white torrent bed, while near Kolonia is a shady garden, the resort of the Jerusalem citizens in the summer.

Wâdy Beit Hanina, as this valley is generally called—although like most of the ravines in Palestine it takes in succession the name of each village it passes—is one of the main drains of the country. It has its head not far from Gibeon, north of Jerusalem, and thence runs south-west, deepening rapidly as it approaches Kolonia, where it becomes wider until passing 'Ain Kârim. Trending west it runs south of Soba and becomes a formidable gorge, taking the name of Wâdy Ism'aîn from a traditionary chieftain of the locality. The course after passing 'Ain Kârim is very tortuous, and the steep hills on either side are thickly clothed with copse. Hermits' caves occur in the cliffs, and the ruin of 'Armah, probably representing Kirjath Jearim, stands among the thickets on the southern brink. As the spurs break down suddenly on the west, the gorge

MOSQUE OF THE FOUNTAIN, 'AIN KÂRIM.
Peasant-women washing clothes by beating them on blocks of stone.

opens into a broad corn vale between rounded chalky hills, and here lie the ruins of Bethshemesh amid its olives, and on the north Sur'ah, the ancient Zoreah, with the white shrine of Neby Samat, the traditionary representative of Samson. This part of the valley is the biblical Vale of Sorek, up which the lowing kine brought the ark in the straight way through the corn-fields from the sandy downs of Ekron.

The present ecclesiastical tradition which identifies Wâdy Beit Hanîna with the ancient Valley of Elah is traceable only as far back as the fourteenth century, and is entirely devoid of foundation. The true Valley of Elah is identified with the present Wâdy-es-Sunt, by the recovery of Socoh on its southern border, and is the next main drain of the country south of the Wâdy Beit Hanîna. It has its head near Hebron, and runs northward and westward past Keilah, Hareth, Adullam, and Socoh, debouching into the Philistine plains at Tell-es-Sâfy, the probable site of Gath. The site of David's victory over Goliath, now shown north-west of Jerusalem, was more correctly fixed in the sixth century by the pilgrim Theodorus between Jerusalem and Eleutheropolis, at a place which he calls Mount Buzana. The real Valley of Elah (now Wâdy-es-Sunt) was the theatre of many of David's adventures, and the hold of Adullam, the copses of Hareth, Keilah on its steep hill, with the white cliff of Gath guarding the entrance to the fruitful corn vale dotted with dark terebinths, were all in turn the refuges which he sought when fleeing from the face of Saul.

The village of Kolonia, which has been mentioned above, is also a place celebrated in Jewish history, although its proximity to the capital forbids us to accept the proposed identification of the place with the New Testament Emmaus. "There was a place," says the Mishna, "below Jerusalem called Mozah: thither the people went down and gathered drooping willow branches, and they came and erected them at the side of the altar with their tops bending over the altar." The Jewish commentators translate the Hebrew name by the Latin Colonia; and as the willows may still be found near the stream of Kolonia, while the ruin of Beit Mizzeh near the village seems to preserve the name of Mozah, there seems good reason to suppose that the modern fashion of making a summer day's excursion from the capital to the little restaurant in Wâdy Beit Hanîna is a survival of the old Hebrew custom of coming down to Kolonia for the willow branches used during the Feast of the Tabernacles, on the 13th of Tizri, and the 21st of the same month, or in the middle of September. It was probably at Mozah also that the daughters of Jerusalem danced in the vineyards on the same festal occasion, when they sang an invitation to the youthful spectators, the words of which have come down to us at the present day: "Behold, O young man, whom wilt thou choose: look not for beauty, but for birth; favour is deceitful, beauty is vain, but she that feareth the Lord, she shall be praised."

'Ain Kârim, the ancient Carem of Judah, is a site now consecrated by numerous ecclesiastical traditions. It contains a Latin monastery founded by the Marquis de Nointel, the ambassador of Louis XIV. of France, and a church dedicated to St. John the Baptist (see page 209), with a white dome, which forms a conspicuous object in the distance, rising beside

FRANCISCAN MONASTERY AND CHURCH OF ST. JOHN AT 'AIN KARIM, IN THE SO-CALLED "WILDERNESS OF ST. JOHN."
On the opposite hill, up which a flock of goats is being driven, there is a school for native girls, presided over by the Sisters of Zion.

the black cypresses of the convent garden. The population of the village is now about six hundred souls, including one hundred Latin Christians. There are also a few nuns of the order of the Sisters of Zion, who assist the Franciscan monks by the education of the native girls (see page 205).

As early as the twelfth century the site of 'Ain Kârim was fixed by tradition as that of the summer residence of Zacharias, the father of John the Baptist, and was regarded as the place of St. John's birth and the "city of Judah" where the Salutation occurred. It was called Locus Silvestris and Domus Zachariæ, and in the fifteenth century John Poloner found there a church in two stories—probably that is with a vault, the upper church having been destroyed by the Saracens. He mentions a cleft in the rock where the ground opened to conceal the infant Baptist during the persecution of Herod at the time of the Bethlehem massacre, and a fountain beside the road where the Virgin rested on the occasion of her visit to Elisabeth. The former tradition now attaches to a chapel built in 1860, and supposed to mark the site of the house of Zacharias (see page 207). The spring near the village is still called the "Fountain of our Lady Mary." 'These traditions are not traceable further back than Crusading times. They belong to that extraordinary system of minute localisation of sacred spots which spread over Palestine under the Latin kings. The number of sacred places in Jerusalem was increased three or four fold after the Crusading conquest, churches and chapels were built all over the land, and each claimed to enclose some sacred spot or to contain some precious relic. The Crusaders were ignorant in many cases of the ancient traditions of the Church preserved in the itineraries and pilgrim journals of the fourth, fifth, and sixth centuries; and the ecclesiastical authorities who determined the sacred sites shown to the devout warriors of the twelfth century can have bestowed but little care on the study of scriptural topography. With the exception of the most important sacred sites, it is rare to find the Crusaders' church standing anywhere near the Byzantine chapel which claimed to occupy the same sacred site. The Byzantine traditions seem sometimes to have been derived from Jewish sources, and are in such cases very valuable; but the Crusading traditions were more remarkable for their startling originality than for their reliability.

But the process of multiplication of sacred sites did not cease in the twelfth century; their numbers grew steadily, and many new ones were added in the fifteenth and even later. Within the last ten years new discoveries in sacred topography have been made in Nazareth and at other places, and every chapel in the country pretends to possess some unique claim to veneration. At 'Ain Kârim the twelfth-century traditions were supplemented by others in the fourteenth century, and the rock-cut cell of St. John, now called El Habs, is a site apparently not dating earlier than the fifteenth century. The fertile valley of Beit Hanina, between 'Ain Kârim and the ridge of Soba, is now known as the "Wilderness of St. John," and supposed to be the desert to which the Baptist retired; which modern scholars, however, identify with the dreary waste west of the Dead Sea.

As we approach the capital the number of traditional sites increases, and the scenes of many scriptural events are grouped at convenient distances round the Holy City. The traveller who crosses the bare ridge behind 'Ain Kârim by the curious cairns which form such conspicuous features on the sky-line from the neighbourhood of Jerusalem, finds his way down to the flat stony valley called Wâdy-el-Werd, the "Vale of Roses," and here on the south we find a fifteenth-century traditional site in the fountain called by the natives 'Ain Hanîyeh, but by the Christians Philip's Fountain (see page 210). The spring breaks out from beneath a kind of masonry apse flanked by Corinthian pilasters, and probably marking the site of an early chapel. A small niche exists in the apse, and remains of masonry are scattered round in the valley bed.

WELL OF ZACHARIAS AND ELISABETH, 'AIN KÂRIM
Near the supposed site of their summer dwelling, where the Virgin is said to have visited them.

It is difficult to understand how the tradition became attached to this site, or how the chariot of the Ethiopian servant of Queen Candace can have been supposed to have escaped entire destruction in the rugged and pathless ravine where the spring breaks out. It is, however, certain that the tradition was transferred at a late period from another site. In the fifteenth century it is first mentioned, apparently in its present position, by John Poloner. In the fourteenth century Marino Sanuto identifies Philip's Fountain with En Hakkore, or the Fountain of the Jaw Bone, famous in the history of Samson, and which was at that period supposed to have been near Beit Jibrîn, at the edge of the Philistine plain. In earlier times the fountain where Philip baptized the eunuch was shown opposite the ruin of Bethsura, on the road from Jerusalem to Hebron. The Bordeaux pilgrim mentions a chapel on this spot, the ruins of which still remain close to the fine spring called 'Ain Dhirweh, under a low cliff above which the village of Halhûl stands on the hill-top.

Wady-el-Werd obtains its name from the cultivation of roses in the valley. The rose is rarely seen in Palestine, but appears to thrive well in this place, and is used for the preparation of the attar of roses. According to the Babylonian Talmud a single rose garden existed in Jerusalem, dating back to the time of "the first prophets," that is to say, to the period preceding the Captivity. The rose will not, however, grow wild in so hot a climate as that of southern Palestine, although the dog-rose is found on Lebanon and on the heights of Hermon. The best authorities are agreed that the "Rose of Sharon" mentioned in the Song of Songs is the white narcissus which grows in such profusion in the maritime plain. The Targums translate the original Hebrew in this sense, and the modern Arabic name of the narcissus (*buseil*) is radically identical with the Hebrew *habutzeleth*, rendered "rose" in our version.

If instead of crossing by 'Ain Kârim to 'Ain Hanîyeh the traveller follows the main road from Kolonia to the capital, he will find scenery fully as picturesque and interesting as that already described. Ascending by a steep zigzag he reaches the edge of the Jerusalem plateau, and will turn to cast a look on the road just past, soon hidden by the brow of the watershed ridge. Beneath him lie the dark gardens of Kolonia, and directly opposite rises the ridge on which Kastal stands, on a high knoll shutting out the view of the maritime plain. The olive-yards of 'Ain Kârim are visible on the left, with bare ridges rising in broad steps like those of an amphitheatre, and due to the regular stratification of the limestone. On the right the same valley is seen winding down from the chalky plateau where stands the curious conical mound called Taliel-el-Fûl, and the ridges beyond are equally rocky and barren in appearance (see pages 188 and 213). The view is here bounded by the hill-crest on which the tall minaret of Neby Samwîl stands out against the sky, and on the south side of the valley the village of Lifta is visible, perched on the edge of a precipitous descent. This village has been identified by some authors with the "Fountain of the Water of Nephtoah," which lay on the border of Judah; but it is far more probably the ancient Eleph, a city of Benjamin.

As the traveller recalls the scenes of this mountain district, he will see in imagination the tall Philistines in their mail coats and bronze helmets flying before the despised herdsmen of Judah, armed only with goads or mattocks. He will recall the handful of ill-disciplined zealots driving back the trained soldiers of Antioch from the hill of Beth-horon. He will see in his mind's eye Judas and his brethren stealing down in the darkness and massing their troops at early dawn hidden among the folds of the chalk downs south of Emmaus. Finally, he will in fancy behold the band of starved but unconquerable devotees who looked down from the rocks of Bether on the impassable girdle of wall and camp drawn round their stronghold by the

ALTAR OF CHURCH OF ST. JOHN, 'AIN KÂRIM.
On the north side of the altar seven steps descend to a crypt, the alleged birthplace of the Baptist. The monks and brethren are chiefly Spaniards.

British legions of Severus. It is the same tale of indomitable courage, constant devotion to the faith, and skill in the tactics of mountain warfare that is repeated at each famous site; but it is ever a tale of struggle and misery, and the festal scene annually witnessed at the willow brook of Kolonia is but one bright spot in the stern history of the King's Mountain.

It has been mentioned in describing the church of Abu Ghosh that the Crusaders fixed on that site as representing Anathoth, the home of the prophet Jeremiah; and since the actual site of this village is not commonly visited by travellers in Palestine, a few words of description may be here added. Anathoth was a town of Benjamin, and is mentioned as re-peopled after the Captivity, the name occurring with those of places north of Jerusalem. According to the Talmud it was built by a giant named Ahiman. The site is described by Theodorus in the sixth century as being near Olivet and six miles from Jerusalem. Marino Sanuto also marks the same place on his curious map, and we can have no hesitation in recognising Anathoth at the modern village of 'Anâta (see page 211). 'Anâta is reached by a road which crosses the ridge immediately north of the Mount of Olives, and which runs down to Jericho by the great gorge of Wâdy Kelt. On passing the ridge the traveller notices some curious stone heaps called Rujûm-el-Behîmeh, "Cairns of the Beast," which seem to be noticed by Marino Sanuto in the fourteenth century who identifies them with the stone of Bohan, which was

'AIN HANÎYEH, IN THE VALLEY OF ROSES.
Commonly called Philip's Fountain, and regarded as a sacred place by the Latins.

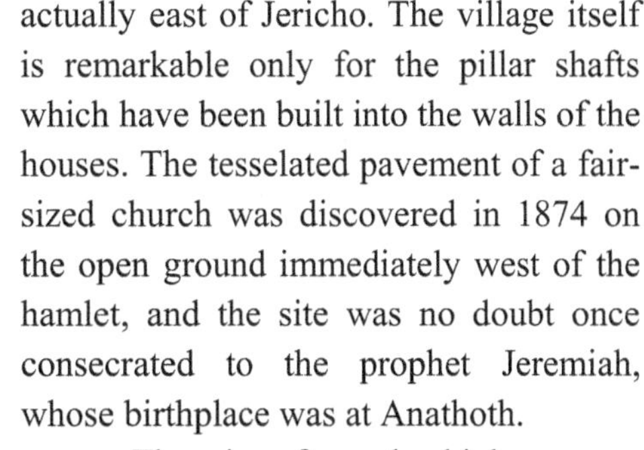

actually east of Jericho. The village itself is remarkable only for the pillar shafts which have been built into the walls of the houses. The tesselated pavement of a fair-sized church was discovered in 1874 on the open ground immediately west of the hamlet, and the site was no doubt once consecrated to the prophet Jeremiah, whose birthplace was at Anathoth.

The view from the high spur on which the village stands is very remarkable, and presents a strong contrast to those which have been previously described. The high ground on the south and west conceals the Holy City from

'ANÂTA, ON THE SITE OF ANATHOTH.
There are the remains of ancient foundations here, and the quarries still supply Jerusalem with building stone.

sight, but on the east and north the spurs falling from the water-shed to the Jordan Valley are spread before the eye. Long, narrow, gleaming ridges of chalk, with curious conical knolls casting peaked shadows on the nearest slopes, mark the action of rain on the softer formation, and contrast with the more rounded outline of the limestone hill west of the watershed.

Wâdy Kelt, a deep chasm rent in the mountains, flanked by sheer precipices many hundred feet high, is unlike any of the ravines which drain the western hills towards the Mediterranean; and the entire absence of vegetation, the sudden disappearance of the dark copses, which are replaced by scattered acacias or by the brown clumps of bellân—a thorny plant of the family of Rosaciæ, which might be called the heather of Palestine—makes a marked contrast between the eastern and western slopes of the King's Mountain. The grey plain of Jericho and the black snake-like line of the Jordan jungle are dimly seen through the hot haze which generally hangs over the valley. The noble ranges of Nebo and Mount Gilead close the view on the east, and the blue-grey mountain of bare rock now called Tell 'Asûr—probably the ancient Baal Hazor—forms the sky-line on the north.

The little dust-coloured villages perched on the slopes and crowning the ridges are nearly all famous in Jewish history. Nearest to the spectator is Hozmeh, the ancient Azmaveth, standing on a hill-top above the curious rude stone monuments called "Graves of the Amalekites"—or "of the Sons of Israel." Farther away is Jeba, the ancient Geba of Benjamin, where Jonathan smote the Philistine garrison, and where the Benjamites were almost exterminated. Michmash, on the opposite side of the great passage, lies low, and is hidden by higher ground; and Parah of Benjamin is recognisable in the ruins above the beautiful pool of 'Ain Farâh, in the gorge east of Jeba. Still farther away lie Bethel, Ai, Rimmon, Ephron, and other sites of minor interest. On a lower spur between Anathoth and Azmaveth is a ruin with ancient wells marking the site now called 'Alnût, and in the book of Ezra, Almon or Alemeth. This place has an interest not generally recognised, for, according to the Targums, Almon was identical with the long-sought Bahurim, famous in the history of David. Of the position of Bahurim we have but little indication in Scripture. It was on David's route from Jerusalem to the Jordan Valley, and apparently in the territory of Benjamin, and certainly beyond the brow of the range of Olivet. It appears that the road ran beneath the hillside near Bahurim, for Shimei "went along on the hillside," casting stones on the patient monarch, who accepted his curses and his penitence with equal dignity. All these requisites are found at 'Alnût. The ancient highway to Jericho descends by the spur on which the city stood, after passing the brow of the hill near Anathoth; the ruin lies well within the limits of the territory of Benjamin, and Jewish tradition identifies the site by the later name which the place still retains. It was then, perhaps, in one of those ancient wells still existing in the ruins that Jonathan and Ahimaaz lay hidden beneath the parched corn spread in the sun in the court of a man's house in Bahurim.

The thirty miles of road between Jerusalem and Shechem are probably better known to the majority of travellers than any other portion of the country; with exception, perhaps, of the high-road between Jaffa and the Holy City. Yet there are many points of interest along this northern route which are unnoticed in even the latest guide-book, but are not the less worthy of attention from all who are interested in the antiquities of Palestine. Some of the most interesting of these unnoticed sites may therefore be briefly described in the succeeding pages.

Passing beneath the arch of the "Pillar Gate," as the Damascus Gate is called by the Moslems—which, with its crenellated parapet and flanking towers, is the most picturesque entrance to the city—the traveller sets out along a stony lane between drystone walls and broad olive groves. On his right are the steep cliff, and the cavern called since the fifteenth century "Jeremiah's Grotto," where the tombs of Sultan Ibrahim and Barukh-ed-Din, Kady of Jerusalem, are shown; which cavern once, perhaps, formed part of the great quarries immediately south. This place, according to Jewish tradition, was once the "House of Stoning," or place of public execution according to the law. Between the cliff and the road is a garden plot, in which remains of a Crusading building of large size were laid bare in 1873. The discovery of a series of stone mangers identifies this ruin with the Asnerie, or Templars'

THE VILLAGE OF SH'AFÂT, ON THE SUPPOSED SITE OF NOB, THE CITY OF THE PRIESTS.
The conical hill in the background is the artificial mound called Taliel-el-Fûl. By some writers Nob has been identified with El Isawîyeh, a village in the same district.

hostelry, described as having been just without the old Gate of St. Stephen, the present Damascus Gate. There are also remains of a hermit's cave and charnel-house close by, and the plot of ground would probably well reward the explorer who could command sufficient funds entirely to clear it out.

The stony lane leads through the middle of the ancient Jerusalem cemetery, lining the slopes of Wâdy-el-Jôz—the Valley of Nuts—and leaves on the right the rock-cut tomb of Simon the Just, the catacombs of the royal family of Adiabene, and many other sepulchres of the ancient city. Traversing the olives, it climbs a long hill and reaches the watershed ridge at a place called Râs Sherifeh, "the high hill top," the crest whence Jerusalem first comes fully in view when approached from the north. Turning back to obtain a last glance of the Holy City, the spectator looks across the dark olives to the long line of grey battlemented wall, behind which rise the tower and dome of the Holy Sepulchre Church, and to the left, and lower down, the great dome of the Kubbet-es-Sakhra, crowned with its gilded crescent and covered with flights of doves. On the extreme right, the ugly Byzantine cathedral built by the Russians, with its white wall and heavy cupola, is the most conspicuous object; and the foreground is formed by

MOSQUE AND TOMB AT ER RAM, THE RAMAH OF BENJAMIN.
A group of peasants in the foreground; the woman wearing a head-dress formed of coins.

the great stone heaps west of the road, which one is tempted to imagine may have formed part of the parapet of the Roman camp at the time of the great siege.

Looking northward, a desolate scene unfolds before the eye. A plateau of white chalk, bare and strewn with stones; a village among olives, a curious conical mound, and distant ridges of hard grey limestone, their sides covered with patches of rich red soil. This point of view is one whence many a famous soldier has first looked down on the Holy City. It was probably on this plateau that Alexander the Great, ascending from Antipatris, met the venerable Jaddua, clothed in his pontifical vestments, and heading the procession of Jewish notables, whom the conqueror received so courteously. It was here that Titus fixed his camp at Scopus, the place whence the great walls and golden facade of the Temple were first clearly seen. It was in this stony slope that the first Crusaders languished under the fierce summer sun, laboriously constructing their wooden towers with materials foraged from a great distance, while man and beast died daily in camp from want of water and of food.

The village immediately to the north is now called Sh'afât, and the name is said by the inhabitants to have been that of a king of Jerusalem—evidently Jehosaphat, as the Arabic word

RUINS OF CRUSADERS' CHURCH AT EL BÌREH, THE ANCIENT BEEROTH.
Nothing is left of this building but its three apses, the north wall, and a fragment of the south wall. The space within is now converted into a corn-field.

contains all the radical letters of that monarch's name. In the twelfth and fourteenth centuries, a village called Jehosaphat is mentioned north of the capital and seems to be the same place. Possibly also the Valley of Jehosaphat, near Jerusalem, mentioned by the prophet Joel, may have lain in this direction, though traditionally identified with the Brook Kedron. Sh'afât seems to be an ancient site, and may perhaps be best identified with Nob, the city of the priests, which lay apparently in sight of Jerusalem, on the main line of the Assyrian advance from the north, if we may so interpret the words of Isaiah, "Yet shall he remain at Nob that day, he shall shake his hand against the Mount of the Daughter of Zion, the hill of Jerusalem" (see page 213).

Another place which must have occupied the same or a neighbouring site is Mizpeh, the "place of view," which was "over against Jerusalem," and possibly identical with the Sapha, or "prospect" whence Alexander first saw the city, and with the later Scopus, or "place of outlook." The name Sh'afât might indeed be thought to be a corruption of Mizpeh or Sapha, although in its present form quite unconnected with those words. There is also some reason for

A HALT FOR THE NIGHT IN THE KHAN OF EL BÎREH, THE ANCIENT BEEROTH.
The village owes its ancient and modern names, which signify "cistern," to the abundant supply of water in its neighbourhood. The khan is near to the chief spring.

supposing that Mizpeh and Nob were different names, used at different periods, for that city in the land of Benjamin where the Tabernacle stood from the death of Eli until the time of the massacre by Saul of the house of Abimelech.

Immediately north-east of Sh'afât, and east of the road, is the curious mound called Taliel-el-Fûl, "the Hillock of the Bean" (see pages 188 and 213). Excavations made in this mound by the Royal Engineers show it to be an artificial platform, supported by rude walls, having originally either a lower surrounding platform or flights of steps leading up. There is nothing to show the date of the structure, nor is there any known reference to it in history; but its commanding position seems to indicate that it may have been intended for a beacon. Jerusalem is plainly seen from the top, and almost all the towns of Benjamin as far north as Bethel are visible. There are no traces of any other buildings round the platform, and the site is that of an isolated monument, not of a former city or village.

BEITÎN, THE ANCIENT BETHEL
To the north-west, in the highest part of the village, are the ruins of a tower with ancient substructions.

It is curious that so cautious a writer as the great Dr. Robinson should have identified Taliel-el-Fûl with Gibeah of Saul. In the first place there is no connection between the two names, nor is the distance between Taliel-el-Fûl and Jerusalem more than two-thirds that mentioned by Josephus as separating Gabaoth Saule from the capital. The latter village was by the "Valley of Thorns;" and we are thus, apparently, directed to Gibeah of Benjamin, standing on the brink of the present Wâdy Suweinit, "the valley of the little thorn tree," which runs beneath the ancient cliff of Seneh, or "the thorn bush." Gibeah also was in view of Michmash, and the latter place is invisible from Taliel-el-Fûl; while, as already noticed, there are no remains of any town nearer than Sh'afat to this curious conical stone heap, which forms so prominent a feature on the barren plateau. Following the road which descends gradually north of Taliel-el-Fûl, a fine view of the rugged ranges round Neby Samwîl is obtained; and the two ancient fallen milestones, one of which is inscribed with the names of the Antonine emperors, are passed. The road here bifurcates, one branch leading towards Gibeon and Beth-horon on the left, the other passing by the village of Er Râm, which is conspicuous for the white domed tomb-house on the hill-top (see page 214). Er Râm is the ancient Ramah of Benjamin; but it seems too far south to represent the more famous town of Ramah, the home and burial-place of Samuel, which was in Mount Ephraim.

The flat depression now gained is the head of the great valley called Wâdy Beit Hanîna, which has been previously described; and the low ridge beyond it on the west conceals from view the terraced hill of Gibeon. A crumbling mound, with traces of ruins, exists beside the Beth-horon road, just beyond the valley-head, and is one of the sites generally overlooked. Its present name 'Adasa, and its position, about thirty stadia from Beth-horon, and the tradition common among the peasantry of a former conflict at the place, are indications which when taken together seem clearly to indicate that this ruin is the site of 'Adasa, where Judas Maccabæus defeated and slew the impious Nicanor, who was advancing from Beth-horon with the avowed intention of destroying the Temple. The bare plateau thus gains interest in our eyes as the scene of one of the most gallant of the battles fought by the great Hasmonian leader.

After passing Er Râm the path leads under the hill of 'Attâra, the Astaroth of the mediæval writers, and thus reaches the village of Bîreh, the ancient Beeroth of Benjamin, a rambling stone hamlet with a fine spring, and ruins of a beautiful Gothic church and of an ancient khan (see pages 215 and 216).

Pausing by the spring which runs out beneath the walls of a little building which forms the village guest-house, we may glance at the history of the village and its church. Beeroth of Benjamin is not a site conspicuous in Jewish history, though probably identical with the Berea where Bacchides collected his forces before the fatal battle of Berzetho, in which Judas Maccabæus was slain.

The church, which was built by the Franks in the first half of the twelfth century, was consecrated to St. Mary, and the town, which boasted of Frankish burghers, was given by Baldwin IV. the Canons of the Holy Sepulchre, with Mezr'ah—not far north—in exchange for Kefr Malik and 'Ain Kinia, villages in the same district. The place was sometimes called Magina by the Franks, and sometimes Grand Mahomery, in contradistinction to Little Mahomery, or Beit Surîk.

A tradition mentioned by Maundrell makes Bîreh to be the place where, after going a day's journey with their company, Joseph and Mary found that the child Jesus had tarried behind in Jerusalem. The story is not, however, mentioned in the Byzantine accounts of the country, nor even in the Crusading descriptions before the fifteenth century.

The apses and side walls, with beautiful carved capitals of various designs once supporting the roof arches, are all now remaining of the church. The walls are of unusual thickness, but the pillar shafts are graceful and slender, unlike the heavy columns which occur in the earliest specimens of Crusading architecture. The khan appears to be partly constructed from ancient materials, and the sloping outer wall has the appearance of mediæval work. During the reign of the Latin kings Bîreh was evidently a place of importance, and was rebuilt by the Canons of the Holy Sepulchre. In 1321 Marino Sanuto speaks of it as "a city of considerable size," although in 1210 it was found lying entirely in ruins.

REMAINS OF A CHURCH AT BEITÎN.
Said to have been erected as a memorial of Jacob's dream at Bethel.

Crossing another valley-head the road now climbs up to a plateau yet more barren than the country already traversed. Nothing more desolate or bleak can be well imagined. On the left a white slope of gleaming chalk, on the right a low cliff, a terraced hill, a miserable hamlet of half-ruinous stone huts, with a central high house or tower. Drystone walls enclose fields scattered with loose stones, while on the slopes the rock is grey and bare, without a single blade of green grass and almost entirely devoid of trees or shrubs. Such is the site of one of the most famous towns of Palestine, for the modern village of Beitîn represents the ancient Bethel, or "House of God" (see page 217).

Only one other city of Palestine, namely, Shechem, is noticed earlier in the Old Testament history than is Bethel. The second altar erected by Abraham stood between Bethel and Ai, and the same site was revisited by that patriarch on his return from Egypt. Probably the altar was still standing when Jacob fled from the south country to Harran and "lighted upon a certain place." He took of the stones of "that place" for his pillow, and called the name of "that place" Bethel; but the name of the city near which the "place" was situate was called originally Luz. Again, the "place" called El Bethel at Luz is mentioned on the return route of Jacob to the south, and the same word "place" is used four times in this chapter in reference to Bethel.

It has not apparently been generally recognised that the Hebrew word thus rendered has a special significance, being the same employed to designate the "places" of the Canaanites, or idolatrous shrines. The word in the original is Makom, identical with the Arabic Mukâm or "standing place," by which a shrine or consecrated spot is now designated. The story gains force when the peculiar meaning of the term is thus brought out. Jacob came to a certain shrine—probably the altar originally erected by his grandfather Abraham—and taking the stones from it for his pillow, slept under the protection of the hallowed sanctuary, which was very probably respected by the inhabitants of the neighbouring city of Luz. Just so at the present day the stranger will find a safe retreat in the vicinity of a Moslem Mukâm, placing himself under the protection of the tutelary deity.

From the sanctuary the name seems, by the time at which the Book of Joshua was written, to have been transferred to the neighbouring city of Luz, and is enumerated as that of one of the towns of Benjamin. There is also in the Book of Judges an unrecognised reference to Bethel in the account of the slaughter of the Benjamites; for by "the House of God," where the ark was in those days, Josephus understands Bethel to be intended, and this interpretation is strengthened by the notice in the same chapter of the highway leading from Gibeah to the "House of God," which from the context was evidently in the immediate vicinity of the Benjamite city. Again, in the time of Samuel we find notice of three men "going up to God to Bethel," an expression which shows that the place was a religious centre in the days of Saul.

Bethel was thus apparently a venerated shrine throughout the earlier period of Hebrew history preceding the building of the Temple in Jerusalem. It was indeed—with exception of the altar near Shechem—the most ancient sanctuary in the land, and there was nothing in the re-establishment by Jeroboam of the same site as a religious centre which would have appeared a striking innovation in the eyes of the Israelites. It was a mere revival of an ancient religious gathering, as the golden calves, symbolic of Jehovah, were the same emblems which had been sanctioned by Aaron in the Wilderness as representing the national deity.

In the later Jewish history the names Bethel, "the House of God," and Beth Aven, "the House of Nothingness," are used apparently as synonymous terms for a single site. Jewish commentators state that the two places were identical, and in the name Bethaun we see perhaps the early corruption whence the modern title Beitîn was derived—a form which was in use at least as early as the fourteenth century.

Barren and stony as the bleak plateau of Bethel is in appearance, it is nevertheless supplied with water from four good springs. To the east is the ruined monastery called Burj Beitîn; to the north is Deir Shabîb, "the monastery of young men" mentioned in the Cartulary of the Holy Sepulchre as forming part of the property of that church. To the south are remains of a fine ancient reservoir about one hundred yards in length, while a great valley is visible running down toward Michmash, and forming probably the hiding-place where the Israelite ambush was set between Bethel and Ai.

Close to the village is the ruin of a little church with a single apse, having the appearance of earlier work than that of the Crusaders, and marking the site where it was supposed that the patriarch's vision of angels must have occurred (see page 219). North of Beitîn is a curious circle of stones, perhaps so arranged by a freak of nature, but having the appearance of a rude stone monument. East of the reservoir is a rock-cut tomb, probably that to which Isaac Chelo refers as the sepulchre of the prophet Ahijah; and, indeed, its position on the side of the mount is one which might not unnaturally be expected for the sepulchre of the man of God who testified against the altar in Bethel—a tomb left untouched by Josiah on the occasion of his destruction of Jeroboam's high place.

In the Middle Ages considerable confusion arose respecting the site of Bethel. In the fourth century the place was known, and St. Jerome speaks of "the House of God, where naked upon the bare ground poor Jacob lay, and, placing beneath his head the stone which is described in Zechariah as having seven eyes, and is called the corner-stone by Isaiah, saw the ladder stretching even to Heaven."

In the sixth century Theodorus mentions the same site, but the majority of the twelfth-century pilgrims pass it over in silence, while many of the more important accounts accept the Samaritan identification of Bethel with Mount Gerizim. Jacques de Vitray, in the thirteenth century, even supposes Jerusalem to be Bethel, and the Sakhra Rock, in the Temple enclosure, to be the stone that had formed Jacob's pillar, and which is traditionally identified with the Lia Fail, or "Stone of Destiny," brought from Ireland to Scotland, and by Edward III. from Scone to Westminster, where it now forms part of the coronation chair. It seems indeed clear that the true site of Bethel was unknown to the Crusaders, although the village was sold by Hugh of Ibelin, in the time of Baldwin V., to the Canons of the Holy Sepulchre.

A short divergence from the main road eastward brings the traveller to the ruin called

THE VILLAGE OF TAIYIBEH FROM THE HEIGHTS OF RUMMAN.
The former is said to represent Ophrah and the latter Rimmon.

El Mukâtir, a Byzantine chapel not improbably marking the supposed site of Abraham's altar; and the view thence extends over the little plateau where stands the modern village of Deir Diwân, close to the ruin of Haiyân, which appears to be the true site of Ai—a city mentioned in Scripture as being "close to" Bethel, which is distant only two miles from Haiyân.

From this détour into a region not generally visited by the traveller we must now return to the main road north of Bethel; and here, as we ride along the watershed ridge, an interesting and picturesque view opens out on the west. A deep valley (Wâdy-el-Jîb) runs northward between steep mountain sides. Terraces of fig-trees clothe the rugged slopes with pale green foliage, and the vine is cultivated on both sides of the

WADY-EL-JIB.
A characteristic example of a valley in the favoured territory of Ephraim. The olive-trees, shading the ancient foot-paths, proclaim that a village is near.

ravine. The Christian village of Jufna lies in the widest part of the basin, and farther north is 'Ain Sinia; while on the western hills Bîr-ez-Zeit is also inhabited by Latins. These three sites are each worthy of a few words of notice.

Jufna, taking its name, which means "vine," from the vine cultivation surrounding it, is the ancient Gophna, the capital of one of the ten toparchies, or counties, into which Judæa was divided about the Christian era. Gophna is unnoticed in the Bible, and this instance, like that of Sepphoris or Taricheæ in the north, and of Bethgubrin in the south, affords a good example of the fact that many of the important towns of Palestine, especially of the later period, are not mentioned in the sacred volume—a fact which should warn us not to be too eager in the endeavour to identify important ancient sites with Biblical towns. Gophna is mentioned in the Talmud, and by Josephus in his account of the march of Titus from Samaria on Jerusalem. It is shown on the Peutinger Tables, the Roman survey of Palestine made in the second century of our era. It contains remains of a ruined tower and a modern Latin monastery. The ruins of the old Byzantine church of St. George are just outside the village.

Bîr-ez-Zeit, a good-sized village on the mountain to the west of Gophna, is probably the Berzetho of Josephus, the scene of the last fatal battle in which Judas Maccabæus lost his life in the year 161 B.C. The patriot had collected a force of three thousand men at Il'asa, near Beth-horon, and advanced to intercept the communications of Bacchides, who had reached Jerusalem by the north road through Samaria. The Greek general had, however, learned caution by former misfortunes, and came back rapidly to Bîreh and to Bethel, which lay within sight of the Jewish army, occupying the high ridge which is visible west of Wâdy-el-Jîb. A furious attack on the eastern wing of the Greeks, directed no doubt against their line of retreat through the narrow pass hereafter to be mentioned, was at first successful; but the forces of Judas had dwindled by desertion during the night to only eight hundred men, and the army of Bacchides is said to have numbered twenty thousand foot and two thousand horse. The left wing closed in on the small band of patriots, and Judas was slain on the rugged mountain side after a short career of seven years of constant fighting.

'Ain Sinia, the third village in the vicinity of Wâdy-el-Jîb, is remarkable for the rich cultivation of fig, olive, and vine which fills the valley and climbs the hillside. In the twelfth century this village, called Val de Curs by the Franks, was given to the Canons of the Holy Sepulchre. It seems probable that the site, which is marked by numerous old rock-cut sepulchres (one having a Hebrew inscription), is that of the ancient Jeshanah, one of the three fortresses, Bethel, Jeshanah, and Ephraim, built by Abijah to guard the three main approaches by which Jeroboam might advance on Jerusalem.

The ancient Roman road runs from Bethel down to Gophna, and so along the valley to 'Ain Sinia, thence climbing the slope of a hill thickly covered with olives, to join the route which runs along the watershed and descends into the narrow pass which formed the natural boundary between the tribes of Benjamin and Ephraim. The region which we leave behind is one of the principal Christian districts of Southern Palestine. Ramallah—the white village so conspicuous from the neighbourhood of Sh'afât and Bireh—contains a Latin convent; Jufna, 'Ain 'Arîk, Bîr-ez-Zeit, Jania, Taiyibeh (see page 222), and Deir Diwân are all Christian villages. In the Middle Ages nearly all this district belonged to the Church, twenty-one villages north of Jerusalem having been given by Godfrey to the Canons of the Holy Sepulchre, while Sinjil, Bethel, Turmus 'Ayya, Mezr'ah, Kefr Mâlik, and others, were acquired later by this powerful body of ecclesiastics.

Traces of the Crusaders are found in all parts of the district, from the two castles which dominate the northern pass, to the rocky fortress of Neby Samwîl on the south; at Bîreh, Beitîn, Jufna, Taiyibeh, Neby Samwîl, and Mukâtir, ancient churches and chapels remain in ruins; and at Arnûtieh and other places there are small forts apparently of Crusading origin.

The narrow pass which we now approach is one of the wildest parts of the road between Nâblus

SEILÛN, ON THE SITE OF SHILOH.
Where the sacred tent and the ark remained for four centuries.

and Jerusalem, which here becomes a mere lane thickly strewn with loose stones. To the left of the road a square building of large drafted stones seems probably to have been a Crusading fort or hostel, and a vertical cliff of hard rock reaches up some twenty or thirty feet, while the steep hill above is terraced and planted with olives. A small spring drips out of the precipice, and is called 'Ain-el-Haramîyeh, "the Robbers' Spring." On the flat rocky bed of the valley a little coarse grass grows near the water, and a group of camels, tawny and dusty, may probably be found reposing in the shade, while their drivers, kneeling on the carefully spread *abbas*, are reciting the afternoon prayer—a ceremony no doubt religiously observed by the brigands from the nearest village, who once haunted the gorge and gave its name to the spring. To the right of the road an extremely steep mountain-side, terraced in places, and in others belted with low cliffs, dominates the pass, rising more

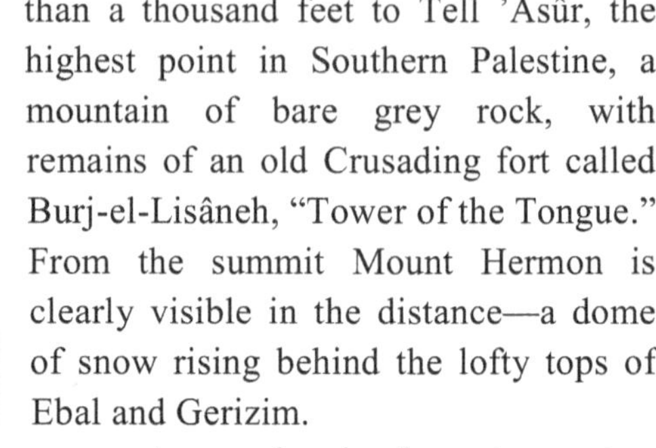

than a thousand feet to Tell 'Asûr, the highest point in Southern Palestine, a mountain of bare grey rock, with remains of an old Crusading fort called Burj-el-Lisâneh, "Tower of the Tongue." From the summit Mount Hermon is clearly visible in the distance—a dome of snow rising behind the lofty tops of Ebal and Gerizim.

A more lonely place at sunset or

ANCIENT DOORWAY AT SHILOH, AND RUINS OF THE "CONVENT CASTLE" IN WADY LUBBAN (LEBONAH).

by night than the Robbers' Spring can hardly be imagined. The dark shadow covers the valley long before the orange glow has faded from the upper rocks; and the cry of the wild hawk, or the howl of the jackal, with the grumbling of the camels, are the only sounds which the traveller hears re-echoed from the surrounding precipices. Looking southward, he sees below the steep path a rock-cut entrance leading to a small tomb-chamber in the cliff, and the view is closed by the terraced hill, dark with olives, on the summit of which stands Burj Bardawîl, "Baldwin's Tower," an old fortress named, no doubt, after one of the Latin kings, and commanding the approach from Nâblus to Jerusalem

A THRESHING-FLOOR.
Peasants winnowing grain with large wooden forks, and oxen dragging a sledge, the under surface of which is armed with sharp flints, to cut up the straw.

through the pass. Even within the last half-century the castle has been the scene of faction fights between the villagers of Yebrûd, 'Ain Abrûd, Selwâd, and 'Ain Sinia.

From the Robbers' Spring the stony lane again ascends towards a fertile plateau, with a steep mountain pass in front. To the left, on the hill, is the village of Sinjil; to the right, in the plain, that of Turmus 'Ayya. Sinjil is one of the few places in Palestine where a

Frankish name has survived; perhaps because the town was founded by the Franks, and had no other title. Fetellus informs us that during the First Crusade, Raymond, fourth Count of Toulouse, "dit de Saint Gilles," advanced by this road, and camped at a certain *casale* on the night before he reached the Holy City. The distances given show that this *casale*—by which word William of Tyre tells us was meant an open village of one hundred houses, paying a tax of one bezant each to the seigneur—was near the Robbers' Spring, and we can have no hesitation in recognising the name of Casale Saint Gilles in the modern Sinjil, a place which, with Turmus 'Ayya (the Thormasia of the Talmud), became church property at a later period.

The region between Bethel and Shechem, belonging to the tribe of Ephraim, is yet more rugged than that round Jerusalem; the valleys are deeper, the mountains steeper and more rocky, and the character of the watershed different—broad, open vales and small plateaux, like that of Turmus 'Ayya, existing close to the central ridge. The country near Jufna is also remarkable for the extent of its cultivation, it being generally observable in Palestine that the Christian villages flourish better than those of the Moslems, partly because the Christians can claim protection from foreign powers, which the Moslems do not enjoy, being left, without any protector, to the tyranny of the Turks. But another reason for the greater prosperity of Christian districts is no doubt to be found in the helpless fatalism and indolent resignation of the Moslems, contrasted with the energy and enterprise of the villagers educated by the Greek and Latin priests.

On the stony ascent near Sinjil, and in other parts of the road, the traces of the ancient Roman pavement are visible. A fence of stone was made along the sides of the highway and huge polygonal blocks of stone were carefully fitted together to form the roadway, as in the streets of Pompeii. From the narrow saddle which is now reached the first view of Gerizim is obtained, a long ridge rising to a blunt summit, with a steep eastern shoulder, not unlike that of Helvellyn seen from near Dunmail Raise. At its feet is the brown plain of the Mukhnah, and Hermon closes the view in the extreme distance; while in the foreground, at the foot of the steep stony winding descent, is the ruined inn and the beautiful spring of Khân Lubban.

The mountains of Ephraim—long spurs covered on the west with thickets of mastic and dwarf pine—are drained by two main watercourses, valleys so steep as to be almost impassable by horsemen, and each indicating an ancient political boundary. The most southern of these—one of the longest valleys in the country—is formed by the junction of Wâdy Lubban with a more northern affluent which rises north of Sâwieh, a place hereafter to be described. The great valley runs down beneath the cliff on which the Byzantine monastery called Deir-el-Kul'ah, "convent castle," is perched (see page 226), and passes through the low chalky hills to Râs-el-'Ain, the ancient Antipatris, the Crusaders' Mirabel. The northern valley, rising at the foot of Gerizim, and flowing south-west, is scarcely less formidable. The southern watercourse formed the ancient boundary between Judaea and

Samaria; the northern (Wâdy Kânah) is probably the brook Kânah, which divided the lot of Ephraim from that of Manasseh. Both valleys form a junction near Râs-el-'Ain, and the great pools beside that ruin are those fed by the rainfall from an area of four hundred square miles of mountain country.

But on reaching the plateau near Sinjil the traveller will probably make a détour to the east, in order to visit the secluded ruin of Seilûn, the Shiloh of the Old Testament.

An ancient causeway leads up the slope of a chalky hill from the open plain of Turmus 'Ayya. Gaining the saddle, the traveller sees in front of him a grey ruin of tumbledown stone huts clustering round the side of a kind of knoll. In the low ground near the approach is a flat-roofed building shaded by a large oak; this is called Jami'a-el-Yetaim, "Mosque of the Worshippers." On the right, higher up, is another square structure, roofless and half ruinous, with some smaller trees. This is called Jami'a-el-Arb'aîn, "Mosque of the Forty" (Companions of the Prophet). A little tank with steps is seen close to the first-mentioned building. The view is restricted on either side by hills, and north of the ruins rises a long barren ridge of grey limestone, with a few scattered fig-trees. Immediately behind the knoll of the ruined village is a deep valley. Several tombs are cut in the rock on either side of the town, and a fine spring, with some rock-cut sepulchres, exists about three-quarters of a mile to the east, near the valley head. The site, remote from the main road, and hidden in the bosom of the hills, is so secluded that it might easily escape the notice even of a careful explorer; and it is not surprising that for so many centuries it remained altogether unknown, though still preserving its ancient name among the villagers who, until quite of late years, inhabited the place.

The "Mosque of the Forty," which is reached before arriving at the ruined village, is a building of puzzling character. It has been constructed at different periods, and used for different purposes. The mosque itself is a small chamber of inferior masonry, built against the eastern wall of the ancient structure, with a small mihrab, or prayer recess, towards the south. The main building is a square of thirty-seven feet side, with solid walls of good masonry, the door being to the north. The doorway is spanned by a flat lintel, having on it a representation, in low relief, of a vase flanked by two wreaths; and the design resembling those on the Galilean synagogues, and almost identical with that over an ancient rock-cut tomb some few miles off at Beita, is of the character which belongs to the Jewish art of the later period, from Herod to Hadrian; and though possibly not *in situ*, we can have little hesitation in identifying the lintel as of Jewish origin (see page 226). The remains of four pillars, which seem to have supported the roof, are visible among the thorns and weeds inside the monument; and a sloping scarp—apparently a later addition—is built against the wall on the outside.

Isaac Chelo, of Aragon, almost the only traveller, Jewish or Christian, who mentions Seilûn, seems very possibly to refer to this building. He speaks of "a very remarkable sepulchral monument where the Jews and Moslems keep lamps perpetually burning," and calls it the Tomb of Eli and his sons, Hophni and Phinehas. The building just described cannot apparently have been a church, the square form being unusual for such a structure and the walls being so perfect as to show that it never had either an apse—which is almost invariably found in Syrian churches—or a western door, which is equally essential. The form would be suitable for a masonry sepulchre, several of which are known in Palestine: and if the building be of Jewish origin, the lintel may perhaps be *in situ*.

There is nothing further of note in the ruins of Shiloh, excepting, perhaps, the sort of sunk

JACOB'S WELL, AT THE FOOT OF MOUNT GERIZIM.
The true mouth of the well is in the floor of a little vaulted chamber below the surface of the ground.

court, four hundred feet long and seventy-five feet wide, which exists on the side of the knoll, north of the houses, and which is thought possibly to have been the place where the Tabernacle stood. In the Mishnah the foundation of the holy house, when erected at Shiloh, is said to have been of stone; but this has of course long since disappeared.

The history of Shiloh commences with the conquest of the country by Joshua, and with the establishment of the Ark in this remote town, which lay within the territory of the sons of Joseph, to whom Joshua belonged by descent. The sacred tent and the Ark remained for four centuries fixed at Shiloh, and only after the death of Eli and the loss of the Ark was the Tabernacle removed to Nob. From that time Shiloh seems to have been completely forgotten, and appears no more in history. Yet even during the period of its fame its position seems to have been thought to require special description, and there is no topographical passage in the Bible which so clearly and distinctly indicates the position of

JOSEPH'S TOMB.
From the north, showing the ruined kubbeh which adjoins it. The cenotaph and one of the pillars appear within the doorway.

a town as that which defines the situation of Shiloh. "Behold," we read, "there is a feast of the Lord in Shiloh yearly, in a place which is on the north side of Bethel, on the east of the highway that goeth up from Bethel to Shechem, and on the south of Lebonah."

In the time of Phinehas—according to the chronology of Josephus—Shiloh became the scene of an adventure which recalls the rape of the Sabines, namely, the forcible provision of wives for the surviving Benjamites. Among the thick leaves of the low vine-bushes the men of Benjamin lay hid, as the Israelite damsels, robed in their holiday attire, marched out to the sound of the timbrel, clapping their hands and dancing, as the bands of women may still be seen to dance on festive occasions among these wild mountains. "And the children of Benjamin took them wives according to the number of them that danced whom they caught." Possibly the name "Meadow of the Feast," which applies to part of the plain south of Shiloh, may preserve the memory of the yearly feast at this place; but the vineyards have disappeared from the hillsides, though it cannot be doubted that the neighbourhood is still fitted for the growth of the vine.

Shiloh was known to that indefatigable explorer, St. Jerome, who places it ten Roman miles from Shechem, in the province of Acrabattene, clearly intending the present site of Seilûn; and in describing the pilgrimage of his friend, Sta. Paula, he says, "What shall I tell of Shiloh, in which the altar is still shown overthrown, and where the tribe of Benjamin anticipated the Sabine rape by Romulus?" But, with the exception of this great writer, no traveller speaks of this remote village except Isaac Chelo in 1334 A.D., as already quoted; while in the twelfth century, and down to the fifteenth, we find the hill of Neby Samwîl regarded as the site of Shiloh, contrary to the most definite language of Scripture. It was left to Dr. Robinson to recover the long-lost site answering so exactly to the account in the Book of Judges of the position of Shiloh.

Passing down the valley westward, we rejoin the main road beneath Khân Lubban, and so follow the course of a flat vale beneath the ancient village Lubban, or Lebonah, the Beth Laban of the Talmud, and the Lepna of the fourteenth century. Beth Laban, it may be remarked, was a place the wine of which was used in the Temple services, but it was so close to the Samaritan border that a doubt arose as to its being sufficiently pure for the purpose. Beth Rima (now Beit Rîma) was another place in the same category; Keruthim (Kerîut) was a third; and these three names thus form valuable indications of the border between Samaria and Judæa.

From the farther end of the open valley of Lebonah we ascend a slope, on which stands the ruin of Khân-es-Sâwieh, named from a neighbouring village. A good spring with a spreading oak-tree near the khan form a resting-place, and the site has an interest not generally recognised.

Père Lievin, the able author of the Catholic guide-book for pilgrims, seems to have been the first to discover that Khân Sâwieh stands close to the ruins of an ancient village called Berkît, a discovery which has since been verified in a satisfactory manner. Now Josephus tells us that Anuath, or Borceos, was the boundary town between Samaria and Judæa; and the distance noticed in the Onomasticon (or Topographical Dictionary of Eusebius and Jerome) between Anuath and Nâblus brings us on the map to the neighbourhood of Khân Sâwieh. East of the road, at some little distance, is a ruin called 'Aina, and this with Berkît represent probably Anuath and Borceos, thus fixing the boundary at this point. When, in addition, we remember the sites of Keruthim, Beth Laban, and Beth Rima, already noticed, and know that Antipatris was also a border town, we are able to identify the boundary between Judaea and Samaria with the great valley already noticed, generally called Wâdy Deir Ballût. Acrabbi, again, is noticed by Josephus as on this border, and is represented by the modern village 'Akrabeh, immediately east of which the valley first sinks from the watershed. At Khân Sâwieh, therefore, we stand at the boundary of Judæa, and as we pass the stony valley immediately north of it, we cross into the region of Samaria and become concerned with Samaritan traditions and topography.

The fine oak-tree near the spring of Khân Sâwieh is one of the few large trees of Southern Palestine, the number of which can almost be counted on the fingers. Three species of oak exist in Syria, of which the evergreen oak attains the largest size, and is called *ballût* in Arabic. The second species, called *sindiân* and *afs*, forms a brushwood of prickly shrubs eight to twelve feet in height; and the third, the gall oak, grows as a small tree twenty feet high, called generally *mallûl*, but sometimes *sindiân*. The large single oaks, like Abraham's oak at Hebron, are rare, but the gall oak is very common in parts of Galilee, growing in thick woods and open glades west of Nazareth, on Tabor, near the sources of Jordan, and in the northern part of the plain of Sharon. The second species flourishes in the copses which cover the hard limestone of the spurs west of the watershed, but never occurs in the soft chalky districts, which are bare of brushwood.

From the oak tree of Khân Sâwieh we now march outward into Samaria, and gain the crest of a ridge whence Gerizim and the Mukhnah plain are distinctly visible. We enter upon a region of sacred tombs, and find the old heroes of the Hebrew invasion lying buried round the Mount of Blessing. Were these sites only venerated by the Samaritans, we might feel doubtful of their authentic character, but Jew and Christian agree in pointing to the same sites for the tombs of Joshua, Caleb, and Nun, Phinehas, Eleazar, and Ithamar, and that of Joseph rather farther north. The modern Samaritans identify Timnath Heres, where Joshua was buried, with the village Kefr Hâris, on the hills south of Gerizim, where are three square domed buildings, sacred respectively to Neby Lûsh'a, Neby Nûn, and Neby Kifl (an historic character of the age of the Prophet). In the fourth century St. Jerome apparently speaks of this same place in describing the route of Sta. Paula, in connection with the other sacred tombs lying in this district, and as being still venerated. "Much she wondered," he writes, "that the divider of the possessions should have chosen for himself a lot so rugged and mountainous." A remark which applies well to the rough mountains round Kefr Hâris. In the fourteenth century Marino Sanuto makes Kefr Hâris and the tomb of Joshua in correct position on his map, but the Jewish descriptions of the place are still more important. Rabbi Jacob, of Paris, in 1258, notices the three tombs of Joshua, Caleb, and Nun at Kefr Hâris. Estori Parchi gives the distance from Shechem as two leagues. Rabbi Gerson, of Scarmela, in 1561, speaks of the monuments over the tombs, and of the caruba and pomegranate trees growing beside them. And finally, in 1564, Rabbi Uri, of Biel, gives a sketch showing three domed buildings with two trees, and lights burning inside the domes. As regards these sepulchres, we have thus an accord between four distinct lines of tradition, and the existence of the name of Mount Heres in the modern form of Hâris.

The plain called El Mukhnah, which we now approach, is a plateau larger than any previously crossed, though smaller than the watershed plains north of Shechem (see page 237). It measures about nine miles north and south, by four miles east and west, and consists of

RUINS ON THE SUMMIT OF MOUNT GERIZIM, ON THE SITE OF THE SAMARITAN TEMPLE.
In the distance, on the right, the snow-covered peaks of Mount Hermon are visible.

corn-land, with small olive groves covering the low rocky swells which rise from the plain and form sites for the villages. The present name Mukhnah is taken from the ruin of the old Samaritan town so called on the slope of Gerizim, and means "the camp." The Samaritans call it Merj-el-Baha, "the Flat Meadow," and identify it with the plain of Moreh, mentioned in the Bible as near Shechem. In the middle of the plain stands the village of 'Awertah, on rising ground among the olives, and well supplied with water. Here in the village itself is the ancient monument called by the Samaritans the tomb of Phinehas; and on the west, shaded by a magnificent terebinth growing in the paved courtyard, is the domed tomb-house of Eleazar, with a Samaritan inscription of the last century. Ithamar is also said to be buried with Abishua not far off. The village mosque is, however, consecrated to a Moslem sheikh. There seems little doubt that 'Awertah represents Gibeah Phinehas in Mount Ephraim, where Eleazar, the son of Aaron, and his family were buried. The Samaritans called the place Kefr Awerah and Abeartha, and the mediæval Jewish travellers all notice the tombs of Eleazar, Phinehas, and Ithamar, the latter as lying among the olives below the village. Rabbi Gerson also describes a vaulted chamber, as yet unknown to modern travellers, where the seventy elders were entombed. Following the path worn in the white chalk along the feet of Gerizim, we pass by the spring of Sarîna, to which a Samaritan legend similar to the story of Susanna attaches, and descend to the Vale of Shechem, west of the little village of Balâta, with its fig garden and clear spring.

Balâta is one of the cities the importance of which is little recognised. Jerome identifies it with the oak of Shechem, which was by the Holy Place of Jehovah; and the Samaritans give to the spot the names Ailon-Tubah and *Shejr el Kheir*, "Holy Oak," or "Tree of Grace." This sacred tree appears more than once in the Old Testament history; first, perhaps, as the oak of Moreh beside the makom, or "place," of Shechem, where Abraham built his first altar; and again as the oak where Jacob hid the teraphim; apparently the same tree which was by the Sanctuary of the Lord, or altar El-Elohe-Israel, erected by Jacob on the parcel of ground which he bought from the children of Hamor. By this oak Joshua erected a great stone, which is noticed later as "the monument" by the oak of Shechem; and the Oak of the Meonenim, or soothsayers, near Shechem, is not improbably the same place. The tradition which fixes the site of this sanctuary farther west, at the little "Mosque of the Pillar," appears to be more modern, and, with several other sites round Shechem and on Ebal, seems to belong to the Crusading topography which connected Ebal and Gerizim with the Dan and Bethel of Jeroboam's calf-worship.

This ancient sanctuary, the site of the first oak-tree beneath which the father of the Hebrews spread his tent in the promised land, and of the first "place," or makom, where he erected an altar, is naturally to be sought in the immediate vicinity of the well dug by his grandson Jacob; and the undisputed site of that well is to be found immediately east of Balâta. Not only is the Bîr Yakûb the only well anywhere in the neighbourhood, but its existence so close to beautiful springs of water gushing out at the feet of Gerizim could scarcely be accounted for were it not for the jealousy with which—as we learn from the Book of Genesis—the old Canaanites preserved their rights to the springs. For his own use, on his own land, the patriarch dug the well, leaving the fountains in possession of the native inhabitants. As we approach the spot we see a dusty patch of ground within a brokendown stone wall. Scattered stones and mounds of rubbish cover the plot, and the shafts of three granite columns stand up in the middle, their bases buried underground. At length we find a hole, in the roof of a little modern vault about twenty feet long east and west, with a pointed arch. The floor is piled with the *débris* of the roof, and the well-mouth is choked, but the well itself, seventy-five feet deep, and seven feet six inches in diameter, is quite clear (see page 230).

The ruins which surround the well are those of an ancient church. In another small vault to the north-west, now closed, the tesselated pavement may still be seen, and the bases of the pillars already noticed. In 383 A.D. Sta. Paula visited the church; in 700 A.D. Arculphus gives a rude plan of it as cruciform. It was standing in the eighth century, and was rebuilt in the twelfth; for Theodorus, in 1172, speaks of the well as enclosed in the church—just as Sta. Paula found it—before the high altar. Even as late as 1550 an altar stood in the vault, and the site still belongs to the Greek church. Looking northward from the well, we see the dome of the little mosque by Joseph's Tomb—a site mentioned from the earliest time by travellers, Jewish, Samaritan, or Christian, and venerated by all sects alike—the companion of Jacob's Well, and probably as genuine a site, being authorised by that rare consent of various traditions which is found especially in respect to places near Shechem. The tomb stands in a little courtyard adjoining the ruined kubbeh, and is surrounded by plastered walls, renewed—as an inscription in English, on the south wall, tells us—by Consul Rogers, the friend of the Samaritans, in 1868. At either end of the rude cenotaph is a pillar on which lamps may be placed; and the monument must be older than, from its rude construction, would be supposed, for in 1564 Rabbi Vri, of Biel, gives a sketch of Joseph's Tomb which would correctly represent the present structure with its pillars. Jew, Samaritan, Moslem, and Christian venerate the site alike, although Josephus says that the bones of Joseph were carried to Hebron, and Sæwulf notices, in 1100 A.D., the same supposed tomb, which is still shown attached to the outer wall of the Hebron haram (see page 231).

On the side of Ebal, above Joseph's Tomb, is the rude hamlet of 'Askar, with its rock-cut channel leading to the spring and its ancient sepulchres. The old Samaritan name for the place is Ischar, almost identical in sound with the Sychar which is mentioned in our version of the fourth Gospel. Jerome and other authorities, indeed, support the reading which substitutes Shechem for Sychar, and Dr. Robinson has proposed the theory that Sychar means "drunken," and was a Jewish nickname for the Samaritan capital. The spelling of the old Samaritan name shows, however, that the derivation was from another root, meaning "to surround;" and Shechem is too far from Jacob's Well to fit the narrative of Christ's conversation with the Samaritan woman. Nor is the expression, "Sychar, a city of Samaria," likely to have been used by a Jewish author with reference to the famous Shechem which is mentioned by name in the Book of Acts. Sychar was well known to the early pilgrims as being near Jacob's Well, and about a mile from Shechem; but the Crusaders confused the two sites, much as modern authors have done when unaware of the existence of 'Askar.

THE VILLAGE OF SÂLIM.
Opposite the eastern entrance to the Vale of Shechem, which is seen beyond the broad plain of Mukhnah. It probably represents the Salem near to which John baptized his disciples.

Here, then, at the mouth of Jacob's Well, we stand on one of the few spots where we can feel any certainty that the feet of Christ must actually have trod. We look round on the same scene which greeted his eyes: we behold the same monuments venerated in his days. The grey olive groves hide Shechem from our sight; the rough rocky side of Gerizim rises to the ruins of that temple where the Samaritan still worships (see page 234). The tawny slopes and precipices of Ebal, the mountain of the curse, where, according to the quaint legends of the Middle Ages, Cain raised his altar and Jeroboam set up his golden calf, appear to the north. On

TOMB OF PHINEHAS.
On the eastern side of the village of 'Awertah, the ancient Gibeah Phinehas.

the white chalk stands the humble hamlet of Sychar, beneath it the rude but ancient Tomb of Joseph; while to the east the eye ranges to Sâlim near Ænon (see page 237) and to the wooded hill of Phinehas, where the great priests of the time of the conquest sleep in hallowed shrines. Long may the venerable well repose in its ruins, set in scenery as venerable in its associations, unspoiled by the jarring inconsistency of Frankish restorations, and hallowed by the memory of the Master who rested once upon its brink!

INDEX TO VOL. I.

www.ingramcontent.com/pod-product-compliance
Lightning Source LLC
Chambersburg PA
CBHW080252030726
47593CB00009B/2463

* 9 7 8 1 5 9 7 3 1 4 5 6 5 *